Understanding Linguistics: The Science of Language

John McWhorter, Ph.D.

THE
GREAT
COURSES®

PUBLISHED BY:

THE GREAT COURSES
Corporate Headquarters
4840 Westfields Boulevard, Suite 500
Chantilly, Virginia 20151-2299
Phone: 1-800-832-2412
Fax: 703-378-3819
www.thegreatcourses.com

John McWhorter, Ph.D.

Senior Fellow, Manhattan Institute

John McWhorter, Senior Fellow at the Manhattan Institute and weekly columnist for *The New York Sun*, earned his Ph.D. in Linguistics from Stanford University in 1993 and became Associate Professor of Linguistics at UC Berkeley after teaching at Cornell University. His academic specialty is language change and language contact. He is the author of *The Power of Babel: A Natural History of Language*, on how the world's languages arise, change, and mix, and *Doing Our Own Thing: The Degradation of Language and Music in America and Why We Should, Like, Care*. More recently, he is the author of *Our Magnificent Bastard Tongue: Untold Stories in the History of English*. He has also written a book on dialects and Black English, *The Word on the Street*; three books on Creole languages; and an academic linguistics book entitled *Language Interrupted: Signs of Non-Native Acquisition in Standard Language Grammars*.

The Teaching Company released his 36-lecture audiovisual course *The Story of Human Language* in 2004. Beyond his work in linguistics, Dr. McWhorter is the author of *Losing the Race*; an anthology of race writings called *Authentically Black*; *Winning the Race: Beyond the Crisis in Black America*; and *All About the Beat: Why Hip-Hop Can't Save Black America*. He has written on race and cultural issues for *The New Republic*, *The Wall Street Journal*, *The Washington Post*, *The New York Times*, *The Chronicle of Higher Education*, *National Review*, the *Los Angeles Times*, *The American Enterprise*, *Ebony*, *Vibe*, and *City Journal*. He provides commentaries for *All Things Considered* and previously appeared weekly on NPR's *News and Notes*; he has also appeared on *Meet the Press*, *Dateline NBC*, *Politically Incorrect*, *Talk of the Nation*, *Today*, *Good Morning America*, *The NewsHour with Jim Lehrer*, and *Fresh Air*.

Table of Contents

Understanding Linguistics: The Science of Language

Understanding Linguistics: The Science of Language

Scope:

As an introduction to linguistic science, this course's main goal is to show that speaking is more than a matter of knowing words and putting them in order. Linguists have discovered that language is an intricate hierarchy of systems, ever changing in surface appearance but ever consistent in organizational essence.

We begin with sounds, of which any language has many more than what the writing system indicates, often even masked in the process (for example, in terms of sound the default English plural marker is not [s] but [z]). Above this level come not words but morphemes, units of meaning, be this *microphone*, *the*, *-ed* in *walked*, or even *-a-* in *came* versus *come*. Then above this is syntax, which as studied by followers of Noam Chomsky has revolutionized linguistics over the past 40 years. The hypothesis is that there is a single innate grammar configured in our brains, with assorted "on-off" switches (e.g., verb first or verb last). Which switches are on and which are off make the difference between, for example, Japanese and English.

Words are, of course, hardly irrelevant to language, and the study of semantics examines how meaning is managed in its journey from a thought to a sentence. Languages differ vastly, however, in how they translate meaning into words; for instance, what is a subject in English is marked in different ways in other languages, depending on whether the subject does something or just feels something. In the same way, languages differ in how they translate into words a speaker's feelings about the topic or which part a speaker wants to emphasize; linguists call this issue *pragmatics*.

Language always changes; thus Old English is a different language from modern English. We examine how 19th-century linguists first proposed that this change happens according to regular tendencies in how words change and then how this developed into a science that allows us to reconstruct ancient languages that were never written and are no longer spoken. We then examine how grammar itself emerges when concrete words like *mind* become abstract bits meaning *-ly*, such as *-ment* in French or *-mente* in Spanish.

Language change is gradual; languages are passed on to new generations of speakers, who can communicate with the older ones. How children learn languages, in all of their complexity, is much more than simply learning words one at a time. We will also examine how adults learn new languages if they have to and how well they manage the task.

The course also covers how social class, gender, and even race determine differences in how we speak a language and how these differences often even determine how the language changes over time (for example, working-class men are the prime changers of language, not Blue Americans, teenagers, or women). We also encounter a burgeoning area of study showing the various processes that result from widespread bilingualism, such as the simplification of a once more-challenging tongue (English is "easy" for this reason). Also, in a social vein, we discover how conversation is guided by rules we subconsciously internalize and how much of conversation consists of using sentences as commands and requests rather than as statements. We will also see that all of the above also differ vastly according to culture: In Malagasy-speaking villages, for example, one asks someone to wash something by saying that "the soap will be used to wash the clothes," without mentioning who will be wielding the soap.

In the final lectures, we meet founding philosophers of language, such as Ferdinand de Saussure, who pioneered the approach to languages as founded on structured interactions between sounds and morphemes, and Edward Sapir and Benjamin Lee Whorf, who proposed that the particularities of one's language channel the way one thinks. We also examine the tension between linguists, who simply describe the way language is used, and much of the general public, who feel that there are ways that language should and should not be used.

Subsequently, we visit how writing emerged in the Fertile Crescent and the proliferation of writing systems since, then the newly burgeoning study of how language began in the first place. For the following two lectures, you get to be a linguist as I show how linguists actually analyze an unknown language's grammar. The first is a Euro-African hybrid of Suriname, called Saramaccan, and the second is an obscure tongue of the Caucasus Mountains in Russia, called Kabardian. Finally, we will survey some of the leading theories about how the language faculty evolved in our species.

Lecture Nineteen
How Class Defines Speech

Scope: This lecture continues the examination of how social factors affect language use. We will review a study that shows that a syllable-final [d] is omitted by Puerto Rican teenagers not in a random variation but at a stepwise, increasing rate depending on factors of accent on the syllable, surrounding sounds, and whether the morpheme is a grammatical one. Also, we will examine Basil Bernstein's hypothesis that working-class people use a restricted code that hampers educational achievement.

Outline

I. In this lecture, we will visit two classic studies that proposed influential theories of how social factors affect how we express ourselves.

   A. The first looks at how levels of grammar and their interaction can be altered according to social circumstances.

   B. The second looks at how language use in a more general way, on the syntactic level, depends on social factors—and what implications have been drawn from that.

II. There are both linguistic (internal) and social (external) constraints on how we express ourselves.

   A. Walt Wolfram, a linguist at North Carolina State University, has shown that final [d] was deleted by Puerto Rican male adolescents at different rates determined by factors both linguistic and social.

   B. There are three basic contrasts in the environment that [d] can be deleted in:
   1. Before a vowel (*food is*) or consonant (*food smells like*)
   2. In an accented/stressed syllable (*agreed*) or an unaccented/unstressed one (*carried*)
   3. As a grammatical ending (*hassled him*) or as the final consonant on a content word (*Harold makes*).

   C. Rates of deletion depend on the three basic contrasts.
   1. A [d] is deleted less before vowels than consonants.
   2. Before a vowel, it is deleted less in accented (stressed) syllables than unaccented (unstressed) ones:

a. In an accented syllable before a vowel, it is deleted less when it is a grammatical item (like a past-tense marker) than when it is a content word.

b. In an unaccented syllable before a vowel, again, it is deleted less when it is a grammatical item than a content word.

3. The result is a gradation of probabilities, and the gradation continues, with the likelihood of deletion increasing in the realm of [d] followed by consonants:

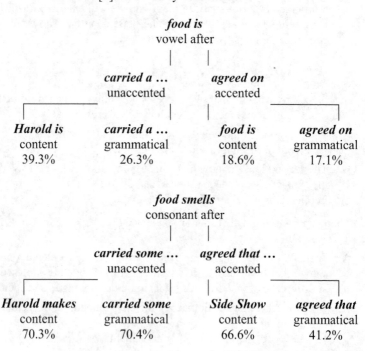

food is
vowel after

carried a ...	*agreed on*
unaccented	accented

Harold is	*carried a ...*	*food is*	*agreed on*
content	grammatical	content	grammatical
39.3%	26.3%	18.6%	17.1%

food smells
consonant after

carried some ...	*agreed that ...*
unaccented	accented

Harold makes	*carried some*	*Side Show*	*agreed that*
content	grammatical	content	grammatical
70.3%	70.4%	66.6%	41.2%

4. This chart shows that the deletion of [d] is not random but patterns on the basis of the content/grammatical distinction, stress (accent), and sound class.

D. These linguistic factors are internal constraints; however, social factors, which are external constraints, also determine deletion rates of [d]. For example, the lower the class of the speakers, the more deletion there is in general.

III. Social factors can influence language on a broader level; the vernacular in a language is not only sounds and endings but also syntax.

    A. British sociologist Basil Bernstein (1924–2000) made a controversial proposal in the 1960s on the topic of how social class may affect how language is structured and what the effects of this might be on children's development.

    B. He proposed that the culture of lower-working-class environments determined the structure of their language (the *Language Deficit hypothesis*), based on the difference between two codes:

        1. *Restricted code*: short, often unfinished sentences; a few conjunctions repetitively; little subordination; dislocated presentation of information; rigid and limited use of adjectives and adverbs; infrequent use of impersonal pronoun subjects; appeals to sympathetic circularity (you know?)—"a language of implicit meaning."

        2. *Elaborated code*: accurate grammatical order and syntax; wide range of conjunction and subordination; wide range of adjectives and adverbs; allows qualification of remarks— "language use which points to the possibilities inherent in a complex conceptual hierarchy for the organizing of experience."

        3. He compared descriptions by a middle-class five-year-old boy and by a working-class one of four pictures showing 1) boys playing soccer, 2) the ball going through a house window, 3) a woman looking out of the window and a man making an ominous gesture, and 4) the children moving away.

        4. The working-class boy's description assumes that the interlocutor knows what he knows and thus uses pronouns where the middle-class boy specifies the referent: *she* versus *the woman* and *there* rather than *window*.

    C. Bernstein argued that the elaborated code conditions broader horizons than the restricted code.

        1. Restricted code serves the purposes of communication within a socially constrained realm of intimates, such as around a dinner table.

        2. Restricted code might interfere with developing a larger perspective on the world and therefore with one's chances of advancement in life.

D. Thus, according to Bernstein, various factors grow out of the distinction between elaborated and restricted codes.

    1. Elaborated code has more room for a difference of opinion that is not an argument, whereas in restricted code the general goal was more toward seeking consensus.

    2. Elaborated code has more toleration of children's questions because the elaborated code encourages you to think broadly, whereas restricted code encourages you to think about the here and the now and perhaps the mundane.

    3. In elaborated code, family roles develop more flexibly, whereas in a family using more restricted code, roles would be more rigidly defined and more basic because the restricted code does not encourage questioning.

E. Bernstein argued that middle-class children master both codes but that working-class children have mostly the restricted code, leading to educational failure, because the elaborate code is used in schools.

F. Various studies suggest that middle-class mothers favor abstract definitions and information-giving strategies, while working-class mothers use more commands, appeal more to maternal or outside authority, or respond with "because I said so."

G. The overlap between the concept of restricted code and vernacular is only partial.

    1. Bernstein observed that it is possible to use relative clauses and passive mood in a vernacular and a less-complex sentence construction in the standard: *The blokes what was crossing the road got knocked down by a car* versus *The gentlemen were crossing the road and a car knocked them down.*

        a. Bernstein's work stimulated others to correct a possible misimpression that vernacular speech must be inarticulate.

        b. For example, William Labov showed in a classic article, "The Logic of Nonstandard English" (in *Language in the Inner City*) that black teens in New York in the 1960s could engage in sophisticated reasoning in restricted code.

    2. Despite speaking in restricted code (features such as *y'know* and unfinished sentences) and heavy vernacular, the conversation can be shown to entail a rational, sequential argument about a larger world.

3. Bernstein's study remains a classic example of an attempt to link social factors with the way language is actually used, and even to draw implications beyond the realm of linguistics proper.

Essential Reading:

Heath, *Ways with Words.*

Supplemental Reading:

Bernstein, *Pedagogy, Symbolic Control and Identity.*

Questions to Consider:

1. It has been said that educated people tend to be more comfortable with open-ended discussions in which participants do not agree with one another, while less-educated people tend, in conversation, to seek agreement. Is this your experience?

2. Basil Bernstein was often accused of dismissing the sophistication of working-class people, while he thought of himself as making a statement about barriers working-class people faced to advancement. Scholars of variation such as Walt Wolfram are sometimes considered by laymen to be apologists for "bad grammar." Have either of these criticisms of this kind of scholarship occurred to you?

Lecture Nineteen—Transcript
How Class Defines Speech

In this lecture, I want to look at how the social world conditions how we use language from the point of view of two classic studies. One of them looks at how levels of grammar and their interaction can be altered according to social circumstances, and then one of them is a matter of pulling the camera back at looking at how language is used in a more general way on the syntactic level, depending on social factors, and what implications have been drawn from that. Part A in this one will be work that has been done showing that the deletion of a final consonant is more complicated and actually more elegant than you might think.

Here's what we might know: We might know that there is a name—Harold—and that if you talk fast, or if you're lazy, or if something, that you might pronounce it as "Harol," and so, "Harol's in the car," "Harol's over there." There's "Harold," and then there's "Harol," so sometimes the [d] falls off. There's more to be said than that, actually. The deletion of a final [d] is conditioned by all sorts of things. There are patterns that you would never suspect just listening to the language going by and thinking, "Hmm, it looks like sometimes people just let the [d] fall off." There is a study by Walt Wolfram, who is a sociolinguist at North Carolina State University, of the deletion of final [d] among Puerto Rican non-female adolescents. He found that it was more complicated than we might think.

In order to get across what he meant, we want to look at our chart here. There are three basic contrasts, in terms of the environment that a [d] can be deleted in. First of all, we can talk about whether it's before a vowel or a consonant. Is the [d] before a vowel, such as in *food is*, or is it before a consonant, such as in *food smells like*? That's one contrast. Then the second of the three contrasts is a matter of what syllable has the accent. For example, are we talking about the [d] occurring in a syllable with the accent as in *agreed*, or are we talking about a syllable in which there is not the accent, and so, for example, *carried*?

A little bit of terminology: I am often in this set saying, "accent," but it's kind of a patch, because linguists call it *stress*. We talk about stress. Stress has nothing to do with how you feel in a traffic jam, but we don't talk about accent. Accent is something different; it's what syllable has the stress. Come along with me, and from now on I'm going to alternate between those two; sometimes I'll give you the accent, but sometimes I'm going to slip and I'm going to use the real term, which is stress. What syllable has the stress? *Agreed* has the stress; *carried* is unstressed.

Then the final context that we want to look at is whether this [d] is on the end of a content word—a concrete word like *Harold*—or whether it's in a grammatical morpheme. So, thinking about the concepts that we've been learning, for example: *Hassled him* is one of these past-tense endings, so that's grammatical. If it's *Harold*, it's just one sound that happens to be final in a content word. You can pick up a Harold and bounce a Harold; it's a concrete thing. Whereas *hassled*, you can't pick that up. You can't pick up a *-ed* in particular; it is a grammatical ending. That means that we're dealing with these three different contexts. What we want to look at is whether we can systematize the difference in terms of how [d] is deleted and when.

Let's look at our chart. We have our vowel after, *food is*, and we have our consonant after, *food smells*. Let's concentrate on vowel after for now. There's a difference between whether when the vowel is after that we're talking about a [d] in a stressed syllable—so *agreed on*—or whether it's in a syllable that's unaccented—so *carried*. Let's look at the one that has the accent stress—See? I'm trying to change you: "stress"—the one that has the stress, so *agreed on*. There are two kinds. There's grammatical, and so *agreed on* is one of those where we're talking about the past-tense ending. What we see is that if we record non-female Puerto Rican adolescents over a long period of time—record everything they say, transcribe it—we find that in terms of the deletion of [d], when we're talking about when there's a vowel after that [d] and it has stress and it's in a grammatical ending, it's very rare that the [d] disappears: only in 17.1 percent of the time. It's hard to imagine somebody saying, "That's something we agree on" and not putting in the [d]; it's odd. On the other hand, when it's a content word, for example, *food is*—food is content; you can bounce it, you can throw it, you can eat it—that is a case where you find that the deletion is actually a little bit more: 18.6. That's not particularly interesting, but nevertheless, the fact is that the number is a little bit bigger. What interests us, though, is pattern. That's what we start to see if we go down the chart (shown in outline section II.C.3).

We're in vowel after: *food is*. We just looked at the stressed case. What about in the unaccented stress—stress, unstressed case—and so *carried*? There's no stress on *-ried*; look at that here. There's the same difference that we have to attend to. Once we have this lack of stress, there are cases where it's grammatical, such as in *carried*. Then there are cases where it's a lack of stress, but it's on a content word, so *Harold is*. The *-old* syllable does not have stress, so we look at that. Here we see something interesting. First of all, in this particular case—when we're in this part of the chart, when we see that we don't have this accent and then we're looking at the grammatical—grammatical is deleted 26.3 percent of the time, as opposed to the 18.6 that we had when we were talking about one with stress where it was a content word. Suddenly there's this jump, and it seems to have something to do—crucially—with stress. The ending tends to go away more when it's not stressed, which is relatively intuitive. But what we wouldn't necessarily expect—if it were just a matter of stress—is that when it's unaccented and it's a content word, suddenly the deletion is 39.3 percent.

It jumps from 26 to 39; remember, we started with just a 17.1. It's much more when it is a content word than when it's grammatical, and it seems that there is a sense. This would have to be unconscious, because it's highly unlikely that these non-female adolescents are running around thinking about this. But it seems that when it's a bit of grammar—when it's something that's going to put something to the past tense—people are less inclined to let it drop than when it's just a matter of saying, "Harold" in a shorter way. Certainly you're not taught that—talk about language acquisition—and certainly those guys bouncing basketballs are not going to be talking about their grammatical endings. Nevertheless, this is the way the language patterns.

All of this is when the vowel is after, but then there are also cases where the consonant is after, so *food smells*. What's interesting is that if we look at the chart here, and we have our four other cases, we can see that in all cases our rates of deletion of [d] are higher than anything that goes on when the vowel is after. Clearly there's a conditioning that's based partly on the fact that it takes a little bit more effort to enunciate consonants in sequence. No matter what's going on—no matter whether we've got the accent or the grammatical versus the content—when the consonant's after, everything is elevated. When we go to the stressed—and so *agreed that*—and we're followed by a consonant; we have our stressed *-eed*, and then we have *th-*: the consonant. Then we have our grammatical versus our content difference: When it's a grammatical ending, it is deleted somewhat less than the content, and so you have 41.2 percent. Nevertheless, that's higher than our bottom level on the chart with *Harold is*, which was 39.3. Then you see in content, and you have 66.6. People are more confident in deleting when it's a content word, such as in *Side Show*. (*Side Show* is the name of a musical, actually, and it's interesting. It's one of these cult hits. It's about

Siamese twins, and I've never understood what was so special about it. The opening number is called "Come Look at the Freaks." I don't really think that's very appropriate. Then the final number has them singing "I Will Never Leave You" to one another. It's kind of obvious, that.) Anyway, so *Side Show*. Then you have the unaccented case. What happens if you have a consonant after, *food smells*, and then you have, instead of the stressed, you have unstressed, so *carried some*, and then followed by a consonant? Here what you get with the grammatical case—and so *carried* (that's a grammatical ending) *some*—is that you've got a deletion rate of 70.4 percent, i.e., most of the time, as opposed to that measly little 17.1 percent that we had in the beginning.

Then we've got a little bit of real life, because when you get down to the bottom of the chart and you have the content, where we would expect there to be an even higher rate of deletion—85 percent or something like that—when you have unaccented, unstressed *Harold* and then followed by a consonant, *makes*, then actually it's 70.3 compared to the 70.4. That's a wrinkle. Generally, when we do studies like this—I say, "we" as if I did it; I had nothing to do with it. Generally, when studies like this are done, you find that the data is never perfect. However, this data is still pretty impressive, because you would never expect this watching these non-female teenage people running around doing what they do. How would you expect this pattern? But what you see is that the deletion of [d] is not random, but it patterns on the basis of the content-grammatical distinction that we've seen and on the basis of what a lot of you think of as accent, but which is really called … and then also sound class. Not something that you would expect. And wait! There's more!

This kind of thing is also conditioned by external constraints. For example, the lower the social class of speaker, it's been found that the higher deletion rate there is in general. Yet these kinds of relationships, in terms of the ranks of the percentages, hold firm. That is [t]/[d] deletion, and there has been a great deal of study of that and analogous cases in sociolinguistics, because something that looks so innocent and random and, frankly, dull at first actually turns out to have a certain kind of underlying beauty. It's kind of analogous to chaos theory. That is that study.

Part B of this lecture is a matter of looking at how social factors might influence language on a broader level. I want to get across in this, partly, that when we talk about the vernacular, we're not only talking about sounds and endings, but we are also talking about syntax; we're talking about the way words are put together. This has been most notoriously analyzed by

Basil Bernstein. Actually, talk about a subtlety of the language: If I say, "This has been analyzed by Basil Bernstein," then that automatically implies that Basil Bernstein is not dead. Whereas, in fact, he is dead, in which case I have to say, "was analyzed by." Did anybody ever teach you that? Nobody ever taught me that. Nevertheless, I just heard that I made a mistake because I realized that Bernstein is not alive. Languages are interesting—there's a subtlety—and that is actually something quite marked about English and European languages, that use of *have*. But that's another story.

Anyway, Basil Bernstein—who died in the year 2000—made a controversial proposal in the 1960s on how social class may affect how language is structured. He proposed that the culture of lower-working-class environments determined the structure of their language, based on the difference between their two *codes*. Bernstein made a difference then between what he called *restricted code* and what he called *elaborated code*. For example, his idea was that elaborated code would be a sentence like *The gentlemen who were crossing the road got knocked down by a car*. Then the restricted-code version of this would be *The guys were crossing the road and a car knocked them down*. The difference between the two sentences is that in the elaborated code you have a relative clause rather than separating the concepts, and so *the gentlemen who were crossing the road* rather than *the gentlemen were crossing the road and a car knocked them down*. Then, in addition to that, you have a use of the passive: *The gentlemen who were crossing the road got knocked down by a car* instead of just saying *the guys were crossing the road and a car knocked them down*.

That wasn't the only difference between elaborated and restricted code; it was a more general notion that the restricted code would be a matter of often short and often unfinished sentences. It would be a way of speaking that used many conjunctions in a repetitive way, especially a lot of *and*. There would not be a whole lot of subordinate clauses—for example, *the gentlemen who were crossing the road*—and things like that, and there would be a dislocated presentation of information in terms of narrative, that a person might be inclined to jump all over the place. In other words, what we might think of as casual speech: That's restricted code. He contrasted that with elaborated code, where you would have what we might call accurate—I would call it more just tidy grammar and syntax, more like writing, there being a way of speaking that is more like writing than another one—that there would be a wide range of conjunctions used, and more subordinate clauses than in the restricted code, and also something which he fashioned as language use which "points to the possibilities inherent in a complex conceptual hierarchy for the organization of experience." That tendency in the way academic prose is written, which had already taken root in the '60s, is truly tragic; that really won't do. What he was saying was that there is a way of talking where you allow that there may be other interpretations of the issue. You're not asserting, but you're presenting what you're saying as one epistemological—to use a kind of word he would have used—one particular take on the situation, the idea being that there are many different ways of looking at things and that there are no easy answers. As opposed to restricted code, where according to his idea you would be more likely to assert, less likely to posit your ideas as equal ones of many in the grand sphere of things.

What did he mean by this? This is what happened when he showed four cards to first a middle-class boy and then a working-class boy. If you feel that these designations sound a little bit stark, it won't surprise you to know that Bernstein was working in Great Britain. These are British boys, and that is a place where class is—or certainly was—something that was more consciously dealt with and felt than in the United States. But there were four cards. One of them showed boys playing soccer—remember that because this is Britain, the soccer does not have that certain middle-class and slightly frou-frou interpretation that it would here; think of them as playing football—but the boys are playing soccer. Then in the second card, the ball goes through a window. Then in the third one, a woman is looking out the window and the man is making some kind of ominous gesture. In the fourth one, the boys are slinking away. A middle-class boy was shown those cards, and then a working-class boy. The middle-class boy described the cards like this: "Three boys were playing football"—i.e., soccer— "Three boys were playing football," in Britain, you know,

> Three boys are playing football and one boy kicks the ball and it goes through the window. The ball breaks the window, and the boys are looking at it, and a man comes out and shouts at them because they've broken the window so they run away, and then that lady looks out of her window and she tells the boys off.

That's what he said. The working-class boy describes it in a different way. This is the full cognition of a human being—I'm sure you can imagine people describing it this way—but it's different from what that middle-class kid just said:

They're playing football and he kicks it and it goes through there, it breaks the window and they're looking at it, and he comes out and shouts at them because they've broken it so they run away, and then she looks out and she tells them off.

That's what he said. All of that was perfectly grammatical English—there's nothing wrong with him—but there's clearly a difference there. The working-class boy is more inclined to use pronouns; he doesn't specify "the woman" and "the three boys." The working-class boy also will just talk about "there," rather than "the window." The working-class boy assumes that the interlocutor knows what he knows. According to Bernstein, this shows that that boy is speaking in what you would call restricted code because it's about the here and the now and the people who he's dealing with, as opposed to positing things in a larger way, like giving a neutral description that anyone could follow. If you look at the middle-class boy's description—or if you listen to it—you can pretty much reconstruct what those cards look like. But the working-class boy's one, that would be a little bit harder. Bernstein called the restricted code "a language of implicit meaning," the idea being that a great deal is assumed.

Incidentally, you should imagine those boys speaking with British accents. I just read them out in American because actually linguists are no better than anybody else at doing accents. It's tough to do a British one because it's very subtly different from the American one; everybody knows what one sounds like. Not too long ago, I made the mistake of winding up in a production of *Arcadia* by Tom Stoppard. I was playing an arrogant British professor, and it was thought that I would be good for the part, spiritually. But I had to use a British accent. Never, never again; that was the most nightmarish experience. But the word *football* would be "footboll." That's my last British accent.

Anyway, Bernstein looked at this kind of difference, and his idea was that the elaborated code conditioned broader horizons than the restricted code. The restricted code was good for talking around the dinner table in your humble home, but that it interfered—if the restricted code was what you were most comfortable with—with developing a larger sense of perspective on the world, and therefore interfered with your chances of advancement in life. As he put it:

> Forms of socialization orient the child towards speech codes which control access to relatively context-tied or context-independent meanings. The linguistic realization of the two orders [i.e.,

restricted and elaborated code] are different, and so are the social relationships which realize them. Elaborated codes are less tied to a given or local structure and take on an autonomy. Restricted codes are more tied to a local social structure and have a reduced potential for a change in principles.

Based on that, Bernstein thought that various factors grew out of the distinction between elaborated and restricted. One thing he said was that in elaborated code there's more room for having a difference of opinion that is not an argument. His idea was that in restricted code the general goal was more seeking consensus. It's interesting: My mother was a child psychologist and a teacher of social work, and she once told me—and I'm not sure why she told me this because I was quite young—but she said that the difference between educated people and uneducated people is that educated people have been opened up to the notion that you can disagree without fighting, whereas uneducated people in conversation seek to always agree. Everybody agrees, and agrees, and that's considered basic social libation. I thought that was interesting, because of course it's a generalization—and she knew that as a social worker—but I suppose she was onto something; it's certainly something worth thinking about.

In any case, this is the difference between elaborated and restricted code in the terminology of Bernstein. His idea was that in elaborated code there's more toleration of children's questions as well, because the elaborated code encourages you to think broadly. Restricted is something that encourages you to think about the here, the now, and perhaps the mundane. His sense was also that in elaborated code people were more flexible in a family in terms of developing their roles, whereas in a family where restricted code is used more, roles would be more rigidly defined and more basic because the restricted code does not encourage questioning.

Bernstein's idea was that middle-class kids master both codes but working-class kids only learn restricted code, for the most part. As a result, they end up being condemned to failure in society just by the kind of language that they are exposed to. Bernstein, I don't think I even need to say, was very controversial. A lot of people thought that he was implying that working-class people only use restricted code and that elaborated code was something that was only available to middle-class kids. But that's not what he was saying, and actually various studies have suggested that middle-class mothers favor abstract definitions and information-giving strategies, while it's more likely of a working-class mother to use commands and to appeal to maternal authority or outside authority—kind of "because I said so," that kind of thing. That's been done in various literatures.

Actually, Bernstein himself observed that the overlap between the concept of restricted code and the vernacular is only partial. For example, we had our sentence: *The gentlemen who were crossing the road were hit by a car.* He noted that you can actually say, "The blokes what was crossing the road got knocked down by a car." Here is vernacular speech that's using the passive and it's using the relative clause. On the other hand, in what is what you would call the elaborated code—the standard language—you can say, "The gentlemen were crossing the road and a car knocked them down," where you undo the relative clause and the passive.

More to the point, Bernstein's work did stimulate people to give a corrective—or to direct people away from a possible misimpression—that what he was saying was that vernacular speech must be inarticulate. That is definitely a case which is worth showing. For example, William Labov showed in a classic article called "The Logic of Non-Standard English" that black teens in New York could engage in sophisticated reasoning in what was definitely restricted code. For example, here is a quotation. This is a kind of joshing conversation about the existence of God, and so this is in the 1960s in New York. I'll read it as best I can.

> Your spirit goin' to hell anyway, good or bad. … 'Cause, you see, doesn't nobody really know it's a God, y'know, 'cause I mean I have seen black gods, pink gods, white gods, all color gods, and don't nobody know it's really a God. An' when they be sayin' if you good, you goin' t'heaven, tha's [expletive], 'cause you ain't goin' to no heaven, 'cause it ain't no heaven for you to go to.

That's what he said. This is heavy restricted code. Lots of "and," for example; lots of short sentences strung together. In terms of subordination, it's there, but not as much as it would be if he were speaking in a more formal way. This was definitely spoken in a context of strong peer-group feeling. That was not meant to be read by starchy me 40 years later in some recording studio; he was just saying it. Bill Labov was good enough at eliciting the vernacular that he actually got these people to talk that way around him, despite the fact that he was an educated and wiry, very white man. This was here.

What's interesting is that we listen—or at least many of us will listen—to the restricted-code cast of this or the vernacular cast of this, and you've got the *ain't*'s and you've got the dropped *g*'s from the *-ing*'s—although again really he's just using a different consonant—and so on. Then you've got also the "boop-boop," and you think, "Well, how persuasive can this speech be? How much of a case can you make when you talk that way?" But it's interesting to realize that a person can be making an exquisitely reasoned case despite the clothing that their speech wears and despite the fact that they might tend to use short sentences strung together.

For example, Labov showed that if you actually look at this guy's statement, then you find that what he's actually saying is, "Everyone has a different idea of what God is like"—that's your first proposition— "Therefore, nobody really knows that God exists. If there's a heaven, it was made by God. If God doesn't exist, he couldn't have made heaven, therefore heaven doesn't exist. You can't go somewhere that doesn't exist; therefore, you can't go to heaven, and therefore you are going to hell." There were lots of *ergo*'s, and there was a lot of reflection in what this person said, despite the fact that he was speaking in restricted code. You could even say that, despite the fact that he was speaking in restricted code and heavy vernacular, that there was definitely a sense of the larger world in what this person was saying. They weren't talking about playing marbles on the pavement that day. They weren't talking about playing the lottery. They were talking about larger issues. They were philosophizing in restricted code.

I think that the general agreement these days is that Bernstein was certainly onto something, but in general one must be very careful in terms of seeing these categories as black and white, so to speak. In any case, Bernstein's study remains a classic example of an attempt to link social factors with the way language is actually used and even to draw implications from it beyond the realm of linguistics proper.

Now we're going to move on to a lecture where we show how a variable will become the language of tomorrow.

Lecture Twenty
Speaking Differently, Changing the Language

Scope: Variation is the source of what can eventually become a new single option; variation, that is, is often a sign that an aspect of the language is changing from one state to another. The working class is the source of most change in a language, as they are less constrained by prescriptive norms and maintain new variants as in-group markers. This process was first discovered through a study of a change in two vowels in the speech of people of a particular age group and social class on Martha's Vineyard.

Outline

I. We have seen that language changes, but only in the broad view. In fact, when we view how language changes from closer in, we see that change happens according to sociological factors.

   A. Namely, working-class speakers are the ones who change language: The vernacular forms are the ones that become the language of the future.

   B. The study of variation is not simply a matter of describing a language in its current form but of zeroing in on processes of change.

   C. Previous perspectives on change attributed change to other, less fine-grained factors.

      1. Imitation of the upper classes seemed intuitively to be a source of change; however, the notion that poor people want to be as much like rich people as possible in their speech has not been scientifically shown.

      2. Principle of least effort does explain some changes; however, looking to whatever is easiest to say doesn't explain different ways of pronouncing *raw* or *singing*.

      3. Free variation was often thought to be the only explanation. For example, the difference between *He's not ready* and *He isn't ready* stays an indicator and seems a mere wrinkle, without any particular meaning.

II. William Labov's study of Martha's Vineyard showed that some variation is not merely static.

  A. Labov noted how people on Martha's Vineyard said, "house" ([haws]) and "light" ([lajt]) differed, with some people saying [həws] and [ləjt].

	standard	Martha's Vineyard
house	[haws]	[həws]
light	[lajt]	[ləjt]

  1. This is schwa plus a glide sound.
  2. Looking at the sound chart, you can see that sounds at the bottom, diphthongs with low vowels, have been raised.

  B. Labov wanted to figure out whether or not there was a *change in progress*.

  1. The most direct method would be to check a population at separate times (unwieldy).
  2. Another method is to rely on historical data.

  C. Labov noted the raising of the first vowel in the diphthongs [aw] (*out, house*) and [aj] (*while, light*) to schwa (*light* becomes [ləjt] instead of [lajt]) was most common in people who fished for a living, lived on the "native" Western side of the island, and were 31 to 45 years old.

  1. The raising had been a vanishing feature in the 1930s, according to the *Linguistic Atlas of New England.*
  2. However, a few decades later the raising seemed to have returned.

  D. Because of the invasion of summer residents, natives were signaling their identification with the island through their speech. This was reinforced by the fact that the variant was more common among people who indicated solidarity with the island: Younger people differed depending on how they felt about the island.

  E. That was how an indicator became a marker: What looked like just a wrinkle or an archaism was the beginning of a change.

III. Working-class people are the leaders in changing speech.

   A. Change was previously thought originate in the upper classes. However, studies have shown that it actually tends to originate in the (upper) working class.

   B. In fact, change never originates in prestige dialects, because prestige speakers resist natural changes because of education and a sense that one is supposed to talk as much like the printed page as possible.

   C. Why the working class?

      1. *Overt* versus *covert prestige*: These groups do not follow the upper classes because there is a covert prestige to their variants, reinforced by involvement in a community.

      2. Linguist Lesley Milroy of the University of Michigan documented that social networks can be *dense* (people interacting largely with one another) or *loose* (social networks extending to all sorts of acquaintances).

      3. Dense networks reinforce vernacular norms.

      4. The middle class has looser networks than the working class.

IV. Labov has taught us that change works in terms of a pair of processes that interact: There's change from below, and then there's change from above.

   A. *Change from below* begins when a variable from an initially distinct sub-subgroup, now irregularly distributed, generalizes to become an *indicator* (for example, [əj] at the time of summer visitors' arrival).

      1. After becoming established in the community, the variable becomes subconsciously perceived as "the way we talk around here" and becomes a *marker*.

      2. The change affects other elements in the grammar ([əw] in Martha's Vineyard was modeled on [əj]).

   B. If the form acquires a stigmatized connotation, this initiates *change from above*.

      1. The variant is suppressed in favor of the prestige model, in accordance with social factors.

      2. If the variant becomes a topic of overt social comment, it becomes a stereotype and may decline (like r-less dialect in New York).

C. However, if the variant does not become stigmatized, it becomes entrenched in the language and instantiates a change.

    1. For example, as late as the 1700s, it was considered "proper" to pronounce the *-ed* in participles like *rebuked* as [ɪd].

    2. In 1712, Jonathan Swift called the pronunciation [rəbjukd] a "barbarous custom of abbreviating words."

    3. However, this pronunciation did not submit to change from above and is now the only way to pronounce the participial ending, except in archaic forms like "blessèd be thy name."

D. Change from above happens most in cultures where there is widespread literacy, as well as writing—only about 200 out of the world's 6,000 or so languages.

V. Language changes happen in a wave. If percentage change is graphed over time, it will look like an S-curve.

A. A change in vocabulary starts with a few items, spreads rapidly to most, and then makes its way through the remaining few. The process is called *lexical diffusion*.

B. Change in sounds shows the same pattern.

    1. In the '70s, a change from [ʊ] to [ʌ] was underway in Belfast: 74 percent of speakers pronounced *pull* as [pʌl], 39 percent pronounced *put* as [pʌt], and only 8 percent pronounced *should* as [ʃʌd].

    2. This showed that the new sound had established itself in *pull*, was only at the halfway point with *put*, and was slowly percolating further as represented by *should*.

C. Other languages show the same pattern: Among Persian speakers, vowel assimilation in imperative verb forms has progressed in implicational fashion.

    1. The process involves the initial of two vowels in an imperative form assimilating to the second one.

    2. In Persian, an imperative or command uses the morpheme /be/. The word *Do!* is /bekon/ on the phonemic level; however, the phonetic form has vowel assimilation, in which one vowel becomes like the other one, and ends up as [bokon].

3. Some speakers never do this at all. Some only do it with the "gateway" word *do*. Some do it with only *do* and *run*. Some very few do it with a range of others.

/bekon/	/bedo/	/bexan/	/begu/	/bekub/	/bebor/
do!	run!	read!	tell!	hit!	cut!
A					
B +					
C +	+				
D +	+	+			
E +	+	+	+		
F +	+	+	+	+	
G +	+	+	+	+	+

4. However, the relationship is implicational: No one only does it with *cut*, and if you hear someone assimilate in the *tell* verb, you can know they also do it with *do*, *run*, and *read*.

VI. Sociolinguists have seen during the 40-year existence of their field that not all variation is a sign of change, but all change happens first as a result of variation.

A. In an Edith Wharton novel, the past tense of *dive* would be *dived*, but today *dove* is more common; this is an indicator, with no social significance, yet it can nevertheless create language change.

B. When you have a marker, with a social meaning connected to it, that marker will—if the language is left to go on about its business—become the language of tomorrow.

Essential Reading:

Wolfram and Schilling-Estes, *Hoi Toide on the Outer Banks.*

Supplemental Reading:

Fasold, *The Sociolinguistics of Language.*

Questions to Consider:

1. We hear often about younger Americans using *like* to qualify their statements much more than was once the case. Is this, do you suppose, a trait typical of the young (age graded), or will older people be using *like* in this way 50 years from now, having internalized it as young people (i.e., is it a *change in progress*)?

2. What do you make of the following observation? One exception to the general rule that change in language comes "from below" involves the stigmatization of *Billy and me went to the store* instead of *Billy and I went to the store*. The *I* construction has been so well internalized by so many English speakers that, although it must be explicitly taught, it could be considered to have become an actual construction in the spoken English language. This would be an example of change coming from above—the prestige variant winning out. However, there is no other externally imposed rule of this kind that has had such success (*fewer books* instead of *less books*, etc.).

Lecture Twenty—Transcript
Speaking Differently, Changing the Language

What I wanted to show in the last lecture is that the study of variation can be applied to figuring out some interesting things about how we speak language from day to day and how social factors influence it. Then I wanted to look at how variation in a broader way, on the level of syntax, can be shown to be linked to larger social factors. Now I want to return to the question that I have hinted at, which is whether or not the vernacular is the source of what language will be like tomorrow.

The way I want to set this up is to say that we looked at how language changes, we looked at historical linguistics, but that was actually, technically speaking, a very broad view. We talked about grammaticalization, we showed how sounds changed in Polynesian and so on, but all of that made it seem as if all of these changes took place at the same time among all speakers of the language, as if somehow these things happen in lock step. Whereas in fact, if we had been able to see these processes of change close up, we would have seen that there were social correlates to what happened. It wasn't just that *going to* started meaning the future—started becoming a future-tense marker—just among everybody at the same rate at the same time. If we could go back to that era with sampling tools and a microphone, we'd surely find that there was more to it than that. Variation study is not only about studying variation currently. As often as not, variation study is about trying to get a sense of what the past or the future of the language is.

A lot of the study of language variation is the study of change. It used to be that change was seen as something much less fine grained. There were many linguists, especially in a more classist America than the one that we've been familiar with since the '60s—of course, America's always been a place where we talked about class rather reluctantly—but nevertheless there was a more delineated sense of levels of society back in the day before we all kind of went informal. Back in the day, a linguist might sit smoking on a pipe and actually say with a straight face that how language changes is that poor people imitate upper-class people. I suppose that seemed vaguely intuitive. There was a notion that poor people wanted to be as much like rich people as possible, so why wouldn't that follow in speech?

But, in fact, scientifically speaking no such thing has been shown. Or it was thought that language changes because of the principle of least effort—whatever is easiest to say. Everything gets kind of run together. There is some point to that. As we've seen, sound change partly involves things becoming easier to say. We saw how the final [d] among our teenagers is deleted more when it's followed by a consonant because consonant clusters can be difficult to pronounce compared to a consonant alone. But that really couldn't be all of it. For example, if you're looking at the difference between [rɔ] at one point in time and then [ra] as a lot of American English speakers started saying at another point in time, is that a matter of a lazy mouth? Or is it really just two different vowels? Or, for example, the difference between *singing* and *singin'*: Is it really so much easier to use your alveolar nasal than your velar nasal? It's the spelling that makes it look like a letter's been dropped, but actually it's just two different equivalent things. Principle of least effort can only take you so far.

It was also often thought that all there was to say about variation was that it was free. You can have something like *He's not ready*, where you contract the *he* and the *is*, versus *He isn't ready*, where you contract the *is* and the *not*. That's just a little wrinkle, as we've seen. It doesn't really seem to be going anywhere, to have any particular meaning. It was thought that pretty much variation was just that; there were more interesting things to look at.

The fact of the matter is that some variation is static, just like the *He's not ready* and *He isn't ready*. Some, however, isn't. It was again William—or as I can say Bill—Labov who discovered this in another one of his classic studies: his study of what was happening on Martha's Vineyard several decades ago. What he was noticing was that if you were in Martha's Vineyard, then you found that there were people who said, "house," and then there were people who said something more like, "hohse." We don't just think of that as a funny way of saying, "house" or the wrong way of saying, "house"; it's just a different vowel. It was, in fact: You can transcribe it as a schwa; and so you see it here. Instead of [haws], [həws]. That was kind of an accent. Some people, instead of saying, "light" ([lajt]) would say, [ləjt]. I don't mean just in those words; I mean that wherever you had that [aw] sound it would come out as [əw]; wherever you had the [aj] sound it would come out as [əj]; and so a dog would [bəjt] you.

There are two things to notice about this: For one thing, what we're seeing is that in one case we've got our schwa plus a "wuh" sound, and then we've got our schwa plus a "yuh" sound. In terms of the sound classes that we're now familiar with, we can see that this isn't just random. What it is, is a schwa plus two things that have something in common: They're both glides. As a matter of fact, they are the glides of English; it's schwa plus glide. That's the way that I think of it in my head, not schwa plus *w* and schwa plus "yuh"; it's schwa plus glide. Also, I could put it as we have [aw] changing into [əw] and the thing where the [əj] comes from the [aj]. But really, if you think about the sound chart, what we're seeing is that the sound [a]—or if the way you really pronounce it is "house," which is the way I pronounce it, and so [a]—those sounds are down at the bottom; those are low vowels, where the [ə], among other things, is higher than them. The way that we would refer to this is that these schwa-plus-glide diphthongs have been raised; it's the raising of diphthongs. That's just some shorthand. I can say that now, and you can know what I mean. There's this raising of these diphthongs in the speech of some people on Martha's Vineyard.

What Labov decided to figure out was whether or not there was a change in progress going on based on this vowel change that he was seeing. How do you figure that kind of thing out? The most direct way of figuring it out, of course, would be to go somewhere at point A and then go somewhere at point B like 40 or 50 years later, after two generations plus have gone by. For obvious reasons, that is rarely the method that is used in trying to figure out whether there is a change in progress going on in the speech of a particular location. Another thing you can do is you can look at historical data if you are lucky enough to be working somewhere where there is any. Labov did that, and he looked at the *Linguistic Atlas of New England*. What he found was that this raising of the diphthong was something that had not been foreign to speech in Martha's Vineyard in the 1930s, but by then it was holding on by a thread. It was something from the past—and it was something some people did, some people didn't—but it was something that was receding from the language. This was something that was on its way out; it was an *archaism*. Whereas here Labov was a few decades later, and people were just [əws]ing and [əjt]ing all over the island. Not everybody, though, but enough people that it seemed to be that something was going on.

He looked more closely. He did sociolinguistic interviews—as we've seen—and he noticed that the people who were saying [həws] instead of [haws] and [ləjt] instead [lajt] weren't just anybody. It wasn't just Mrs. Tinsley up the road with her 17 cats, and then Jake the 14-year-old with the square jaw, and then old Zeke the fisherman over here. It wasn't a random distribution. It was people who were in their 30s and early 40s—not late 40s, but early 40s. These were people who were of that age, and there was something else about them: When you talked to them, you found that they were people who had a particular solidarity with the island. That was something which was really important at this time, because this was the era when summer residents had started invading Martha's Vineyard. As soon as I say Martha's Vineyard, I think naturally most of us think about people going for the summer and having good times, but of course the island was inhabited before then, and it was by a contingent of mostly working-class people. There was a certain resentment of the change of the character of the island with all of these often rich people—where there are certain social barriers between them and these tourists—coming and changing the character of things, and changing the economy, and giving people a sense of the outside, which meant that some people were leaving the island in larger numbers than they had been before. There was a contingent of people in their 30s and early 40s who had a choice: Either they could leave the island and join the world beyond Martha's Vineyard, and therefore become history on the island, or you could stay even though your existence would probably be relatively modest, but when you stayed you knew who you were and you were keeping the local community of Martha's Vineyard—the original indigenous community—alive.

What he also found was that younger people than being in their 30s were not as uniform in displaying this raising as the people in their 30s and early 40s were but that you could tell whether or not somebody who was, say, 17 was going to say [həws] or [ləjt] depending on how they felt about the island. If they were just itching to get off of the island: [haws] and [lajt]. If they were the kind of person who was going to stay, then [həws] and [ləjt]. What's interesting is that this is subconscious; certainly nobody was walking around shaping their diphthongs to fit their social identity. But part of speaking—part of shaping your vowels subconsciously—was doing this raising of glide diphthongs on this island at this point in time. This was an indication that the following thing had happened: Way back in the day, this raising of diphthongs in Martha's Vineyard had been an indicator. Some people had done it; some people hadn't. It didn't look particularly interesting; probably some people did it beyond Martha's Vineyard, too. It was just there. Indicators can spread and hold on fast, kind of like the [dʒan], [ʃan], [dan], [ran] vowel. Or indicators can just kind of flutter away, and that one seemed to be the kind that was just going to go away. But then there was an intervening factor, which was this influx of summer visitors. As a result—and this was a subconscious process, but as a result—there arose a sense that there was a way of speaking that was indigenous to Martha's Vineyard. Certainly the people themselves on the conscious level would refer to a few terms, just like Rhode Islanders will commonly refer to *bubbler* for *water fountain* and other things. But that's the folk conception of language being just a big basket of words, which is understandable.

Something else that people did—which certainly they did not discuss fondly when talking to outsiders—was that they raised these glide diphthongs in their speech, so that words like *house* were pronounced [hǝws] and words like *light* were pronounced [lǝjt]. This was something that would have been done below the conscious level, but as such it was no longer an indicator, this variable; this was now a marker, because it had a social significance. If you say [hǝws], you're one of us. You're one of the people on the island doing what we do, and you're not going to leave. If you say [haws], you're one of the visitors, or you're somebody who's probably going to go off and go to college and wind up in some split-level in Lenox, Massachusetts, drinking yourself to death—something like that.

That was how an indicator became a marker, and it spread. It wasn't just a matter of something that happened for a few summers: It took hold among the entire young-adult population of people who had an allegiance to the island. Because, of course, people who left the island therefore were no longer part of the island; that was a change that happened in this microcosm of American speech. We had that raising happen. It's something that was created by working-class people. It wasn't created by the summer visitors; it wasn't created by whatever local elite there was on Martha's Vineyard. This raising was something that happened as a marker of vernacular working-class—even underdog—identity. The fact of the matter is that is the usual case in how a change takes place in a language's structure. It was previously thought that it was the upper classes who took the lead, but in fact that is almost impossible. Finding a change in a language that was driven by successful people is quite rare. That's because, especially in a literate Western society, prestige speakers—people who are middle class, upper middle class, or wealthy—generally have a sense that you are supposed to resist changes in the language. There's always the sense that we're supposed to talk as much like the printed page as possible.

For example—to take a very innocent little wrinkle—there's a word, and this time we need the spelling: It's spelled *o-f-t-e-n*. It's spelled that way because there was a time when everybody said [ɔftǝn], because it's a derivate of a word *oft*, which is now for us just poetic. At least, I don't use the word *oft*. But it used to be *oft-ten*. Now the word has evolved. When consonants come together, often one of them falls away; we've seen that. You could look at the word *often* and you could almost know that as time goes by, just like *capicola* is going to become "gabbagool" in nonstandard Italian, [ɔftən] is going to become [ɔfən]. People vary; many of you probably say [ɔftən]. The world will keep spinning, but in that, you're holding back the language from changing. There's a sense that it's not supposed to do what it would normally do. You're putting a spoke in the bicycle wheel, because really, it wants to be [ɔfən] because that's what languages do. For example, there's another word: *c-l-o-t-h-e-s*. The way that I pronounce that word in terms of IPA is [kloz]. The word is [kloz]. It's very similar to what you do to a door if you're not opening it. You open it, you [kloz] it, and you wear [kloz]. It's as simple as that. I know people who say, "clothesss" and kind of stick in the *-thes* sound. I can see why, because you have that thing on the page, but the truth is you probably have to be taught to do it, or you make yourself stick that voiced interdental fricative in there—[kloðz]—when really, we don't even think of them as cloths anymore. It's probably occurred to you that you're donning your body with cloths, but we don't think about that very much. Just like the word *sloth* comes from "slowth." That's what it is—I just told you that—but you don't think about it. I personally don't put on my clothes thinking, "I'm putting textiles—cloths—on me." I don't think most of us do, yet *-thes*: [kloðz]. That's because people who are middle class and/or literate and/or educated tend to retard change.

It's different in the working class. In the working class, of course, there's overt prestige; we've seen how that can work in terms of the hypercorrection that a person might display when they are asked to read a word list of words that have minutely contrasting sounds. There's a sense of what "proper language" is. But then there's covert prestige. There is a sense that "the way we talk around here"—the way we raise our diphthongs or whatever—is us, and we're OK. The contrast between that and the way the high muckety-muck speak is actually something that we're rather proud of; we don't want to get rid of that. We saw how that kind of covert prestige became attached to that raising of diphthongs on Martha's Vineyard. A lot of time has gone by since that study. I think that today, in the America that we live in, the most vibrant example of covert prestige attaching to a nonstandard variety is—you know what I'm going to say—what is now unfortunately known as "Ebonics." (I prefer "Black English.") In terms of the wonderful influence that, for example, hip-hop slang—or at least some hip-hop slang—has had on the way relatively young people use English in the country today, I think it's painfully obvious to see that nobody who is fluent in that dialect is thinking that there's anything wrong with it compared to the standard English that one is being taught in school. There is a pride in the dialect; nobody is ashamed. There is almost a sense that it would be better to talk that way than to talk the way the Olsen twins talk— not that I've ever met them. There is a covert prestige.

There is work by Lesley Milroy at the University of Michigan that documents that social networks among people can be either dense or loose. There can be people who interact largely with one another and have relatively little interaction with the outside world, and then there are people whose social networks extend to all sorts of acquaintances and formal relationships. In terms of where their relationships are dense, that really might not extend that much further than beyond their home and/or some of their extended family. The fact is that covert prestige is more likely to emerge when groups are relatively dense and tight and there's all the interaction with one another. The interaction with one another is the norm, and then outside is seen as something different and—because we're all human beings—even maybe relatively threatening, certainly alien, certainly nothing that we would want to imitate in our moments of comfort. The middle class often has looser networks than, for example, what we would call in sociolinguistic study the working class.

Labov has taught us that change works in terms of a pair of processes that interact. There's change from below, and then there's change from above. On Martha's Vineyard, there is this raising of diphthongs that arises randomly. Some people do it; some don't. It's just an indicator. Then it becomes processed as the way we talk around here, and it becomes a marker. As it happened, actually it was originally the schwa plus [j] that happened. The first kinds of words were ones like [lɘjt], [bɘjt], and [fɘjt]. Then, because if you're dealing with one glide there's a sense that to make things tidy—analogy: remember that?—to make things tidy, you might want to go to the other glide. Then came the ones with the *w* sound, so [hɘws], [mɘws], and things like that. This new marker established itself even more because it applied to more words—because now it applied to [ɔw] as well as to [ɘj]. That is the first stage.

At this point, two things can happen. One thing that can happen is that there is a countervailing change from above. In the change from above, this nonstandard variant is suppressed in favor of the prestige model. We saw how that happened with r-less dialect in New York. That became stigmatized after World War II, this business of leaving out the [r]'s and saying, "drivah, drivah," instead of, "driver, driver." As a result, something that was a very natural process—and we've seen how final sounds tend to erode, and I didn't mention it to you, but just like [h] is a sound that gets beat up a lot, so are liquids, and in particular [r]—if you see an [r] that's final after a vowel, you know that stuff is going to start happening to the [r]; it's going to melt into the vowel and make the vowel something different. It's going to fall off. In terms of a language where there are words like *corner*, just like *capicola* is going to become "gabbagool," you know it's going to become something like "cawnah" after a while. That was natural. Of course, it started as something that people who were not attending to prestige did, and so it was a working-class variant. It was doing pretty well, but there's this countervailing process which stereotyped it, and as a result it started declining. Now the number of people in New York who speak pure r-less dialect is shrinking all the time. I am not sure I've ever heard anyone use that dialect under 20 in New York, for example. I could be wrong; I haven't studied it, but it's nothing like it was in the old days.

On the other hand, if the variant does not become stigmatized, then it becomes entrenched in the language. For example, you can read Jonathan Swift in 1712 in all seriousness claiming that if somebody says, "rebuked" ([rəbjukd]) instead of "rebuk-ed" ([rəbjukɪd]) that it's a barbarous custom of abbreviating words. He really means that. That's 1712, which is really only about 10 minutes ago, if you think about it. That means that he saw what he considered lowly people using this barbarous custom and he, as a person of means and influence, would never do such a thing. But, clearly, now we're all barbarous. It's spread, and now we just have archaisms like "blessèd be thy name," but nobody would say, "rebuk-ed." That's because the change came from below—it was not stigmatized—and then it became part of the language.

Change from above happens most in cultures where there is widespread literacy as well as writing. But that is, of course, only about 200 out of the world's 6,000 or so languages. The vast majority of the world's languages are not written; they're just spoken; they're just mouthfuls of air. To see them written on the page is either never or seen as almost comical or peculiar because they're just spoken. Especially if you are a monolingual Anglophone brought up in the United States—in terms of what you were brought up speaking—like me, it can be hard to imagine what it would be like to speak a language that you did not have any written representation for. But that's how most languages are spoken, and so change just happens. It starts small, and it's initially processed as, "Well, some people do that." Then, if you check up on the language 500 years later, that's the way everybody does it. That's how language changes.

Generally, the changes that you see in a language do not happen overnight throughout that module of the language. We saw how with the raising of the diphthong, first it was [əj] and then it spread to [ɔw]; it spread through the language. That is something that we often see. As a matter of fact, it happens in a wave. It happens first slowly; it happens to a few—you'll see for example a sound change in a few words—then there'll be this big flood and it will take care of most of the words in which it could appear, but not all of them; it will go up to like 80 percent. Then slowly it will close it up, and it will occur in every single word that it possibly could. You see a kind of an S-curve—and that's what this chart is—and that's how what's called *lexical diffusion* happens.

For example, in Belfast in some decades ago, there was a change from the [ʊ] sound to the [ʌ] sound. We think of them as different kinds of *u*'s, but now we know from the IPA that they're different sounds: phonemes. You can *put* something; that means that you've placed it somewhere. But if you *putt*, that's obviously something different. But the vowel was changing. In the '70s, 74 percent of speakers were pronouncing *pull* as [pʌl], but 74 percent of speakers were not pronouncing *put* as [pʌt]; only 39 percent were. Then only 8 percent were pronouncing *should* as [ʃʌd] This change was proceeding slowly. Or, in the same way, there was something interesting that happened in Persian. In Persian, to make an imperative—in order to make a command—you use the morpheme; it's spelled *b-e*, and so *be*. For example, if you want to tell someone to do something, then you say /bekon/. The /be/ is the imperative morpheme, and /kon/ is the *do* form. There's the phonemic level, which is /bekon/; then, for a lot of people, on the phonetic level, the surface form has vowel assimilation. What that means is that one vowel becomes like the other one. In this case, the imperative morpheme's vowel—/e/—ends up becoming like the vowel of the verb that it comes after. So instead of saying [bekon]—although that was in your head—you say [bokon]. You have two [o]'s; that's how you might say, "Do!"

What's interesting is that at a given point in time you could look at Persian and you could see that there were some people who never did this at all. They kept their /be/ nice and neat on all their verbs. There's no such thing as going [bokon] because there's an /o/ in the next syllable. They did not do that at all. Then there were some speakers who did it with the verb for *do*. They would say instead of [bekon], [bokon]; but then everywhere else their imperatives would just have a nice [be]. Then if you kind of trolled around and did sociolinguistic interviews, you could also see that there were people who did it with both *do* and with the verb *run*. The verb *run, do!* You could say, "Run, little Jimmy!"—except his name would be "Run, little Farouk!"—and so /bedo/, but you'd actually say [bodo], because you have that /o/ following. Then you had some people who did it with *do* and *run*, and then they also did it with the verb *read*; and so, "Read, little Mahmud." Instead of [bexan], it would be [baxan]; and so you have this assimilation. It went like that.

The thing is, if you ever heard anybody say [baxan], then they also did it with *run* and with *do*; there's no such thing as somebody who did it with *do* and who did it with *read*. Or, in other words, it was another one of these implicational hierarchies, and it went all the way out to the verb *cut*. Some people actually did it with six different verbs, and the most extreme would be people where when they said, "cut," they wouldn't say [bebor]; they'd say [bobor]. But there's no such thing as just chaos. It's not that some people do it with some verbs and some people do it with others; rather, what you could see in looking at the distribution is that this change—this vowel assimilation in these Persian imperatives—began with the verb *do*. Then people started hearing a pattern and it started spreading to other words, but it spread to the other words in a certain order. You might do three, you might do five, you might do six; but with everybody, if it's five, it's always the same five verbs. These sorts of things happen in a systematic way.

What we've seen, and what sociolinguists have seen, in about the 40-year existence of the field is that not all variation is a sign of change, but the fact is that all change happens first as a result of variation. Some things just stay indicators and they're just little fluttering, free-variation matters of choice. Sometimes, though, an indicator can develop into something that really takes over. For example, the verb *dive*: If you were in an Edith Wharton novel, you would probably think that the past tense of *dive* is *dived*. I think most of us today—I know most of us today—have the past tense of *dive* as *dove*; that is particularly in the North. There's no social significance. Nobody listens to someone say, "dove" and thinks, "Don't invite him over, we're his betters." But it's just an indicator. Nevertheless, that one has created some change. But certainly when you have got a marker and there's a social meaning connected to it, you will find that the kind of social meaning that it has to the working classes is such that if the language is left to go on about its business, that will become the language of tomorrow. That was something that was discovered in a clear way by William Labov working on Martha's Vineyard.

Lecture Twenty-One
Language and Gender

Scope: Gender has a significant affect on how we speak. In many languages, the sheer choice of what word endings we use depends on whether we are men or women. Studies have also shown that women tend to speak more "properly" than men, using the prestigious or "standard" alternatives of variables, worldwide— likely out of a drive to express legitimacy through speech, which men feel less need for because of their historical status as breadwinners. Men also dominate women in taking the floor conversationally.

Outline

I. Men and women, in all societies, use language differently.

    A. This includes not only how people of different genders converse but, in many languages, even which grammatical forms they use.

    B. A truly complete description of a language—or language in general—must include the fact that the language of men and the language of women are different in many ways.

II. Gender differences in language exist at the structural level, and there are more differences than we might imagine from English.

    A. Gender of the speaker can determine form.

        1. In Russian, the past-tense verb ending differs according to the gender of the speaker. For example, "I knew" for men is *ja znal*, but for women it is *ja znala*.

        2. In many languages, these differences are more elaborate. According to research by Mary Haas, in the Koasati Native American language of Louisiana, the entire conjugation is different depending on the gender of the speaker:

	men	women
I am saying	*ka:hás*	*ka:hâl*
you are saying	*i:sks*	*i:sk*
he is saying	*ká:s*	*ka:*

B. Gender of the addressee can determine form.

    1. In Hebrew, gender of the speaker determines the form of the first-person singular when speaking in the present, such as "I love." However, in the past, the gender of the addressee often determines the ending; for example, "you loved" addressed to a man is *ahavta* but addressed to a woman is *ahavt*.

    2. But again, this differentiation is more elaborate elsewhere. We know from Francis Ekka that in a language of India called Kurux, endings differ according to whether a man is addressing a woman, a woman is addressing a woman, or either a man or a woman is addressing a man!

	woman to woman	man to woman	anyone to man
you come	*bardin*	*bardi*	*barday*
you came	*barckin*	*barcki*	*barckay*

III. Foundation of the study of language and gender is fairly recent.

    A. University of California, Berkeley linguist Robin Lakoff's classic book *Language and Women's Place*, published in the early 1970s, argued that women's identities are submerged because they are encouraged to use expressions that connote triviality and uncertainty and are discouraged from using strong expression.

    B. Her argument included a variety of examples.

        1. Women are encouraged to use adjectives that are subjective rather than neutral, such as *adorable* and *charming*. Neutral adjectives like *terrific* and *great* connote de facto, rather than subjectively determined, importance.

        2. Women use more tag questions: *Aren't they? Isn't it?*

        3. Women use softer *directives* (request forms) than men.

        4. Women use more question intonation in statements: Husband asks, "When's dinner?" Wife answers, "Six o'clock?"

    C. Lakoff's paradigm had problems.

        1. Lakoff's observations apply to America before the feminist revolution and thus are now dated.

        2. Data was introspective rather than collected in a survey.

        3. However, her observations stimulated the now-thriving field of language and gender study.

IV. Since Lakoff's work, sociolinguistic gender patterns have been found through scientific research.

    A. It has been resoundingly confirmed in various studies over the decades that there is a strong tendency for men to use socially disfavored forms—the more colloquial, vernacular, and even stigmatized ones—more than women.

        1. For example, University of Sydney linguist Barbara Horvath noted that among William Labov's interviewees, men were much more likely to use [d] instead of [ð], regardless of class.

        2. Similar patterns have been found in Detroit; Montreal; Norwich, England; Belfast; and elsewhere.

    B. This is reflected in the differences between male and female grammatical forms in other languages as well.

        1. In Japanese, women are more likely to say, "*watashi*" for *I*, while men are more likely to say "*washi*."

        2. *Washi* is a shortened form of *watashi* and thus emerged after it, as an alternate, just as [d] emerged after [ð] in English pronunciation of *them* and *those*.

    C. Linguist and psychologist John Edwards at St. Francis Xavier University in Nova Scotia studied children in Dublin in 1979. Children of both sexes were recorded, and listeners were asked to identify their gender.

        1. Where there were mistakes, class mistakes were made.

        2. Boys misheard as girls were from the middle class; girls misheard as boys were from the working class.

        3. People had an expectation that "vernacular" was male and "proper" was female.

    D. University of Mashhad, Iran, linguist Nader Jahangiri found a difference in Persian that tracks neatly down the class scale, alternating between men and women.

        1. In Persian, there is a process of optional vowel assimilation in words, as we saw in Lecture Eighteen.

        2. Assimilation is most likely among men with no education, a little less among women of no education, then men with primary school education do it a little less than women with none, women with just primary education a little less than them, and so on.

E. Speculations have been offered to explain why women speak more properly.

    1. It may be because men are rated by what they do, women by how they appear.

    2. Women are possibly more attentive to norms because of child-rearing.

F. This tendency changes in societies where women are acquiring more power.

    1. In Norway, accent on first syllable of loan words (such as *avis*, "newspaper") is nonstandard but is on the rise in young women as opportunities for them have increased.

    2. It is used less than 10 percent of the time among women over 63, only 25 percent in women between 37 and 62, and 60 percent in younger women (similar to men's 66 percent).

G. There is also a sociolinguistic gender pattern in language usage.

    1. University of Chicago anthropologist Susan Gal showed that in Oberwart, Austria, German is the prestigious language and Hungarian is the less prestigious one.

    2. Women prefer Germans as husbands and only speak German among themselves, whereas men speak Hungarian among themselves.

V. When we think of language and gender on the lay level, we often think about conversations between men and women.

A. Sociologists Don Zimmerman and Candace West showed that in 10 same-sex conversations, there were 7 interruptions, but in 11 cross-sex ones, there were 48 interruptions and the male was responsible for 46.

B. Linguist Pamela Fishman showed that:

    1. Men used statements rather than questions twice as often as women.

    2. Women used minimal response as a *back channel*—a short utterance of moderate volume used to support the speaker and show that one is engaged—while men used back channels as devices to end a topic.

    3. Out of 76 topics introduced in normal conversation, women attempted to initiate 45, of which 17 were taken up; all 28 of the men's were taken up.

C. Georgetown University linguist Deborah Tannen has argued that women are given to using what she terms *rapport talk*—asking questions, talking about inner feelings—while men are given to using *report talk*—establishing social status and imparting information.

D. In Japanese, the use of the particle *ne* is typical of women; it translates roughly as *you know* but solicits agreement or just checks for solidarity in a particular fashion associated in the culture with females rather than males.

VI. Despite popular belief, women do not talk more than men.

    A. Louann Brizendine, neuropsychiatrist at the University of California, San Francisco, said in her 2006 book *The Female Brain* that women use 20,000 words a day while men use only 7,000.

    B. But University of Arizona psychologist Matthias Mehl and his assistants tracked 400 students over six years with recording devices and found that both men and women average about 16,000 words a day, and variation among individuals is large. Other studies have long suggested similarly.

Essential Reading:

Tannen, *You Just Don't Understand.*

Supplemental Reading:

Lakoff, *Language and Women's Place.*

Questions to Consider

1. In *Language and Women's Place*, Lakoff observed that women are aware of finer color terms than men, such as *cerise, aquamarine, puce, mauve*. This appeared to most an accurate depiction of gender differences in language use among mature Americans in the early 1970s when the book first appeared. Do an informal survey of male and female friends and examine whether it is still true today. (This is not a loaded question: Your findings could go either way.)

2. In her book *You Just Don't Understand*, Deborah Tannen argues that women use *rapport talk*, exploring feelings, while men use *report talk*, giving information and establishing pecking order. Think about this in your workplace or social life, and examine whether this seems an accurate depiction of how women use language differently from men. Again, not a loaded question: Naturally, linguists wary of Tannen's public success have been known to say that she does not attend to academic research. But the academic research might be biased itself, and how well her books sell must reflect a certain consonance with reality. So, discuss.

Lecture Twenty-One—Transcript
Language and Gender

When we talk about language and how it varies according to social factors, of course gender is one of those factors. This is not only about how people of different genders converse but also often in what grammatical forms women use as opposed to the ones that men use. What this means is that a truly complete description of a language has to include how gender figures into the way that language is spoken and used. In this lecture, I want to talk about some of the research that's been done on language and gender.

In part, the study of language and gender involves observing that there are gender differences on the structural level in many languages—and a lot more than we might imagine from English. Of course, in English we have things like *actor* and *actress*, and of course we have a distinction in our third-person singular pronoun between *he* and *she*, but there isn't much more than those kinds of brute indications in terms of nouns of whether or not something is male or female. Then the occasional pronominal distinction like *he*/*she*—*his* and *her*—but that's partly because, as languages go, English is a relatively *telegraphic* language. Compared to most languages in the world, there's an awful lot that you don't have to say in English. That tends to be true of large, geopolitically dominant languages. It's the smaller languages that tend to be more complex.

That complexity includes indications of gender that we would never think about in English. For example, even in Russian—which is itself a dominant language—in the past tense, the sex of the speaker determines the form. To say, "I knew," you'd say, "*ja znal*" if you were a man; if I were a woman, I would say, "*ja znala*." That is something that you absolutely have to do. There is nothing political about it; that is what one does when one speaks Russian. That sort of thing is true in a great many languages. In a smaller language like the Koasati language—which is one of the indigenous Native American languages that happens to be holding on by a thread in this country; it's spoken in Louisiana—you find that actually there are full tables of forms that are different in terms of whether you are a man or a woman speaking. For example, if you are saying, "I am saying," "you are saying," or "he is saying," then if you are saying, "I am saying" and you're a man, then you say, "*ka:hás*"; if you are a woman and you're saying, "I am saying," then you say, "*ka:hâl*." There's a difference. If you're saying,

"You are saying," and you are a man, you say, "*i:sks*"; if you are a woman, then you say, "*i:sk*." In fact, as you see here, the difference is that there is an ending that men use that women do not. I'm not sure how we're supposed to feel about that; that might imply that men are derived and women more basic, or it might imply that women are somehow lesser. But in any case, you see that there is this difference, and of course it's not just with these three forms; this is the kind of difference that permeates the grammar.

Then, on the other hand, you can also see languages where the sex of the addressee determines the form. For example, in Hebrew: On the one hand, it can be your sex that determines the form when you're talking about first-person singular. If "I love" in Hebrew, *ani ohev*; if I'm a woman, *ani ohevet*. But when you're addressing someone, for example in the past, if you want to tell a man that he loves somebody, then you would say, "*ahavta*"; if it's a woman, then it's "*ahavt*." All of these things are indications where gender determines how we express ourselves on the grammatical level.

It can get almost counterintuitively baroque in some languages. There is a language spoken in southern India called Kurux. In Kurux—it's very interesting—you have forms that are used when a man speaks to a woman, and then you have forms that are used when a woman speaks to a woman; there are endings. Then you have different endings if anyone speaks to a man. The grammar is very different in terms of anything we would think of. These are the things that one learns as a child when one is learning Kurux. To them, that is a perfectly ordinary way to use language. It's a matter of form determined by gender, and there's a lot of this in many languages.

However, in terms of language and gender as a field that's attracted a lot of attention—particularly since the 1970s—generally, what people are thinking about are differences in how women use language or differences in how language is used upon women. The person who can be said to have founded this kind of study is Robin Lakoff, who is a linguist at the University of California at Berkley. She wrote a classic book, *Language and Women's Place*, in the early '70s—1973—and she made an argument that women's identities are submerged because they are encouraged to use expressions that connote triviality or are particularly subjective and that they're discouraged from using strong expression. This book and the paradigm that it influenced have been very successful and have attracted a great deal of attention. Professor Lakoff's examples included adjectives. Her claim was that it was more typical for women to say that something was *adorable* or *charming*, rather than saying that something is *terrific* or *great*. According to Lakoff's idea, *adorable* and *charming* are subjective; they invite someone to agree, and they possibly convey a certain sense that there's a question as to whether something is adorable or charming. The sense is that you see a cat, and you say, "Oh isn't the cat adorable?" as if there was maybe some doubt about it before, and you're mentioning now that as a matter of fact this thing is adorable; isn't that remarkable. As opposed to somebody saying, "That's terrific" or "That's great." That's just a statement; it sits, it's concrete, and there's no argument about it.

Lakoff argued that women are more likely to use tag questions: "It's a nice day, isn't it?" or "These are good parsnips, aren't they?"—inviting this sort of confirmation, as if she wasn't sure about what she was saying at first. Or there is the idea in Lakoff's early work that women are more likely to use softer directives than men. For example, a man might say, "Move that chair"; the woman would be more likely to say, "Would you mind moving that chair?" or "Could you please move that chair?" Then there was the idea that women use more question intonation in statements. The prototypical scene was that the man walks in and says, "When's dinner?" The wife says, "Six o'clock?" instead of another scenario—which Robin Lakoff imagined could happen, would be preferable to happen—which would be, "When's dinner?" Then the wife says, "Six o'clock," like that.

This was the paradigm: the idea that women's disempowerment is reflected in the way women speak. The fact of the matter is that when one puts forth these ideas today—in our era; it's been a very long time—often people have a sense that these claims do not exactly fit the era that we're in. There's a perplexity, particularly among younger people. That is because I think that today there's a problem with *Language and Women's Place*, which is simply that it was a very, very long time ago. It was written about, basically, women of the 1940s and the 1950s. That was perfectly reasonable then. It has been suggested by many people that, since the feminist revolution, these observations are somewhat dated. That might be true. For example, I personally don't know any women who would talk about something being adorable or charming. That sounds to me like somebody who's in a hat with a flower on it and is in an old movie at a garden party or giving a speech before the Junior League or something like that. It's a different world. Women probably spoke more like what Robin Lakoff was talking about back in the bad old days. Today's modern woman, I think, is less likely to talk that way, and a lot of studies have suggested that. The study was perfectly relevant and probably on the nose in its time. It might be that, blissfully, times have changed in such a way that these things are not as true. It's also been said that the data in that book was collected by introspection and by observation. That's a good thing in its way. It's kind of like being a good journalist or just being a very intelligent person. Technically, the field of sociolinguistics has moved since then toward a general requirement that conclusions be built upon formal surveying, and that is not what this book was based on. The study of language and gender from that particular perspective has been formalized quite a bit since the early '70s, and the conclusions have been questioned. But as an opening statement, Robin Lakoff's work was very important. The language and gender field would not be what it is today if weren't for her work.

Since then, it has been found through scientific research that there is a strong tendency in the way women tend to use language, and that is that it's men who use the socially disfavored forms—in terms of the markers that we talked about—rather than women. Women tend to be more, as we call it, *prescriptive* in their speech; women tend to be more proper in their speech. Not all the time, but there is a very strong tendency. It's been confirmed in quite a few studies. For example, the University of Sydney in Australia linguist Barbara Horvath noted that among Bill Labov's—William Labov's—interviewees, in terms of people who were more likely to say [d] instead of [ð] in words like *those*—and so "those"/"dose"—this was something that was much more likely of men than women. You can see in this chart how that works.

Of course there are women who will say, "dose" to a certain extent, but men vastly surpass them. If you think about it, that's intuitive—I mean, we don't walk around thinking about that sort of thing consciously—but if you think about who's more likely to speak in a "dem," "dese," and "dose" way, the first thing that comes to mind is a guy. That's not because it's a stereotype; it's because that really is the case. You can imagine a woman talking that way, but it's the secondary thing. I think our first image is of men speaking in that way. That's been found in terms of actual scientific study. It's been seen in Montreal, it's been seen in Detroit, and not with that particular variable, but with many others in terms of socially disfavored versus socially favored variables. It's been found in Norwich in England; it's been found in Belfast. One study after another shows that there's this tendency among women.

You can see this even in terms of the grammatical forms in a language. For example, if there are two ways of saying something, and one of them is shorter than the other—you can tell that one of them is the shorter version of the other—then you know that the shorter version came after the longer version. The shorter version is most likely the product of natural phonetic evolution, where there is always erosion. If you know that it's the new form, then you also know that probably—if it's an ordinary human society—the shorter form is going to have some sense of stigmatization about it. At least, it's going to be considered something that you do when you talk fast, and then, most probably, it will be thought of as more colloquial or even incorrect. In Japanese, to say, "I"—as in me, myself, and—there are two forms: The full form is *watashi*, and then you can also say, "*washi*." If you look at those two words, you can see that *washi* is a shorter form than *watashi*. As you would predict—based on this pattern that you see with the "dem," "dese," and "dose" in English and so many other instantiations of that—it is women who are much more likely to say, "*watashi*." The male form is *washi*, to the point that you can say that there is a female form and a male form. A woman is not supposed to say, "*washi*"; she would say that to imitate a man. *Watashi* would be kind of a prissy way of speaking for a man; that's what a woman says. The lines are not that firmly drawn, but it is a very strong tendency in the language in terms of subdivision of labor. If the new forms are slightly stigmatized, they are less likely to be used by women than by men.

Even in our perceptions, you can find that in our brains we process a sense that the woman is more likely to speak properly. There was a very interesting study done by John Edwards at St. Francis Xavier University in Nova Scotia. This was a study done in the late '70s. He studied kids in Dublin, and he recorded children of both sexes—so that means boys and girls—and then he asked listeners to identify the genders of the kids. Remember that we're talking about kids who are at such an age that the boys' voices have not broken; it can be amazing how much like girls boys can sound. (On *The Simpsons*, all of the boys are actually done by women. Bart Simpson is done by Nancy Cartwright, and all of his friends are done by a small passel of women. No man could really sound like a boy; it's a woman who has to.) All of these kids were recorded, and then people were asked to identify their gender. It was interesting: Where people misidentified the gender, it was about class. If someone heard a boy and thought that it was a girl, then that boy was always middle class. If someone heard a girl and thought that it was a boy, then that girl was always from the working class. There was a sense that disfavored forms—colloquial forms—were somehow male and standard forms were more female. We internalize this because there is a certain reality in it.

Or, talking about the Persian imperatives that we saw recently before, those pattern in terms of women being more prescriptive than men as well. The people who have the vowel assimilation in the imperatives the most are the lowest-class men with the least education; then people who use it a little bit less are the lowest-class women with no education, but the women do it a little bit less than the men. Then it's done a little bit less by men who would be above both the lowest-class man and woman in station, and then a little bit less by women of that same position, and so on. It's a stepwise chart. The question becomes: Why is it that women are more prescriptive than men? Why do women speak more properly? Why is it feminine to use longer forms? What is the reason for that?

There have been speculations—I don't think it's really ever been nailed—but one speculation was that men are rated by what they do: what they do for a living, or what they happen to be prominent for. Women are rated more by how they appear, and so there's a sense that one must speak properly. There's an argument for that, I suppose. It was an argument that I think had a little bit more sway 30 years ago to many people than it does now, but it's still there. It's also been said that women are more prescriptive in their speech because they're conscious of modeling their language for children who are growing up. I'm inclined to doubt that one, but it has been taken very seriously. Nevertheless, the tendency is definitely there. You can see that how women speak actually changes more toward the way men speak as opportunities open up for women in a society.

For example, in Norwegian, if you put stress on the first syllable of the word *avis*—that's *newspaper*—then that is the sort of barstool, nonstandard way of saying it. If you say, "*a-VIS*," then that's a more standard way of saying it. Actually, that can give you a sense of how arbitrary our sense of what sounds right and what doesn't sound right is. We don't speak Norwegian, I presume; at least I don't. I see this *avis* and it looks like something about car rental; it happens to be *newspaper* in Norwegian. Apparently to them if you say, "*a-VIS*," that's proper, and if you say, "*A-vis*," that's crude. That's as arbitrary as the fact that the little thing that goes "woof" is called a *d-o-g* in our language and a *chien* in French; it has no meaning.

Let's think about that, when you're thinking about what you don't like in a language. I can't stand when people say, "Can I get a Coke?" The first time I heard that when I was about 11, I thought, "This is not a world that I want to be in sometimes." It just rubs me the wrong way. "I'd like a Coke." "May I have a Coke?" "I would like a Coke." "Can I get a … ?" What do you mean "get"? It's crude. That is completely arbitrary. There is no reason to dislike that; it's just in my DNA. Anyway, back to our topic. *A-vis* is nonstandard. It used to be that you could survey men, and it was practically two in three who said, "*A-vis*," whereas with women it was used much, much less. When this was surveyed in the 1970s, it was found that women over 63 only said, "*A-vis*" 10 percent of the time; so only a few, 10 percent of women, 10 percent of the time did that. Whereas women between 37 and 62 only did it 25 percent. Then in women younger, it was 60 percent. Younger women were talking more like men on that word and others, and this seemed to be indexed to widening opportunities for women in society, and therefore a change in how gender lines were seen.

Go south in Europe to a little town called Oberwart in Austria. In Oberwart, it is a bilingual area because the Hungarian language spreads beyond the boundaries of Hungary, which are in some ways rather arbitrary. There is a great deal of Hungarian spoken to the east in Romania in Transylvania, and there are also people in Austria—next door—who speak Hungarian; there are about 20,000 Hungarian speakers there. It's interesting. There was a study done in Oberwart. In Oberwart, German is the prestige language because that's the language of Austria; it's associated with progress. Hungarian is seen as the peasant language, because that's what it was before German ended up coming into Oberwart and taking over. Hungarian is the language of peasants, and crude, and home, and oatmeal—I don't know if they eat oatmeal, kasha, whatever the equivalent is there—whereas German is thought of as the language that's on TV, etc. As you would expect, based on this general tendency in how men and women use language, the women in Oberwart who are of Hungarian ancestry prefer Germans as husbands, and they speak German among themselves. The men speak Hungarian—which is thought of as the low language—among themselves. We see this pattern again and again and again.

These days, I think, because of the popularity of Deborah Tannen's work—Deborah Tannen is a Georgetown University linguist who has written various books on conversations between men and women, or conversations between various people, and the pitfalls therein—when we think of language and gender on the lay level, I think we think about conversations between men and women. There's been a great deal of study of that kind of thing done. They tend to make it look, again, like a world we don't always want to be in. Don Zimmerman and Candace West did a study where they showed that in 10 conversations between people of the same gender, there were 7 interruptions. But in 11 conversations between people of different genders—which of course means between men and women—there were 48 interruptions, and the male was responsible for 46 of the interruptions. That's really kind of sad.

Or Pamela Fishman showed, in her corpus, that men used statements rather than questions twice as often as women. There was a difference in what *back channeling* meant among women and men. Back channeling is when somebody who is being spoken to gives some kind of indication that they understand what's being said and that they're in on the thread. A common back channel in English is "mm-hmm." For example, one can imagine—I can imagine—my wife back channels. I'll be talking about how, "We sat on the tarmac all this time, and everybody was talking on their Blackberries, and nowadays you don't get any peanuts." She'll go, "Mm-hmm, mm-hmm, mm-hmm, mm-hmm." That's what she does; I think that's what a lot of people do. Men often back channel differently. Just imagine: Think about two guys talking and one guy is sounding off about Blackberries and peanuts and things like that. Is the guy going, "Mm-hm, mm-hmm, mm-hm?" It doesn't feel right; he might, but it doesn't feel right. Often, men use back channeling as a way of very politely trying to put a halt to the other person's conversation so they can talk. I remember this guy; it was when I first started graduate school, and there was this guy who was complaining about the department, and he liked to try to take people in and make them bitter like him. He was trying to do that to me—people tend to do that to me—and I remember he was talking about his miserable life, and all these people were around him. Every time someone else tried to say something, he'd go, "Mm-hmm, uh-huh, uh-huh, uh-huh, uh-huh." He just wanted to talk; he was this bullish person. It wasn't that he was really trying to encourage them to talk—"Oh yeah, mm-hmm, mm-hmm, mm-mm"—he wanted them to stop it. That is something that men often do. All of these things are not absolute, but they're tendencies, and this was shown in Fishman's work.

In terms of initiating topics, there was a corpus that she had where there were 76 topics introduced in this cross-sex situation. Women attempted to initiate 45 topics; 17 of them were taken up. The men tried to introduce 28 topics; all of them were taken up. A woman tries to push in, and she might be taken up, but just often will not be, whereas the men just jumped right in there.

Deborah Tannen herself has argued that women tend to do what she calls *rapport talk*, where the focus is on asking questions and talking about inner feelings, whereas men do *report talk*, where they establish social status and they impart information. That is definitely something to think about, because I don't think that it's absolutely counterintuitive. I would definitely say that I noticed that in college, and I didn't know from Deborah Tannen that there was a difference in the way women spoke to one another and men spoke to one another.

These, of course, are not absolutes. There are women who are different from these tendencies; there are men who are different from these tendencies. Individuals participate in these things to differing extents. I would certainly say that in a great deal of male conversation, the idea is to compete. There is a constant sense of figuring out pecking order, and the joshing, and the teasing. Women do that, but there is more talk about feelings, etc. For example, a group of women—and this has been shown in some quarters—are more likely to talk about the intricacies of how a woman might feel about a person she's dating. Men are much less likely to have that particular kind of conversation: "How do you feel about her, Justin?" "Well, she makes me feel …" No, not usually. That's a weird Justin. That's more likely for people who are not men.

Or there's a particle in Japanese: You spell it *n-e*; it's *ne*. Technically, it has a glottal stop on the end of it. What *ne* means is roughly "you know?" But you can say it in a way to just kind of indicate "You okay? Everything fine?" A Japanese woman might say, "*Ne?*" to her husband: "Is everything all right?" *Ne* is a very female particle in Japanese; it's not used as much by men. That it is because it has a kind of a function that might be considered part of Deborah Tannen's rapport talk rather than the report talk.

One last thing to get in, though, is that there has always been a stereotype that women talk a lot, that women are gabby. Like in *Music Man*, that number where all the women are walking around: "Pick a little / pick a little / talk a little / pick a little / pick a little / talk a little / pick pick pick / talk a lot / pick a little more." Women are these gabby hens; you see it in old cartoons. Not long ago, the media went crazy. (Blogs spread crap around in ways that are really disturbing sometimes.) In 2006, if you were a linguist, you kept being asked about Louann Brizendine's book, *The Female Brain*. It said all sorts of things, but what made it into the media was that women use 20,000 words a day, while men only use 7,000. It's not true at all.

For one thing, it doesn't correspond to intuition. Intuition is not science, but, if you really think about the lives we lead, are women that much more talkative than men? I don't see it. Think about going to the airport; think about being at a supermarket; think about a party. The men aren't standing around not talking while the women are gabbing. If you actually study this sort of thing scientifically, you can confirm in this case the intuition. There was a University of Arizona psychologist, Matthias Mehl, and he had a team of assistants. They tracked 400 students over six years—so not just sitting a bunch of people in a room or something like that—but over six years, they tracked these poor 400 students with recording devices, and they found that, really, both men and women use about 16,000 words a day and that there is variation among individuals. Some people aren't very talkative; some people are especially talkative. But there is no visible evidence that the people who are especially talkative are more likely to be non-male. There have been many other studies suggesting the same thing. But because it's so sexy to imagine that women have this tendency to talk more, and because that's fun to talk about on talk shows, that's the sort of thing that will make it into the media, rather than this very lengthy and authoritative study and others which have shown that if there is anything dramatic to be said about differences in how men and women speak, it is not that to be female is to be a chatterbox. I just wanted to report that in case you have been misled by reports of that.

In any case, this has been a lecture on language and gender. We've seen it in the various grammatical forms in the language; we've seen it in terms of conversation. We've seen that this is a field of study which has been seen as having great promise, and it has revealed quite a bit, but it has also cut through various stereotypes.

Lecture Twenty-Two
Languages Sharing the World—Bilingualism

Scope: At the present time, 6,000 languages coexist in just 200 or so nations. Bilingualism and multilingualism are norms rather than oddities. This lecture examines the results of bilingualism according to social context.

Outline

I. There are 200-plus nations in the world and about 6,000 languages.

    A. Although fewer than a quarter of nations recognize more than one official language and only a few recognize more than two (Bolivia, Comoros, India, Luxembourg, Papua New Guinea, Peru, Rwanda, Seychelles, Singapore, South Africa, Spain, Switzerland, Vanuatu), clearly in most nations more than one language is spoken.

    B. On the small island of Timor, more than a dozen languages are spoken.

    C. There are about 800 languages spoken in New Guinea, 300 in Nigeria, etc. In nations like Nigeria, as many as 90 percent of people are bilingual.

    D. The tendency for us to be monolingual English speakers in the United States is actually something that is odd compared to the way most people experience language.

    E. Thus the proper topic of a lecture, in terms of what is remarkable, would be monolingualism!

    F. Bilingualism can have various effects on the languages in question.

II. Transitory bilingualism is a situation where two languages meet but there is no permanent effect on either language.

    A. Typically in America, for instance, first-generation immigrants learn the new language to varying extents but prefer their native one, the second generation is bilingual, and the third generation has passive knowledge, little, or none of the first generation's language.

    B. Composer Irving Berlin's mother barely ever learned English; Berlin himself was bilingual in English and Yiddish; his children speak only English.

C. The second generation's command of their parents' language is often fluent but not as complete.

    1. Take "I know another person who listens to Rush Limbaugh" in Russian.

> Parent: *Ja znaju eščjo odnovo čelovek-a, kotorjy slušaet Raš-a Limbo.*
>
> I know else one person who listens Rush Limbaugh.
>
> Child: *Ja znaju drugoj čelovek i on slušaet to Rush Limbaugh.*
>
> I know one person and he listens to Rush Limbaugh.

    2. Here, the second-generation speaker does not use case properly and uses simpler sentence structure, avoiding a subordinate clause.

III. Languages tend to borrow a lot of words from each other; this is called *lexical borrowing*.

    A. If speakers of a second language are especially numerous and/or powerful, then the new language they are learning may take in a great many words from the second one.

    B. In English, this happened during the Norman French rule, when French contributed about 7,500 of today's English words, often having to do with formal realms such as government, cuisine, and the arts.

    C. Because French was the "high" language, *hearty* from English is a less formal word than *cordial* (from French *coeur*), a *house* is less formal than a *mansion*, etc.

    D. This mixture in English is not unusual. Over half of Japanese's words are from Chinese; half of Urdu's are from Persian and Arabic; Albanian is 60 percent Greek, Romanian, Turkish, Serbian, and Macedonian.

    E. In the United States, "Spanglish" is the result of this process in reverse: Spanish spoken in the long term by people bilingual in English has many English words (*lonchar* instead of *almorzar*, "to have lunch") and English-influenced usages of Spanish words (*carpeta* is *carpet* in Spanglish, rather than *folder* as in Spanish).

IV. When languages come together, sometimes there will be a slight simplification due to bilingualism.

   A. If so many adult immigrants speak their new country's language that even native-born children hear the language spoken incompletely as often as not, then the result is often that the new country's language becomes somewhat less complex.

   B. In China, starting in A.D. 618, hundreds of thousands of foreigners were relocated into the country permanently as the result of wars. They lived among the native Mandarin speakers and often married them.

   C. It has been argued that this is why Mandarin Chinese is less complex grammatically than the several other Chinese varieties like Cantonese and Taiwanese. For example, Mandarin syllables change meaning according to four tones:

mā (high)	mother
má (low-high)	hemp
mǎ (middle-low-high)	horse
mà (high-low)	scold

   D. But Cantonese ones change according to six:

yāu (high)	worry
yáu (high rising)	paint
yau (middle)	thin
yàuh (low falling)	oil
yáuh (low rising)	have
yauh (low)	again

   E. Cantonese also has many more pragmatic particles to indicate attitude than Mandarin, which leaves much more of this aspect of expression to intonation and context.

V. Bilingualism is a norm worldwide, and it has various effects, but it never leaves a language disabled. Given how bilingualism works, we can understand some things we see happening in our modern society in a different way.

   A. Often in American history, people have been nervous about the idea that English seems to be being overrun by speakers of other languages.

1. The basics of transitory bilingualism show that there is no foundation to the concern that the presence of foreign languages is a threat to an official language.
2. By 1920, only one in six New Yorkers were native-born whites. It was said in the 1880s that in lower Manhattan "the U.S. language was a hard find." Discomfort with this led to a requirement in 1906 that people admitted to the United States speak English; Theodore Roosevelt declared, "We have room for but one language here."
3. On the prevalence of German in early America, Benjamin Franklin warned against Pennsylvania becoming "a colony of aliens."
4. Alarm about the German language peaked during World War I, and in 1923 a teacher was brought to court for teaching German. The word of the court was that allowing children to be educated in another language would "naturally inculcate in them the ideas and sentiments foreign to the best interest of this country."
5. In Iowa, a governor once ruled that no one could use anything but English in public, even on the phone.

B. Bilingual education receives more criticism than it should.
1. It has been proposed by many educators that reading comes more easily without the need to translate and that other skills come more easily when taught in a child's native language.
2. Thus the Bilingual Education Act of 1968 was enacted to protect Spanish-speaking children's heritage while ushering them into English.
3. Bilingual education programs are often unpopular, even with luminaries such as Ronald Reagan.
4. However, when run by competent school systems, bilingual education works well worldwide, such as in Norway (Turkish, Urdu, and Vietnamese), England (Punjabi), the Netherlands (Turkish, Arabic), Sweden (Finnish), and Mexico (Tzeltal, Tzotzil), where the programs have been proven to result in faster learning.

Essential Reading:

McWhorter, *Power of Babel*.

Supplemental Reading:

Winford, *Introduction to Contact Linguistics*.

Questions to Consider:

1. Children raised by parents born in another country often learn their parents' language at home but then reject it after being in school for a time and no longer speak it by the time they are teens. Have you raised children who retained bilingualism into adulthood or seen other parents do this? If so, what was the factor that kept the children from rejecting the "foreign tongue"?

2. If your parents speak another language natively and passed that language on to you, would you say that your version of their language is "complete"? Or do you speak what linguists term an "immigrant version" of the language?

Lecture Twenty-Two—Transcript
Languages Sharing the World—Bilingualism

Welcome back. As we further discuss how societal factors affect how language is used, one topic that we will want to discuss is the fact that with a great many people, they live their lives in more than one language; that is, there's a great deal of bilingualism and multilingualism in the world. There are 200 or so nations—I think the official number is 212—and there are about 6,000 languages. You can see that there are some countries that recognize more than one language as official. There are even some—a dozen or so—that recognize several. Nevertheless, that clearly does not account for the 6,000 languages in the world, and the fact is that in most nations a great many languages are spoken. It certainly isn't that these languages are spoken exclusively by particular groups who don't speak anything else; there is a great deal of sharing of languages in one person going on around the world. It's the norm.

For example, look at this language map of the island of Timor, which is way, way, way, way down near Indonesia. It is shared by actually Indonesia and itself; the eastern part is independent. You can see that there are more than a dozen languages just spoken on Timor. There are only 3,000,000 people on the island of Timor; that is less than half of the number of people who live in New York City. Timor is about the size of this room; nevertheless, you have all of those languages. In fact, last year, two more were discovered on little Timor that were thought to be extinct. The fact is that this is perfectly ordinary. If you're doing a bird's-eye view of the world, this is how languages are distributed. There are really a great many, and as you can imagine, there's a great deal of bilingualism and multilingualism on Timor. For example, the dominant languages there are Indonesian and Portuguese. Then one of the indigenous languages, called Tetun, is the indigenous *lingua franca*; everybody knows Tetun. Then there are all of the other ones, and some people know two of them, some people know three of them; that is typical. In New Guinea, there are 800 languages. New Guinea is just an island; 800 languages in New Guinea. In the country of Nigeria, you hear about Yoruba and Hausa and Igbo; those are the big three. Then, of course, there's a great deal of competence in English, but the fact is that there are 300 languages spoken in Nigeria. The ones we hear about are just the *lingua francas*, but there are a great many more. In a nation like Nigeria—in many African countries—90 percent of people can be documented to be bilingual, because that is what you have to do to function. If you're born speaking a language that only 500 or 5,000 people speak, if your life is going to go beyond that village, obviously you're going to have to learn another language—bang, you're bilingual. In fact, most people you know are bilingual.

What this means is that in terms of a lecture, the proper title would really be not "Bilingualism" but "Monolingualism." Monolingualism is actually rather odd. The tendency in the United States for us to be monolingual English speakers is actually something that is odd compared to the way most people experience language in the world.

Bilingualism has various effects upon the languages that people are using. It depends on the situation. One thing that can happen is that when two languages meet, there is no effect upon one or the other. There can be what's called transitory bilingualism. For example, typically in America, the first-generation immigrant learns the new language to varying extents, but they prefer—they always prefer—their native language. Then the second generation is bilingual; and so they can talk to their parents, but they also function in the wider society speaking English indistinguishably from everyone else. Then the third generation will have passive knowledge of the old language; maybe they'll know some words and some expressions, but they won't really speak it. At best they'll understand it fairly well, but it won't actually be their language. Of course, they do not pass it on to the next generation at all. That is perfectly typical.

Irving Berlin, the song composer, was born in probably Russia in 1893, and he was brought over to the United States as a child. His mother, Leah, was a very nice woman. She spoke Yiddish when she came to the United States. She never really learned English; she could go out and buy bananas or something—probably not bananas. She could go out and buy rolls—well no, she'd make her own rolls. She could go out and buy fish, but other than that she didn't really speak English. She lived a Yiddish life, and that was rather typical. Irving Berlin spoke perfect American English, he spoke very good Yiddish, and he had a relationship with his mother in Yiddish and a relationship with the United States in English. Irving Berlin's children do not speak Yiddish; they just speak English. That is a typical kind of progression.

If you zero in a little bit closer, you see that even with that second generation, often the command of the "old country" language is not exactly 100 percent. Talk about second language acquisition: You can learn a language as a first language but nevertheless incompletely. You'll have signs of the sorts of things that we've seen in terms of how languages are often acquired as second or third ones. For example, there are many people in this country right now who are second-generation Russian immigrants. They often speak Russian—you can hear them speaking Russian with their parents, etc.—but if you dig, you find that actually there's a difference between their parents' Russian and their Russian. Their Russian is kind of like schoolboy or schoolgirl Russian—a little better than that, but still obviously less Russian than their parents. For example, if someone says, "I know another person who listens to Rush Limbaugh"—just that statement, "I know another person who listens to Rush Limbaugh." This is from that study where somebody was asked about that. In real Russian, the way that sentence goes is like this up on the screen: You have "*Ja znaju*," "I know"; "another person," "*eščjo odnovo čelovek-a*"—and you see that this is how it goes in the standard. "Who listens," "*kotorjy slušaet*," and then "Rush Limbaugh," "*Raš-a Limbo*." If you don't know Russian, that just looks like some stuff.

Now let's compare it to the kid's Russian; this is how a second-generation Russian speaker rendered that same sentence: They said, "*ja znaju*," now that's "I know"; you got that part, that's pretty easy. But then where the parent says, "*eščjo odnovo čelovek-a*"—which is proper Russian meaning *one more person*—this person uses a different word: "*drugoj čelovek*." I don't need to get into why that's wrong; it's not completely wrong, but it's not very felicitous. It's the sort of thing that, for example, I would say. It's the sort of thing that a second-language speaker pulls because they're not fully at home in the language. Then, also, this person is using a relative clause. They're saying, "I know one person who listens to Rush Limbaugh." The child is actually saying, "I know one person and"—and that's the *i* here—"he listens to Rush Limbaugh." This person is unwrapping the sentence. It's kind of like the difference that we saw between restricted and elaborated code. Then there's a cheat. We have the child saying, "*Ja znaju drugoj čelovek i on slušaet* to Rush Limbaugh." It kind of does this little switch. That's perfectly comprehensible to a Russian person who's living in the United States and happens to know who Rush Limbaugh is. But then if you look at the actual native version, then it's not "*slušaet* to Rush Limbaugh"—because "to," for one thing, is not a Russian word—but Rush Limbaugh has a case marker: *Raš-a Limbo*. That makes *Rush Limbaugh* an accusative—it's actually technically genitive; that's a complication we don't have to worry about—but notice that he has a case, whereas when the child does it, *Rush Limbaugh* doesn't have a case; the child kind of gets out of that by just sticking in *to*. What the child said is Russian, but it's the kind of Russian where that child's grandmother will say, "You're not really speaking the language properly." That's called immigrant Russian or an *immigrant register* of the language. That's typical in terms of how the second generation often speaks a language.

In any case, what we do see when languages affect one another—when bilingualism, languages in the same mouth, means that languages start taking on one another's traits—what we do see is that languages tend to borrow a lot of words from each other. It's called *lexical borrowing*. If speakers of a second language are especially numerous—especially powerful—then the new language that they're learning might take in a great many words from this second one. The classic example of that is what happened to English during the Norman French rule, which was for about 200 years. During the time that England was run by the French, French contributed—depending on how you count it—about 7,500 new words to the language. They had things to do mostly with the formal realm, like government and cuisine and the arts, and that was because French was the high language. French was the language of government and the court. For example, there is the word *cordial*, and we get that from French, and the root there is the word that's now *coeur* for heart. There's *cordial*; then we do have an English word: *hearty*. If you think about it, *cordial* conveys a kind of formality; you think about Edith Wharton. *Hearty* is Vikings or somebody sitting in a chair watching a football game; it's lower than *cordial*, and that's because French was the high language. *Mansion* is from French—mansions are big and expensive—and *house*, that's English. A *house* can be a hovel or something like that. That's something that we find.

That's a story that's often told, but this is the place to dispel a myth. There are things that get around, and they just hold on and they just hold on. For example, the idea that Al Gore said that he invented the Internet: He never said that. You can readily confirm it, but people just love to talk about that. It makes some people feel so good to imagine that poor man claiming that he invented the Internet. The myth never dies. Here is another myth: that English has been uniquely receptive to words from other languages. We are always patting ourselves on the back about that. You hear that again and again; it sells some books. That is a complete street myth. If you get in a plane, and you're flying around the world looking at all the world's languages, like for example if you flew over Timor—if you could manage to get your plane to stop in it, it's so small—then you would find that words are mixing around in languages around the world, and they always have been.

It is perfectly ordinary for a language to have a highly mixed vocabulary. That's part of what the influence of languages upon one another is. Lexical borrowing is rampant. Language is like sex, you could say; that's just what happens when languages are next to each other. Over half of Japanese's words are from Chinese. Nobody runs around in Tokyo talking about how receptive Japanese is to anything. Or, for example, Urdu of Pakistan is basically Hindi with a lot of Persian and Arabic in it. Urdu wasn't receptive; Urdu developed under certain circumstances where naturally words would be shared. Little Albanian—I call it little only because the country is small, not because it isn't a wonderful and mighty language—but Albanian's vocabulary is 60 percent Greek, Romanian, Turkish, Serbian, and Macedonian; 60 percent. Albanians have all sorts of concerns; they are proud of themselves for various reasons, but they do not walk around talking about how receptive Albanian was to anything because that kind of word mixture is quite normal. The fact that the French ran England for a pretty long time and, as a result, English was left with French words is really rather mundane. It's something that happens all around the world. That's just something to think about.

It also sheds light on something else: You get constant newspaper reports about the idea that there is this new language emerging in the United States that's a mixture of Spanish and English. Actually, we're in a position to see that that's not really framing the issue right. "Spanglish" is the result of the fact that there are an awful lot of people who have come to this country who speak Spanish as a native language, and keep speaking it, and also speak English. What would you expect under a circumstance like that? Certainly you wouldn't expect that the Spanish would stay the way it was in Mexico or Puerto Rico or wherever else. That would be very odd. What you would expect is that the Spanish would—big surprise—take on a lot of English words. For example, there is the word *almorzar* for *lunch*; that's the real Spanish word. Many people say, "*lonchar*"; that's kind of what you would expect. Then there are other things. For example, in Spanish itself, the word *carpeta* means *folder*. Predictably among people, especially born here, *carpeta* ends up often being used to mean *rug* or *carpet*.

These are the sorts of things that happen all the time, but what we know, our precious knowledge, is that a language is not just words. We know now that language has a grammar, etc., from this course. Spanglish is still Spanish. People who are speaking Spanglish are still using the full conjugational paradigms; the nouns that they're using still have gender, etc. What's going on with Spanglish is not the birth of a new language; it's just good, old, ordinary, Wonder Bread, kitchen-sink lexical borrowing. For example, Yiddish is really German. It was spoken in a context where people used a lot of Hebrew words and a lot of Slavic words. As a result, it has a large lexical component of Hebrew and Slavic, but the core is German. That's what happened to it. There's nothing miraculous about that sort of thing; that's what Spanglish is.

In any case, the fact of the matter is that when languages come together, sometimes there will be a kind of slight simplification of the entire language in the vein of the immigrant Russian that we saw. This has happened in various languages throughout the world. For example, suppose that there are so many immigrants to a country or a region that even native-born children start hearing a language spoken incompletely as often as not; then the result is that the whole language can end up becoming less complex.

One place this happened, most likely, is in China. In A.D. 618, there were hundreds of thousands of foreigners who were relocated into China, mostly as the result of wars—people from surrounding areas. A great many of them were settled among native Mandarin speakers, often married them, and stayed there forever. The place was overrun with people who could only speak Chinese in a nonnative way. It's been argued that that's why Mandarin Chinese is grammatically less complex than any of the other Chinese varieties like Cantonese, Taiwanese, and "Shanghai-nese." It's strikingly less complex, and there is certainly some connection between that and the history of the language. For example, in Mandarin, you have syllables that change their meaning based on four tones. *Mother* is *mā* for high; *hemp* is *má*, and that's low-high; then when it's middle-low-high, something like *mǎ*; then *mǎ* means *horse*; then if it's *mà* then it's *scold*. (I don't speak Chinese. It's always scared me, so what I just did, I probably sound like a complete idiot to a Chinese speaker. I actually bought the Rosetta Stone set for Mandarin Chinese at Dulles Airport the other day, because I figured it's time to actually jump in. But I haven't used it yet, so sorry about that for you Chinese listeners and viewers.) In any case, it is a four-tone distinction. In Cantonese, you have six tones, and so here you see that the syllable *yau* can mean *worry*, *paint*, *thin*, *oil*, *have*, or *again*. That's only some of the meanings, based on which of the six tones are used. If you're looking at the Romanization and noticing that the fourth, fifth, and sixth word have the *h*, that's actually something that indicates in the Romanized form that you've got a low tone. That's not an actual [h] sound;

so really this is an indication that it's the same syllable *yau* with six different tones.

This example of Mandarin and Cantonese with the tones is given so much, and I think we're in a position to see something other than just the ding-dong tones. Remember the pragmatic particles from German that we talked about like *auch*, *schon*, *doch*, and *denn* that convey these quiet meanings of mood and orientation and attitude? Chinese languages have a great many of them too, or most of them do. In Mandarin, for example, let's say that you want to say, "I still have to write a dissertation." What you mean is *mind you*—like you're almost implying that this isn't true—*I still have to write a dissertation*. In English, the way that we indicate that is with a certain intonational pattern (high-low). That's kind of it, except you have to apply it to words. In Chinese, there is that, plus there's a particle. Here in Mandarin, when someone says, "I still have to write a dissertation," then there's this final particle *ne*. This is not the Japanese *ne*—completely different—that we saw in the last lecture, but you have this particle that kind of lends it that "mind you" tone. Mandarin Chinese has a few of these particles.

In Cantonese: Cantonese has so many of these particles that if they were physical objects, you could put them in a bowl. That didn't make sense; but there are a great many of these particles in Cantonese. You have to use more of them, which makes it a more complex language; mastering Cantonese is harder. For example, here's the same kind of sentence: This is someone saying, "And she got first place, you know." It's not somebody saying, "She got first place." That's not how you talk; there's some attitude in it. "She got first place, you know"; it's that (high-low) again. In Mandarin Chinese, that would be one of these *ne* sentences. But in Cantonese, you have these four particles: The first one is evaluation (*tìm*); the second one is what you use to assert your point (*ge*); the third one indicates that we're talking about something with current relevance (*la*); and the final one—the *wo*—indicates that the whole issue is newsworthy. No one could tell you what those things meant if you asked—these things are done subconsciously—but that is what all those things contribute, and they're used in various combinations. The reason that Mandarin doesn't have that is because long-term bilingualism has shorn it of its initial complexity.

Bilingualism is a norm, and it has various effects, but it does not leave a language disabled. It will not just kick English to the curb; it might leave it different, but it will not leave it disabled. Given that that is a reality of how bilingualism works, there are some things that we see happening in our modern society that we might look at in a different way. For example, often in American history people have been nervous about the idea that English seems to be being overrun by speakers of other languages. There's a sense that if we hear too much of another language or other languages, then there's something wrong—that there's some unpleasant result that's going to happen. But the fact is that, as we've seen, transitory bilingualism means that people who speak other languages generally were either born in that country and will not live forever or they're people who speak both English and the language of the old country and their children will just speak English.

You can see that that is the case by just looking at what happened in the past and then realizing that today is not all that different in terms of, for example, the concern that is often expressed about the number of Spanish speakers who are in this country. In 1920 in New York, only one in six whites were native born; everybody else was from somewhere. This is the era when a great many of the immigrants were—the newer ones were—Eastern European, and then there had been a great many immigrants from Germany and from Ireland. Today, only one in five white New Yorkers are native born, actually; it hasn't changed that much. But in the 1880s, it was said that in lower Manhattan it was hard to hear English. That was an exaggeration by journalists, but that was the impression that one could get just walking around.

In 1906, there was a requirement put forth that people admitted to the United States had to speak English. This was seen as something very urgent. Theodore Roosevelt actually made a speech where he mentioned it. He even said—can I imitate Teddy Roosevelt? I've heard him. I'm going to try.

> We have room but for one language here, and that is the English language, for we intend to see that the crucible turns our people out as Americans, of American nationality, and not as dwellers in a polyglot boarding house.

He really sounded like that. There are recordings—cylinders—of him; it's like, [makes static noise]; that's him. That's what he said, and he really believed that. Theodore Roosevelt—people did not call him Teddy—Theodore Roosevelt was not an idiot; he just thought that there must be something wrong. He didn't know anything about transitory bilingualism; he hadn't taken linguistics. But really, the only result of this possible "polyglot boarding house"—if you think about it—is what we now call diversity in terms of where people are from and what their ancestors are. In New York, it's still a polyglot boarding house, and I don't think that we worry about the Amharic speakers and the Polish speakers and the Italian speakers—we think that that's just OK—and the Chinese, etc. It doesn't threaten anything, because eventually everybody's descendants learn English. The people who are not speaking English are people from somewhere else. They don't live forever.

Or German: It used to be that German was considered the problem. There were many, many, many Germans here who actually still spoke German. Back in the 1700s and well into the 1800s, there were a great many—literally hundreds—of German newspapers in the United States. There were coherent German communities. Benjamin Franklin, of all people, didn't like this—just hearing too much German around. He said (I'm going to spare you my Ben Franklin imitation),

> Why should the (Germans) be suffered to swarm into our settlements and, by herding together, [herding!] establish their language and manners to the exclusion of ours? Why should Pennsylvania, founded by the English, become a colony of aliens, who will shortly be so numerous as to Germanize us instead of our Anglifying them?

What really was the problem? Was there really any danger that there was going to be this "Germanization"? This got even worse during World War I, where there were certain tensions with the Germans. It got to the point where German became almost like a bad smell. It was subdued; it was suppressed in this country. As a matter of fact, there was a teacher who was brought to court for teaching German in school. The way the decision went down was:

> To allow the children of foreigners, who had emigrated here, to be taught from early childhood the language of the country of their parents was to rear them with that language as their mother tongue. It was to educate them so that they must always think in that language, and, as a consequence, naturally inculcate in them the ideas and sentiments foreign to the best interests of this country.

Serious people were saying things like this about German. Really, what were they talking about? If you read, say, Sinclair Lewis's novel *Main Street*, where he's writing really about growing up in Minnesota and he's writing about the situation there as it was in the teens—it's different people, but he's writing about his hometown. There are German immigrants who are still German dominant and not really comfortable in English. In that life that Carol Kennicot leads in *Main Street* and Sinclair Lewis had lived, you hear of German around you a lot. It wasn't threatening, because the people who spoke German natively and dominantly, their lives ended eventually; their children were English dominant, and so it really wasn't a problem. Now the only places where German is still dominant are, for example, tiny communities like Amish communities, and I doubt that anybody considers them a threat. Yet there was a time when the governor of Iowa was actually laying down a law that nobody could speak anything but English in public, even on the phone. Clearly there is a sense sometimes that hearing a whole lot of another language is a problem, when really it's just a transition to a situation that will be just like it used to be in the past, which is that English remains dominant in this country and in other countries their official language remains dominant. Transitory bilingualism is generally the same everywhere.

In the same way, bilingual education is something that gets a harder rap than it really should. Many people have proposed that when you're teaching children how to read, it's more effective in their native language, and that other skills—basic skills—come more easily when taught in children's native language. In 1968, there was the Bilingual Education Act, and it was enacted in particular to help Spanish-speaking immigrants' children to learn. Bilingual education programs today are very unpopular in some quarters. For example, when he was governor of California, Ronald Reagan at one point said,

> It's absolutely wrong and against the American concept to have a bilingual program that is now openly, admittedly dedicated to preserving their native language and never getting them adequate in English so that they can go out into the job market and participate.

(I used to be able to do him, but I guess my voice has changed.) In any case, that's what he said.

Reagan was not insane, because the fact of the matter is that bilingual programs as practiced in this country have often been disasters for all kinds of reasons. They end up not teaching children effectively and keeping children for too long in such programs. But that is not to indicate that bilingual education itself must fail. In fact, it's something else, like lexical borrowing that is a norm worldwide. Actually, there are a great many studies showing that where it's done it can be very effective, and more effective than systems where children are just kind of dumped in to sink or swim. For example, in Norway, believe it or not there are many Turkish-, Urdu-, and Vietnamese-speaking kids, and it's been shown that they learn better and faster if they are started with their native languages and then move on. The same sorts of things have been shown with Punjabi-speaking kids in England, with Turkish- and Arabic-speaking kids in Holland, with Finns in Sweden—more than once—and with some indigenous languages in Mexico. These things work, and if you go to many countries where it would be germane, you find that there is bilingual education. There might not even be a term for that, because you just assume of course with small children you start them in their native language and then usher them in to the dominant language. But giving them their basic skills in the native language is considered wise, important, and effective, because it is. That's another way that bilingualism can be seen as a threat when actually it is not.

The point of this lecture has been that bilingualism and multilingualism are norms worldwide. They can have a range of effects upon the languages in question, but bilingualism is never, at least to my knowledge, a problem.

Lecture Twenty-Three
Languages Sharing a Sentence—Code-Switching

Scope: Bilingualism and multilingualism are norms worldwide. People often use two languages within one conversation, often switching between the two within sentences. This does not occur in a random fashion but according to traffic rules. The rules are determined by the difference between concrete and grammatical morphemes as well as social factors. This phenomenon is called code-switching.

Outline

I. *Code-switching* is a symptom of bilingualism.

   A. When people switch between one language and another in code-switching style, they have full command of both languages and could speak either one of them at open-ended length if necessary.

   B. There are no hesitations during code-switching as if the activity were an effort or stunt, nor are there any metalinguistic comments about the activity itself; it is largely subconscious.

   C. Code-switching is so entrenched into a context—and so typical— that, for example, Spanish speakers from different communities can tell one another apart by differences in their styles of switching.

II. Code-switching is not a random mixture of two languages. It is constrained by aspects of the workings of grammar.

   A. There have been various theories as to how this works, but a leading one is that of Carol Myers-Scotton, formerly at the University of South Carolina. It is called the *Matrix Language Frame hypothesis* (MLF).

   B. There are three main principles of the MLF conception of code-switching.

      1. A code-switching speaker is always basing the speech on a *matrix language*, even if there are many words and even phrases from the *embedded language*. Therefore, the basic rules of syntax are from the matrix language. An English-Spanish code-switcher using English as the matrix language would not say, "a car *nuevo*," because this would recruit Spanish's word order.

2. Grammatical morphemes—such as conjugational suffixes, prepositions, or articles—come from the matrix language, not the embedded one.

3. Grammatical items may be expressed briefly in the embedded language if a word used in the embedded language can only be situated into the sentence by using embedded language material. The following is an example that Myers-Scotton published in 1993.

    a. For example, when English is embedded and Swahili is the matrix:

    > *Niende nika-***check for you**.
    > I'll go and **check for you**.

    b. The way to express *for you* in Swahili is with a suffix meaning for-ness and with *you* stuck before the verb, such that the speaker here would have had to say:

    > *Niende nika-**ku**-*check*-**ea***
    > I'll go and **you check for**.

    c. Since there is no way to "backtrack" once the speaker has uttered *check*, *check for you* is expressed as an entire package.

III. The obligatory resort to the embedded language's structure is one reason for switching. Otherwise, the switching is determined by social factors.

A. Code-switching is often used to connote authority.

    1. Someone speaking Hungarian in Oberwart might switch to German when trying to discipline a child.

    2. Under similar circumstances, someone speaking Taiap in Papua New Guinea might switch to Tok Pisin, an English-based Creole language.

B. Degree of code-switching correlates with social orientation toward the two relevant cultures.

    1. Among "Nuyorican" speakers, there are three kinds of code-switchers.

        a. Some switch to English mainly in tag questions and interjections, which suggests an orientation highly oriented toward the Latino.

        b.   *Intersentential* switching indicates a healthy but less absolute Latino orientation.

        c.   *Intrasentential* switching indicates a bilingual, bicultural orientation.

   2.   In Belgium, bilinguals in Flemish and French who came of age before social tensions arose between the two languages code-switch intrasententially; younger speakers code-switch more intersententially.

   3.   In Montreal, code-switching is not especially common, and intrasentential code-switching is rare. This is because the "Anglo" and "French" identities are still separate.

IV. Code-switching can have historical results.

   A.   There are many languages that are likely the result of code-switching in the past.

      1.   For example, in the Michif language of Canada, North Dakota, and Montana, the verbs, question words, and demonstratives are in Cree, while nouns are French.

      2.   Angloromani is a hybrid of English and the Gypsies' (Roma) native language, Romani.

   B.   Code-switching happens when bilingualism is relatively stable, but language can also come together in a way that pushes one of the languages out, known as *language shift*. This may be due to migration, industrialization, school pressure, urbanization, prestige, or small population size.

      1.   In Oberwart, peasants had been bilingual in German and Hungarian since 1500, using German in business transactions. In the 1800s, monolingual Germans came as merchants, artisans, and government officials, and the province became Austrian in 1921, adding prestige to German.

      2.   At first there was no shift necessary, since agriculture flourished and was more lucrative than working for Germans. After World War II, the economy developed and led to job opportunities with Germans.

      3.   By the 1970s, German words had been borrowed into Hungarian but not vice versa.

         a.   Young people used more German: German was used in schools, and those speaking German were more fluent in it than their ancestors were.

b. Oberwart Hungarian was considered a "bad" variety and lacked even any covert prestige.

  c. Very old people still used Hungarian in a wide variety of contexts, while the youngest people used Hungarian only in church and little elsewhere.

C. Code-switching between languages looks chaotic on first glance, but it is controlled by systematic processes that are going on in countries all over the world.

Essential Reading:

Myers-Scotton, *Duelling Languages*.

———, *Code-Switching*.

Supplemental Reading:

Milroy and Muysken, eds., *One Speaker, Two Languages*.

Questions to Consider:

1. Given the vast numbers of immigrants and their children living in the United States today, you may well be a code-switcher yourself. To your mind, what determines whether you switch from one language to another during the same utterance, or even within the same sentence? Do you find that the rules listed above apply to the way you code-switch?

2. Code-switching is less exotic than a worldwide norm, given that there are 6,000 languages sharing space in only about 200 countries. However, code-switching is not exactly a folk term, and thus people tend to process it as abnormal or impure. If a Hungarian tourist asked you "Can't those Mexicans speak any single language instead of mixing up English and Spanish?" what would you tell them?

Lecture Twenty-Three—Transcript
Languages Sharing a Sentence—Code-Switching

It was 1985. I moved to New York for the first time, and I was an impressionable lad of 19. I kept a journal, and I still have it. One of my first impressions of New York after about a week was an impatience; I will openly admit that I was annoyed by something. What bothered me about New York was that it seemed that there were so many people who kept switching between English and Spanish and then back to English and back to Spanish, sometimes in the middle of the sentence, that they didn't really speak either language well. I didn't like that; it just got on my nerves.

What I was hearing was this kind of thing—we're going to put it up on the screen so that you can follow—but this is somebody who would be saying, "Why make Carol sit in the back so that everybody has to move so she can get out?" What somebody would be saying on the subway would be, "Why make Carol *sentarse atras para que* everybody has to move *para que se salga*?" It's this mixture. Or you'd hear somebody saying something like, "He was sitting down *en la cama mirándonos peleando*, *y* really, I don't remember *si él nos separó* or whatever, you know." It's this mixture. To me—because I'm the kind of person who keeps the steak and the macaroni and the peas separate—I thought, "Either speak one or the other. Don't switch, or not in front of me." I just found that kind of disorderly.

I was quite wrong. What I was seeing was how bilingualism often happens up close. There's a word for what these people in New York were doing—and for what people all over the world do—and it's called *code-switching*. It's called that because, big surprise, people are switching codes. This is what happens when people speak two languages at a time. Very often—naturally, just like languages share words—people will switch between one and the other because both of them are expressions of their identities. It's a matter of what happens when you speak two languages at a time; it is a symptom of bilingualism.

The important insight on code-switching is that when people do this code-switching, they actually have full command of both languages. The people I would see on the train who were kind of getting on my nerves by not keeping the peas separate from the meat could have spoken to me in fluent English and never needed to resort to any Spanish words. They also, I'm sure, could speak to their elderly relatives in Puerto Rico or the Dominican

Republic in full-blown Spanish and not need to use English words. It's not a matter of deficit; it's actually very much an endowment. It's something to be jealous of. It is a true bilingualism. There are no hesitations during code-switching. It's not a stunt or something like that. It doesn't require effort, and people who do it during all the times of their lives don't usually talk about it much. When somebody comes in—in a suit and tie—and says, "Why you are code-switching?" generally the response is, "Yeah, I speak this and I speak that. Yeah." To them, that's not interesting. It's just a perfectly normal thing. It's not a stunt; it's not a game; it's just a way of living.

It is so entrenched—and it can become so idiosyncratic in a community, just like a language's collection of phonemes, morphemes, etc.—that Spanish speakers from different communities can identify where someone comes from often by the way they code-switch. It ends up being a very nuanced thing that people do. The fact is, if you listen to people doing it—like I was in the train back during the Reagan administration—it can sound very sloppy. It's kind of like, "Why don't you just pick one?" It seems like a radio station is going in and out or something like that. But actually there are rules in code-switching. Code-switching is actually constrained by the basics of grammatical structure that I've been showing you in this course.

There have been various theories as to what those rules are, and you would be surprised how angry people can get about this sort of thing. What's interesting is it's mostly people who don't code-switch between anything and anything else; it's just Anglo linguists. I have seen people almost in tears at conferences over fighting over how code-switching works. It can be a nasty little business, and they're like wars in the world. Nevertheless, that is the way academia is.

It seems to me that the person who has contributed the most useful and generalizable model of what the rules of code-switching is Carol Myers-Scotton, who was at the University of South Carolina. Her hypothesis had the rather intimidating name of the *Matrix Language Frame hypothesis*, and because that's ugly, I'm not going to say that again; we're going to call it the MLF. The MLF acronym does not mean anything except Matrix Language Frame hypothesis.

There are three main principles of the MLF conception. That is that, first of all, a code-switching speaker is always basing their speech at any given time on a *matrix language*. They might switch matrix languages, but basically, even if there are words and phrases popping in from the other language, they are speaking one of the languages at that time in terms of grammar. There is a matrix language at all times, and then the other language popping in—the kind of different radio station—is called the *embedded language*. The basic rules of syntax are always in a particular language. That means that somebody on the train in 1985—or actually any time—in New York who's code-switching would not say, "I just bought a car *nuevo*"—*nuevo* meaning *new* in Spanish. If you've ever heard people code-switch, you know they don't do that. The reason for that is that if they're talking about, "Well, I bought a car," then they're using English's grammar—not only its words, but its grammar—and in English, we don't put adjectives after nouns; so that would never happen.

Then that means that grammatical morphemes—this is the second principle—grammatical morphemes like conjugational suffixes, prepositions, or articles come from the matrix language and not the embedded one, even during code-switching speech; *-iendo* is the progressive affix in Spanish. Nobody would ever say, "I was eat-*iendo*"; it's ridiculous. People code-switch—they mix the languages—but that wouldn't happen. If you want to say, "I am speaking with my mother," then you say, "*Yo hablo con mi madre*." But if you want to talk about it in the past, you would never say, "*You* habla-ed *con mi madre*" using the English past marker. That's because the morphology—the grammatical morphemes in general—have to be from the matrix language. There is the switching back and forth, but typically that would be between—for example—sentences. It is not done within words in that way.

There are situations—and this is because if you just use those first two principles, you hear all kinds of exceptions in the way people actually do code-switch—there actually is a way that you will find grammatical items being expressed in the embedded language briefly. The way that happens is in an example like this. What we're going to have on the screen is some Swahili, and we're going to have this indication. This is somebody who is code-switching between English and Swahili—very common in some African countries. The person was saying, "I'll go and check for you." How this works here is "*Niende*" is "I will go," "*ni*" is "I," and "*ende*" is "go." Then they say, "*nika*"—now "*ni*" is repeating the "I" again. Never mind why; I don't think that sounds so strange, that's just what they do. The "*ka*" is a suffix that means that we're talking about something sequential; so we say, "I'll go and check." You can think of the "*ka*" as kind of meaning *and*; it has "and-itude." "*Niende nika*-check for you." What's interesting here is that all of a sudden we have grammatical morphemes. This "for" is in

English, and that's not the way it's supposed to be, but the reason this happens is because there's some kind of train wreck between the languages. Here's "I'll go and check for you."

Now look here at how Swahili works. The fact is that it is a different language from English—as we knew—and therefore there are things it does that English would never do. The way that you would have to say, "check for you" in Swahili is that you have to have, for one thing, the "you" is a pronoun, but it's an affix and it goes before the verb. You can look here, you can see this: "*Niende nika-ku*-check ..."; you have to have it back there, plus "for-ness"—the way to say, "for." There is no word in Swahili separate for "for"; I am 96 percent sure that that is the case. The way that you indicate "for-ness" is with a suffix (*-ea*). You have to say, "I will go and you check for." That's how it goes in Swahili; that's not odd in Swahili and other Bantu languages.

What happened to create this violation—where you've actually got "for" in English, when the person is supposed to be in the Swahili matrix language and grammatical morphemes would be from that—is that once the person said, "check," they were stuck, because you can't then go back and put the pronoun affix "you" before it. You didn't do it. "*Nika*-check," and because in English we say, "check for you," that was the unit that was in the person's mind. But once the person says, "check," you can't have that *ku* thing; you didn't do it. Therefore, you just finish it out with "for you," then you go back to the Swahili. So code-switching is a matter of switching, say, between sentences or between clauses. You can drop in words, but generally you are, at all times, using the grammar of one language. People have looked at this in many situations in the world, and there are definite consistencies in how code-switching works. Obviously people don't think about these things, but this shows that the basic underlying representation of grammar that we've been proposing does exist in people's minds.

Then of course there are the social principles of code-switching, like why do people switch? What makes somebody switch? Is it just completely random, or are there factors involved that would make somebody switch to a different code? It's found that to an extent there is a randomness; there's an extent to which listening to people switch from one language to another, you cannot say that at each point where they switch that there's a particular reason. That's one of the things that people fight about at conferences, because ideally we'd like to be able to say that person switched because of this grammatical factor or this social factor, or because the planets were aligned differently, or because they ate a black olive, or something like that, but you can't; I mean, life is always a little bit messy.

But there are some tendencies, and for example code-switching is often used to connote authority. Somebody will switch into another language in order to underline what they're saying and to give it some weight. For example, here is somebody who is speaking Hungarian—we have that up on the screen—and they are somebody who is bilingual in Hungarian and German, and they do a switch. This is somebody who's trying to discipline a child. Here they are saying, "Come here, put all this away both of you, well now!" Then, "*Kum her*! Now you don't get supper!" It's something like "*Szo! Ide dzsüni! Jeszt jerámunyi mind e kettüötök, no hát akkor! Kum her!*"—that's the German. Then "*Ném koapsz vacsorat!*" That's how code-switching works. That's one example.

Or we can go to a tiny, tiny, tiny—I mean tiny—village in Papua New Guinea where they speak a language called Taiap. Taiap must be … 2,500, maybe? Intuitively, I would think it was spoken by seven people; this is one of these tiny, tiny languages. In Papua New Guinea, as I mentioned in the previous lecture, there are 800 languages spoken—not in Papua, but on the whole island of New Guinea; Papua New Guinea is one half of it—but there are 800 languages spoken on that island. As a result, you can imagine that there must be a *lingua franca*; there must be several, and there are. One of them is the unfortunately named language Tok Pisin. Tok Pisin is not a reference to what it sounds like. Another word for what it sounds like is micturition; there's your word of the day. But it's not that. "Pisin" actually means *business*; that's how it comes out in the language's phonology.

Tok Pisin is an English-based Creole language. It has the bizarrest history. It started when white people went to Australia and had to talk to the Aboriginal people. Then this new way of speaking English was taken out into the ocean to the east and used with various indigenous people who were used to collect sea cucumbers (disgusting creatures), sandalwood, and whatever else they were doing. Then it was brought back to the coast of Australia as a plantation language in Queensland. It was also used on Samoa, and the Germans picked it up and started using it in New Guinea. Anyway, that language now exists today. It is a simplified but full-language version of English, highly influenced by Aboriginal languages and the Melanesian languages spoken by the sea cucumber guys. It is now something very useful in Papua New Guinea for allowing people who speak these languages to communicate with one another. It is also the language from above. There's actually a newspaper in it called *Wantok*, "one talk."

Here is somebody speaking Taiap, and once again this is a child being disciplined. Because I know just what somebody's going to write in from Taiap-land and complain that I was pronouncing their language wrong, but I think this is so unlikely that I'm just going to pronounce it the way it's written. It's "*Ɔretukun. Ɛaryŋarana. Ɔretukun. Lusim em! Ɛne nda tawairunak.*" Now "*Lusim em!*" is the Tok Pisin, and that's like "loose"—never mind the *-im*—and the *em*, and that's "Let her alone," so "Let her alone. She better not cry. Let her alone. *Lusim em!* I'm gonna smack you." It's used to connote this kind of authority.

Something else that's been seen is that code-switching comes in different flavors and that it correlates with social orientation toward the two relative cultures. For example, the people I saw on the train, we call them "Nuyorican" speakers. That's not pejorative; that is the term that's actually used in the literature. Among the Nuyorican speakers, there are actually three kinds of code-switchers. There are people who switch to English mainly just to do tag questions and interjections. Those people are very Latino in their orientation, their life experience, and in their spirit. Those are people for whom English is something that is very much outside. For example, one quotation—this is a genuine quotation from an actual human being; this is not me making it up—is that someone was saying, "My mother had to go sign and [boop] to get me out, you know?" The "boop" stands for this expletive, which you can see on the screen. I will not utter it, but you can see what it is. The actual utterance was in Spanish with quick resorts to English, so "*Mi madre tuvo que ir a firmar y* [boop] *para sacarme*, you know?" That's what the person said. That's just dabbling English in.

Then there are people who do what's called *intersentential* switching. This is somebody who has a very healthy Latino orientation but is also very assimilated in terms of how they feel about their place in the English-speaking society. This is a beautiful example of that, which is somebody talking about smoking. They are saying, and we can see on the screen:

> *Tu no fumas, verdad? Yo tampoco. Dejé de fumar* and I'm back to it again. And they tell me, "How did you quit, Mary?" I didn't quit; I just stopped. I mean, it wasn't an effort that I made. *Que voy a dejar de fumar porque me hace daño o* this or that, no. It's just that I used to pull butts out of the wastepaper basket. *Se me acaban los cigarros en la noche.* I'd get desperate *y ahí voy al basurero a buscar, y sacar*, you know?

That's intersentential, because it's between sentences. This person is using whole sentences in both languages. This is not dropping English in as a kind of dusting; this is really indulging in it. But this is still not *intrasentential* switching, which is something different altogether.

The intrasentential switcher is somebody who really is a person of a fully bilingual, fully bicultural, neither one nor the other orientation. That goes back to "Why make Carol *sentarse atras para que* everybody has to move *para que se salga*?" That's where you have—within the sentence, where it can happen between clauses—you have these switches. That is a particular kind of person as well.

We see around the world that the difference between intersentential and intrasentential is something that marks cultural orientation. There have been major tensions in Belgium between French and Flemish. People who came of age before that happened code-switch between French and Flemish intrasententially. People who came of age afterwards keep the languages separate, and they code-switch, but it's more intersententially. Or there's something interesting about Montreal: You go to Montreal, and you know that both English and French are spoken there. You imagine that when you get on the train in Montreal, you're going to listen to people doing the intrasentential code-switching routine—familiar from, say, Nuyoricans in New York—and you don't, actually. You really don't hear that much code-switching between English and French. If you do, it is intersentential; people running around doing it intrasententially is vanishingly rare. I personally have spent a certain amount of time in Montreal. I never heard it, and was always listening for it because I thought it would be kind of neat. There's a reason that people don't do that, and it's because obviously there is a separation between the Anglo culture and the French Canadian culture there. There aren't that many people who feel that they are both of those things; you are one or the other. Of course there have always been the political and cultural tensions. As a result, you don't see that kind of code-switching.

What's interesting about code-switching is that it can have some historical results. There are languages that are the result of clearly very intense code-switching in the past, which children grew up hearing and actually made into a language. It's happened a lot more than once. For example, there is up in Canada, and today North Dakota and Montana, a language called Michif. Michif was created when French Canadians were running around up there, and they were hunting furs, and they were not women, and they got tired of that, and so there were unions between them and Native American

Cree women. Those unions produced children. The children grew up as half French Canadian, half Cree. They ended up creating a language that split the difference between the two, and that's Michif, which is still spoken today.

In Michif, you see that verbs and question words and demonstratives—like *this* and *that*—those are in Cree, but the nouns are all in French. You can see this is "Her brother died when she was a little girl." If you know French, you can see in the Michif example that there is "*son frère*," which is "her brother," and "*la petite fille*," that is "the little girl," and then there's all the rest of this stuff. Here's the French: "*Son frère est mort quand elle était une petite fille.*" Then here's the Cree. I'll just let that go, but you can see that on the screen [*Kînipiyiwa ostêsa aspin kâoskinîkîwit*]. Michif is a cross between the two [*Kînipiyiwa son frère aspin kâ-la-petite-fille-iwit*]. That is the result of a code-switching, where people were using Cree as the matrix language but using lots of drop-ins from French. Now it is just a separate language altogether, where the nouns actually are French—you don't use the Cree nouns at all—and it has a system of its own.

Another example of this is Angloromani. Romani is the language of the people often known as Gypsies—more properly Roma—in Europe. Their language is actually an Indian language. Romani is related to Hindi and Gujarati and Bengali and the gang. Romani clearly definitely gets around. There is a language called Angloromani, and Angloromani is the result of code-switching. This is a situation where the matrix language was English, but one dropped in a lot of Romani words. "The Devil came and said, 'Come with me.'" In Angloromani, it's "The *Beng wel'd* and *pen'd*: *Av* with *man-di*"—which is this peculiar kind of mix to us that to people who speak this language is perfectly normal. It's often used as a kind of an in-group code, especially by Romani, who are actually losing actual pure Romani, but they still have this as an in-group language. You can see in Romani what it would be [*O Beng vi-as. Yov pen-das: Av man-tsa*], and the words that I used just now that were unfamiliar are in this Romani. Then in Angloromani, you have this mixture. That is something that can happen to code-switching; code-switching might just continue forever or it might freeze into what becomes a brand new language entirely.

Finally, we want to observe that code-switching is not what always happens when there is bilingualism; code-switching is something that happens when bilingualism is relatively stable. But the fact of the matter is that sometimes languages come together in such a way that one language is going to be on its way out. One language will just take over another language, and then code-switching doesn't happen. That is a language-contact process as well, and it is called *language shift*. I wanted to touch briefly on language shift just to give you a dollop of flavoring of that in our course, because language shift is studied by a lot of people and there's been a lot of good work done on it.

One example of this would be in Austria. I talked about Oberwart, Austria. This is somewhere where peasants had been bilingual in German and Hungarian since about 1500, and German was just used in business transactions; German was just a language for the outside world. Then, in the 1800s, monolingual Germans came in as merchants, officials, and things like that, and the province itself became officially Austrian in 1921. Now here German is the prestige language. Oberwart is where that Hungarian-German code-switching quote came from, and so it does happen. However, the fact is that what's really been happening in Oberwart for the most part is that Hungarian has been being overtaken completely by German. This has been especially after World War II when the economy developed and it meant that there were lots of job opportunities with Germans. You could see this switch going on in the 1970s, where you saw that, for example, there were lots of people who were speaking Hungarian as a matrix language and dropping in some German. But with German, German would always be spoken pure, and so there's no such thing as code-switching there. There was a sense that German was itself; you don't mix it with what came before. Young people were using more German, and German was being used in the schools. People speaking German were more fluent in it the younger that they got. The Hungarian variety of Oberwart was being rejected as bad Hungarian, rather than there being the covert prestige of it being "the Hungarian that we speak here."

All these things were seen as evidence that Hungarian was going away. You could even be very systematic about it. For example, you could find some people who were speaking Hungarian with a very wide range of people and in a very wide range of circumstances. For example, you could find a person who used Hungarian in prayer, who used Hungarian with their grandparents, with their parents, with their friends, with their siblings, with salespeople, with their spouse, and with children. If you found anybody like that, then that was somebody who was very, very old. In fact, technically, that person probably did not have grandparents or parents, but you take my point. Or you could find somebody who only used Hungarian in prayer. That person would generally be the very youngest people. There were people in between; you might use Hungarian in prayer and then with your grandparents, but then with nobody else. You might use Hungarian in prayer, with your grandparents, and with your parents, but then with nobody else. You could actually make a grid where you could see that young people tended to restrict Hungarian to prayer, if that; very old people were using Hungarian everywhere, and the younger you get, the fewer contexts you're using Hungarian in. Basically, German has rendered Hungarian all but extinct in this area. That is the way language shift generally goes. You can see different effects on people of different ages where the language is used in fewer and fewer contexts. That's just one example of language shift.

But the main point of this lecture has been that there is code-switching between languages, that it is one of many things in language that looks awfully chaotic on first glance but it's actually controlled by systematic processes, and that it's something that is typically the way bilingualism actually works. For people to keep the languages completely separate is actually a rather unusual case; if you speak two languages, then just as often you're going to switch between them. Code-switching is going on in all sorts of countries all over the world. It's often not particularly documented, because nobody thinks of it as anything particularly interesting. It's something that linguists happened to have noticed and to have systematized. However, the fact is that it is done, it is normal, and it's actually—I've always thought—quite interesting. I hope you did too.

Lecture Twenty-Four
The Rules of Conversation

Scope: Spontaneous conversation between people is not a mere matter of people speaking deferently in turn, exchanging information. It is also a matter of people interrupting one another almost necessarily. In conversation, we are concerned as much with verbal rituals as with conveying data and impressions. This lecture is about conversation analysis, which posits that there are rules behind conversation just as there are rules to phonology and syntax.

Outline

I. Holden Caulfield of *The Catcher in the Rye* noticed that conversation has rules.

    A. When Caulfield sees a play in New York, he notices that the actors' lines overlaped when they spoke.

    B. Caulfield was astute in noticing that this is, indeed, the way real people talk. In general, human conversation is something different from the way it is usually depicted on the page or the way we think of it deliberately.

    C. Linguists and sociologists have discovered that conversation is guided by subconsciously controlled rules, just as syntax is—and just as code switching is guided by the combination of morphology and syntax known as *morphosyntactic structure.*

II. Conversation is defined as unplanned speech and is quite different from planned speech.

    A. Casual speech is much less tidy than written language, even among educated people, and has several typical traits.

        1. Repetitions, false starts, and hesitation noises are in talk the world over.

        2. No human being can avoid rapid speed and casual enunciation.

        3. Inexplicit vocabulary in response to memory and attention lapses are also universal in how human beings use language on the everyday level; i.e., *whatchamacallit.*

        4. Active sentences are more common than passive sentences.

5. What could be called restricted code features clause stringing with *and*, *but*, or simple juxtaposition.

6. Casual speech is composed of utterances, not "sentences."

B. Taking a sample of college students speaking casually, we can notice the frequency of *and*, the hesitations with *uh*, the rarity of the passive. This is typical *casual*, or *unmonitored*, speech.

C. This is the object of study in the investigation of conversation. No actual human beings have ever conversed casually in the fashion of Caspar and Isabel in Henry James's *The Portrait of a Lady*.

III. We are now in a position to look at a model of conversational systematics.

A. The most influential model for how we manage conversation was created by the sociologists Harvey Sacks, Emanuel Schegloff, and Gail Jefferson. Their insight was that conversation is guided by rules that are not conscious ones of the "Don't interrupt!" kind.

B. Conversations are divided by changes of turn between *units*. The changes of turn happen at a *transition-relevance place* (TRP). There are three rules, which apply in order.

1. The current speaker selects the next one explicitly by soliciting a response, upon which the selected person has right and obligation to speak.

2. If the current speaker does not select, then the first person to self-select has the floor.

3. If neither rule applies, the current speaker may continue.

C. In our example, no one self-selects after first TRP, so the speaker continues, stops, starts again, but then her companion self-selects. The first speaker self-selects again, *projecting* the end of the second speaker's unit (at the word *fault*) while the second speaker was about to select the first, producing an overlap.

D. If there are no overlaps, then something peculiar is going on; there is probably even hostility.

E. Another source of overlap is simultaneous self-selection, which produces exchanges with no overlaps or only slight ones, because within a unit the speaker has exclusive rights to talk.

F. There are also strategies for keeping the floor (maintaining one's unit).

1. Avoidance of eye contact is a way of keeping the floor, while looking someone in the eye often is a way of indicating that the speaker is finished.
2. Many people string their utterances together seamlessly, without pauses analogous to periods in written language.
3. Gestures and postures, such as the hands in the air, can discourage others from taking their turn in conversation.

G. Speakers signal the end of a turn in other ways besides looking someone in the eye.
1. Prolonging the final stressed syllable invites someone to come in.
2. Dropping pitch level on the final syllable is another invitation.
3. Closing the utterance syntactically, with a "period," is not nearly as common as supposed.
4. Using tags such as *you know* and *or something* is more common for female speakers.

H. A gap is socially undesirable in many cultures and will tend to be filled even when there is no content.

IV. *Adjacency pairs* are set exchange routines that wouldn't make sense if you only uttered one member of the pair.

A. Much of how we actually engage in exchange with other people consists of adjacency pairs:
1. question/answer
2. greeting/greeting (*How are you? Fine.*)
3. request or offer/acceptance or refusal
4. complaint/apology
5. statement/recognition
6. compliment/acceptance or rejection
7. farewell/farewell.

B. Preclosing signals, which gently end an exchange, are composed of series of adjacency pairs.

V. Cultural differences also affect conversational style.

A. Deborah Tannen has shown that among some people in some cultures, overlaps are standard; simultaneous talk is valued, even required.

B. In this kind of conversation, speech rate is rapid, overlap is cooperative, and silence is avoided. Overlaps are positive, gaps are abhorrent.

VI. Topics are not generally fixed before a conversation but are continually renegotiated (note how hard it is to sit down and talk about one thing in an informal setting).

A. Much of conversation tends to be brute sociological reinforcement, not topic coverage at all.

B. If there are topics, they float in and out, just decoration to the basic acknowledgement of each other's presence, goodness, and friendship, such that it is easier to say what *was* talked about than what *is* being talked about (note the pause one would make before explaining what is being talked about).

C. Having a set topic is relatively uncommon and involves sponsoring an event where everyone knows in advance that a topic is set. That is the marked case, to use our distinction between marked and unmarked.

Essential Reading:

Tannen, *Conversational Style.*

Supplemental Reading:

Wooffitt, *Conversation Analysis and Discourse Analysis.*

Questions to Consider:

1. Record you and friends having a casual conversation, and leave the machine on for a good half-hour so that any self-consciousness about the recording wears off. Take a look at the final 20 minutes or so of the recording and marvel at how choppy and full of interruption normal speech actually is. This is why some scholars have been moved to seek regularity amidst the apparent chaos.

2. Is there a person you have trouble communicating gracefully with, who in terms of this lecture flouts one or more of the rules we have seen? Which rule have they failed to master, or which rule do they abuse in some way?

Lecture Twenty-Four—Transcript
The Rules of Conversation

It's my favorite moment in *The Catcher in the Rye*. I think a lot of people's favorite moment is the hard stakes or various things that Holden Caulfield talks about, but I remember when I first read it just being taken by one passage of his. It's when he sees a play in New York, and he is watching The Lunts. For those of you who have only been around for a certain period of time, The Lunts were a couple—they were a man and a woman, Alfred Lunt and Lynn Fontanne—and they played in a lot of theatrical productions where they generally played a couple—or people who wanted to be or used to be. They were quite famous at the time. When Holden goes to New York to see a play, of course he gets to see The Lunts—that would be with a capital *T* and a capital *L*. Holden describes something about The Lunts; this was a trademark of their performance. He says:

> When one of them got finished making a speech, the other one said something very fast right after it. It was supposed to be like people really talking and interrupting each other and all. The trouble was, it was too much like people talking and interrupting each other.

Holden picks up on something very particular and very real about the way people talk. In general, human conversation is different from the way it's usually depicted on the page, and therefore different from what I think a lot of us imagine conversation to be, as opposed to what it is. The upshot of all of this is that linguists, sociolinguists, and sociologists have discovered that conversation is guided by subconsciously controlled rules, just like syntax is. Just as we've seen that in code-switching there are rules that grow out of the basic—I'll give you a word here—*morphosyntactic structure* of the language (morphology, syntax, put them together, and it's morphosyntax; so that's what we say: morphosyntax), conversation has rules as well.

What we first have to realize, in terms of how conversation works, is that we're not talking about the idealized form of language that we see on the page. Conversation is unplanned speech, and that's something quite different from planned speech. Casual speech is much less tidy than written language, and this is even among educated people. This is not a matter of class; this is not a matter of education. This is a matter of me; this is a matter of you. It is everybody.

For example, repetitions, false starts, and hesitations—noises and hesitations—that is the way human beings talk the world over. For example, Hillary Clinton is someone who says, "you know" a lot; she's a very articulate person, but when she's putting her thoughts together, she says, "you know," like many articulate people. There's one interview with her where she's talking about how she used to go duck hunting. She says, "I remember standing in the cold water. It was so cold, you know, at first light." That's what she says, an articulate, intelligent person; lots of "you know." Another one is Barack Obama. If you actually watch his interviews in transcription: a lot of "you know's." It's actually rather reflective; it's a way of pausing before thinking. At one point Obabma said, "Well, you know, there are a lot of companies that have been around a lot longer than Google, but Google's performing." He puts in the "you know." That is perfectly normal in speech.

Or something else that is common in unplanned speech is that you have rapid speed and you have casual enunciation. This is something that no human being can help. It's a lot of what drives sound change; that's the way words are actually pronounced. There is a wonderful example of that, actually, in an expression that has become particularly popular among black young men over what I'm told is the past 15 or 20 years. That is the expression "You know what I'm saying?" to elicit sympathy or to elicit understanding. "I went down to the store looking for Tahitian Treat and they didn't have any and that really bothered me, you know what I'm saying?" But of course it's not said the way I'm saying it. Nobody says, "Do you know what I'm saying?" You say, "Know I'm sayin'?" Or you might say, "'M sayin'?"

Really, the fact is, linguists have studied "You know what I'm saying?" and the way it's actually pronounced in the phonetic stream often is [nmsɛ̃]. Really, we've got this new word based on rapid enunciation. We can even put it up on the screen. Look at the way that would actually be transcribed. It would not be, "Do you know what I'm saying?" It would actually be this one word: It would be [n], [m], [s], and then we're going to have the ɛ symbol, and in order to get that it's "'m sayin'," that "enh"—there's a difference between "eh" and "enh"—so we make it a nasal, and so we're going to put our little tilde on top. That's how you would transcribe "'m sayin'." that's it. That has become kind of a pragmatic particle in Black English. If a Martian came down and just wrote down what he or she saw— a Martian could be a woman—so a Martian wrote down what they saw (but of course you're not supposed to do that), then you would have in their dictionary of the English language this [nmsɛ̃] as a pragmatic particle. That's just the way things go.

There is inexplicit vocabulary, and also memory lapses, and therefore words like *whatchamacallit* and things like that. That is more and more the case as you get older, and I mean older like my 42. Over the past four years, I've been doing that more and more. I'm afraid of getting old because it happens a lot, but that is a normal way of speaking.

Active sentences more than sentences with the passive, and so one might say, "The gentleman was deported." That's something you might have in English, particularly in written language; and we might have it in oral language. In many languages, that would immediately be rendered differently. You would ask somebody, "How do you say, 'the gentleman was deported'?" and they would say, "They deported the gentleman." That's common in many languages around the world, and that's more common in unplanned speech. Then there is lots of clause stringing with *and*'s and *but*'s, and so we're talking about what could be called restricted code again. In that light, "The guys crossed the road and a car knocked them down and someone said, 'Hey what did you do that for?' and then they saw that the car kept driving." That is the way people speak in a normal way.

Importantly, the whole notion of "sentence"—the idea that we speak in sequences of subjects and predicates neatly qualified and ending with periods—is of course not the way people really talk. Really, when we talk about the study of conversation, we talk about utterances—not sentences in terms of parsing and the like, but just utterances, what is a coherent packet. Like in a previous lecture, when I talked about what topic prominence is and I talked about the topic-comment structure, I talked about a woman who was saying, "Me, I was so tired yesterday I couldn't make change." Actually, I'm tidying that up. I for some reason remember that very vividly, partly because there was something notable about the appearance of the person in question, and partly because it was a very beautiful cloudy morning in San Francisco and I was buying my favorite sausage. (Saag's brand sausage. Order it from California; it's actually worth it—the "Louisiana Hots.") But this woman said—and I can still smell this moment—what she said precisely was, "Me, yesterday, I was so tired I couldn't even make change." Where are the sentences in that? The "me" was all by itself; "yesterday" was all by itself; then "I was so tired I couldn't even make change," and really what she said—because it was in a conversation and I was getting my change—was, "Me. Yesterday. I was so tired." And then she got interrupted. That's the way conversation actually works; she didn't finish. Language is messy. She was going to talk about change, because that's what the conversation had been about, but she was not dominant in the conversation.

What I mean is, here is a sample of some college students in the early '70s just talking. This is people just talking, and there's a tape recorder, and they're just going. They're not performing; they're not extraordinary; they're just students. For the record, they were at UC Berkley. You can see in the text here, one person says, "They've had quite a bit of trouble with trying to get established. They want to establish a Synanon in, I think, Malibu, and, uh …" Synanon was a drug-rehabilitation program, and it was established in 1958. If you were around then, you will remember that they came up with the really important catch phrase—I've often thought about this, and I wasn't even there then, but it's gotten passed down—"Today is the first day of the rest of your life." Because it is, if you really think about that. In any case, that's what this Synanon they're referring to is. Let's start it again:

> "They've had quite a bit of trouble with trying to get established. They want to establish a Synanon in, I think, Malibu and uh …"

> "Yeah, they, they, uh, they want to move the Synanon that they've got now at, at the beach to Malibu. Uh … and they're having a rough time with the planning commission and nobody seems to want them. And no matter where they go they're not wanted."

> "Well, from what I've heard I think they've done a, a fair job. I think they should be given a chance."

> "They've done a tremendous job and it's true but the people, uh …"

> "Well, the people in the surrounding area worry about it because they're …"

> "They're afraid that they'll have dope addicts running around, I think."

That is the way people actually talk, and so that's what conversation study is. What it is not is the way that people talk, for example, in an Edith Wharton novel. I just saw the film of *House of Mirth*; do not rent it. Really, one of the worst films ever made. Or, more to the point, *Portrait of a Lady* by Henry James—really bad movie. It should be given to film students.

Here is an exchange in *Portrait of a Lady* between the Caspar character and Isabel Archer. It starts with Isabel:

> "I told you just now that I don't wish to marry and that I almost certainly never shall."

> "I know you did, and I like your 'almost certainly'! I put no faith in what you say."

> "Thank you very much. Do you accuse me of lying to shake you off? You say very delicate things."

> "Why should I not say that? You've given me no pledge of anything at all."

> "No, that's all that would be wanting!"

> "You may perhaps believe you're safe—from wishing to be. But you're not," the young man went on as if preparing himself for the worst.

Nobody talks like that. They don't talk like that now; they didn't talk like that then. No human being could. *The House of Mirth* film has people talking like that. It's quite shameful. That's not the way it goes.

With that in mind, we're in a position to look at a model of conversational systematics. The most influential model for this—the traffic rules of conversation—was formulated by sociologists, namely Harvey Sacks, Emanuel Schegloff, and Gail Jefferson. Their insight is that conversation is guided by a structure that is not just conscious ones along the lines of "Don't interrupt." That's obviously something that we teach people. The little girl who lives next door to me is under the misimpression that I imitate Bugs Bunny well, and she always wants me to do Bugs Bunny and just falls on the ground. All I have to do is say one sentence. She will walk up to me talking to grownups and just tug on my shirt and say, "John, can you imitate Bugs Bunny?" Her parents teach her, "Don't interrupt." But in fact, that is just a fraction of what having a conversation's about, and the truth is that really we do interrupt, and all the time.

According to the Sacks, Schegloff, and Jefferson model, conversations are divided by changes of turn between *units*. The changes of turn—i.e., when a new person starts talking—happens at what's called a *transition-relevance place*, or a TRP. There are three basic rules, and they apply in order. It's either (a), the current speaker selects the next one explicitly—that can happen by soliciting a response—and then the selected person has the right and actually the obligation to speak. If they don't speak, then something very strange has happened. A conversation involves, in the social sense, a kind of obligation—an unsaid obligation—that you don't just stand there looking at each other for any long period of time. Then (b), if the current speaker does not select, then the first person to self-select has the floor; and so somebody can do it themselves. Then (c), if neither (a) nor (b) happens, then the current speaker may continue.

The fact is that usually it's (b) that happens, where someone self-selects and breaks in, and not always in tidy fashion. Here is a conversation between Claire and Chloe: Claire says, "So then we were worse off—and she went down four. But uhm ... uh" Then, Chloe says, "Well then it was her fault, Claire." Then Claire says, "Yeah she said one no trump, and I said two."

What happens here is that Claire starts off saying, "So then we were worse off and she went down four." No one says anything: "But um ..." Now actually someone could have come in there, but they don't, and so Claire continues: "uh." But on the "uh," Chloe then self-selects. She says, "Well then it was her fault, Claire," and the "uh" and the "well" overlap. People don't just wait politely like in a Henry James novel or in a lot of novels. Then Chloe says, "Well then it was her fault, Claire." Then, at this point, Claire self-selects again. She ends up overlapping on the enunciation of her name, because the way Chloe says "fault"—when she actually says, "Well then it was her fault"—implies with its intonation that she's soliciting Claire to come back in. What Claire is termed to have done is that she *projected* that she had been selected, even though technically she had not been in words by the intonation of "fault" and the context.

What happens in something like what you see on the screen and what you've just heard is that there are overlaps, and that is something that is standard in normal human conversation. If there are no overlaps, then something peculiar is going on; there's probably even hostility. The way that people jump into a conversation is by overlapping with final syllables. Also, there's simultaneous self-selection. Here are three guys: There's Mike, and then there's Vick and James. Mike says, "I know who the guy is." Then Vick says, "He's ba-ad," at the same time as James says, "You know the guy?" They say it together. (Notice how I'm talking to myself in these. Isn't that neat? You can hear all of my voices together; just wanted to call attention to that.) That's what happens. This system produces exchanges with only slight overlaps. It's not that people are biting all over each other—constant but slight overlaps, because within a unit, a speaker has exclusive rights for talking.

Beyond that, there are things going on that allow people to keep the floor. For example, people will avoid eye contact. Think about how little you actually look someone in the eye when you're conversing with him. If you are seven years old and you're going to draw a conversation, you're going to have two people with their little noses pointing at each other and kind of talking at each other. But think about how unnatural that is; that's not what you do. Often when you're talking to someone, you make all sorts of excuses to look in the other direction, to look past them. You're reflecting; you're looking somewhere else. Often, when you do that, it is a way of keeping the floor. Part of looking someone in the eye often is a way of indicating that you are finished and calling on them, so to speak.

Then there is the fact that many people string their utterances together seamlessly. The whole notion of a period is something rather artificial. There weren't always periods in terms of how language was punctuated, because we don't really talk in periods most of the time. We might close out our utterance, but the fact is that usually we just kind of keep on a-going. If you ever have done the trick of turning on a tape recorder and recording you and your friends talking for a half hour and then playing it back, you'll notice that it can be very difficult to actually identify sentences. People don't sit around saying things like, "Armadillos are very peculiar animals." That's just not the way people talk. You just string various utterances together seamlessly: "Me. Yesterday. I was so tired." That's the way people talk in general.

Or there are gestures and postures. I remember I had a friend once, and she had a gesture that I found extremely annoying. When she would discourage anybody from taking their turn in conversation, she'd go like that; so she'd say, "Well I blah blah blah blah blah blah and blah blah blah." In the pictorial sense, this was kind of—I'll use a Robin Lakoff female word—adorable and charming; it was kind of cute. There's a symmetry to it; I'm sure an art student would have liked to draw it. But really, what this meant was *shut up*. It was like "I'm talking now," and she talked a lot. She knew nothing about me after … anyway, that was one version of that. One that's more common is this one; you know: the hands. "Well, all I know is Chipwiches were very popular in the early '80s, and now nobody seems to eat them anymore, and I can't find them," and you kind of go like this. This seems innocent enough, but really it means *don't you talk*. But that's what many people do, and that's the way that you indicate that you are maintaining your unit. The idea is that the other people are not supposed to break in. If you do this a lot, it means that you're actually kind of a dominant converser.

How do you signal the end of a turn? You could look someone in the eye; that's one way of indicating it is your turn: to do something rather unusual, which is to look at the person. You could prolong the final stressed syllable, so you could say, "And that's when I decided I'd just spend the night up in the treeee." That invites somebody to come in. You would be less likely to say, "And that is when I decided that I was going to spend the night up in the tree." *Boom*. That's not how people talk; "up in the treeee" and then you're done, and then somebody will break in. Or you might drop your pitch—gradually—and so you say, "And that's when I decided I was going to stay up in the tree and besides, there's [mumbles] ..." and that's an indication. Lower intonation is an invitation for people to jump in. You might close the utterance out with a period, but that is not the usual case. When you're finished watching this lecture—you know, when you go off to do the rest of your life—try to see how many periods you actually utter, and I don't mean literally saying, "period," but how many things you say that could really be said to have periods after them, especially subject-predicate sentences that are nice and tidy. It's not nearly as common as you would think.

Then of course there are the tags such as *you know* or *or something* or *type-thing*, which is one that I find non-male people seem to use a lot: "Oh, it was a party-type-thing," and then the person comes in. I remember one person who was talking about how—it was someone who was not usually given to being nostalgic—but she was looking at pictures, and she was saying, "You have to keep these pictures, because after a while that's all there is, you know." The "you know" was a solicitation for me to say something. There was more than that, actually—this sort of thing gets left out of discussion of language—but sometimes inappropriately. There's facial expression. I remember what she said was, visually—in addition to what she said verbally—"You have to keep these pictures" (I'm going to try to make the exact same face she made) "You have to keep your pictures, because after a while that's all there is, you know." That expression that she made was also an invitation to jump in.

Gaps are noxious in most cultures in terms of how you have a conversation. You don't just sit; you actually sometimes even say awkward things just to keep a gap from happening. When I was in grad school, I used to play cocktail piano for pocket money. Usually it was for rich people—and that was good because then I would get tips—but sometimes you would get kind of weird gigs. I had a job at a fraternity, and they were trying to connote some kind of note of formality. They had me playing the piano, but it was the same frat guys. I remember during the preparation for the party, there was nothing to say. I mean, I'm sure they had a party every weekend; they all knew each other; there was nothing to say. But you can't be quiet, and so basically there was this constant cacophony; it was almost rhythmic. There was lots of clapping for no reason, just to kind of put energy into the air, and then "Woo!" "Yeah!" "Let's do kegs!" "Woo!" "Yeah!" "Let's do kegs!" They did that for like a half hour; there was nothing to say. There was no content, but you can't have a gap. They can't just walk around the way cats would. You've got to make this noise, and you have to say those same three things over and over. They were being absolutely normal human beings.

Something else that is often seen is that a lot of language is not having careful observations in sequence like in *Portrait of Lady* but just *adjacency pairs*. Adjacency pairs are a matter of set exchange routines that wouldn't make sense if you only uttered one member of the pair. For example, there's a question, and then there's an answer. You put a question mark—so to speak—at the end of something, and then it solicits an answer. Then there's set questions and answers, or adjacency pairs. For example, in greetings: "How are you?" "Fine." "What is your condition?" We don't even hear it that way. What it really means is *you exist*, and then *fine* is *thank you for acknowledging it*. It's not really a request for any kind of content. Or, for example, you can have a request followed by an acceptance or a refusal: "Would you like a sandwich with mayonnaise?" I personally would say, "No, I would not." Things like that. It has to come in pairs. You have your apology and acceptance thereof; you have goodbye/goodbye.

There's an awful lot of that kind of thing. As a matter of fact, when you're ending a conversation—when you're ending an exchange—a great deal of it is composed of a series of adjacency pairs, which together really do not have a whole lot of content. You can imagine two people ending with something like, "So that's agreed?" "Yep, agreed." "Good, I knew you would." "Yes, no problem, really." "Thanks for the help." "Don't mention it." "Okay, I'll be back soon." "Okay, then bye." "Bye." Not a lot of that really meant anything; it was kind of a little game that you engage in—a little ritual that you engage in—to just do a kind of social libation to show that there's no tension, and it's a matter of pairs. The most important thing in all of those pairs was that the person who put out the first half of it was answered by something else that corresponded. What they're actually saying has all probably been discussed before.

Of course there are cultural differences in conversational style. For example, Deborah Tannen at Georgetown has showed that among people in some cultures, overlaps are richer and more standard than they are in some other varieties. Simultaneous talk actually is valued. I've given you kind of a vanilla, middle-class, white, American version of how conversations go—and that's true in many parts of the world—but Tannen has shown that conversational rules can be very different in, for example, the New York culture of talk that she grew up in, New York City. For example, if people are talking about trying to locate a building on Columbus Circle in New York, then Steve will say, "The Huntington Hartford is on the South side." Then Deborah will say, "On the other? Across." This is during what Steve has said. Or people request and give verification within the same utterance overlapping riotously. "Right where Central Park West met Broadway, that building," and then Deborah says, "By." Then Steve says, "Shaped liked that?" Deborah says, "Columbus Circuit? ... that Columbus Circle? Steve says, "Right on Columbus Circle. Here's Columbus Circle, ... here's Central Park West." Deborah says, "Now it's the Huntington Hartford Museum." Peter says, "That's the Huntington Hartford right?" You can see on the screen, and you can hear how I did it, that you have all of these overlaps there. All of that is perfectly, perfectly normal.

Something else that's normal that is not always obvious is that not only are topics not usually set before a conversation, but very often conversation is not about much of anything. Topic is constantly renegotiated, and it's very hard to sit down and talk about one thing. Say you're going to sit down and talk about politics; you very often will end up talking about what schools you want to get your children into. The topic tends to float. Much of conversation—as I mentioned—tends to be just a matter of group sociological reinforcement and not topic coverage at all. Topics just—if there are topics—float in and out; they're really just decoration to the basic acknowledgement of each other's presence, goodness, and friendship.

I was at a party a while ago, and these are people who know a lot about various topics, and I found it interesting during that party to notice we never really talked about anything. It was a dinner party; it's not like anybody was dancing. Nobody was drunk or anything like that. It was a dinner party with good food, and we never really talked about anything. One thing that kept coming up was I write a weekly column, and I had said to my wife, "You know, I don't feel like talking about politics tonight, so when we meet these new people, how am I going to discourage them from asking me about politics?" My wife said, "Well, just say that you're a journalist," and I said, "Well then they're going ask me what I write about." She said, "Well, tell them that you write about the issues of the day." I said, "That sounds like something Margaret Dumont would say in the Marx Brothers' movies, 'The issues of the day.'" People heard me say, "The issues of the day," and it was picked up; everybody at the party kept saying that. That was one topic. Then another guy—a very smart guy—was talking about eating horsemeat in Japan. He's one of these funny people; he's professionally funny. So he made it very funny, and a catchphrase came from that. We talked about Margaret Dumont, horsemeat in Japan, and everybody's walking around saying a couple of catch phrases. The only real topic that came up at the party was that that was the party where I recorded the word *oil* backwards that we used in that early lecture. For a while we did talk about phonology, but it was only something I really wanted to talk about.

Topic is something that is really not as central to human conversation, orally, as it is to our writing. Having a set topic is something that is relatively uncommon. It involves sponsoring an event where everyone knows in advance that you are to set a topic and you are not going to talk about horses in Tokyo; you're not going to talk about the issues of the day in a high, fluty voice. But that is the marked case, to use our term marked versus unmarked again.

There are rules to conversation—not the ones that we might think, but there are rules. Overlap of varying degrees is normal; it is not rude. Topic is extremely fluid. We are none of us characters in books. And because it has been told to me that sometimes I look rather severe at the end of these lectures, I'm going to end this one with a smile.

Lecture Twenty-Five
What Is This Thing Called Language?

Scope: In his signature work, *Course in General Linguistics*, Ferdinand de Saussure established linguistics as a discipline concerned with language in a present-tense sense rather than as a historical procession. De Saussure's philosophy is based on oppositions between units of meaning—now known as phonemes and morphemes—where the link between the sounds used to express the units and the actual meanings of the units is arbitrary. De Saussure inaugurated the study of language as a human activity, rather than as something recorded on paper.

Outline

I. In the next several lectures, we will examine various schools of thought as to how and why we use the conglomeration of language to be human—regardless of class, race, or gender—and whether there is any advice on whether we should do that in a different way.

   A. Our focus will be on what language, overall, accomplishes and how it relates to human thought or the nature thereof.

   B. We will first examine a signature work in what is termed the *philosophy of language*.

II. The linguistic philosophy of Ferdinand de Saussure (1857–1913) was the foundation of how linguists—as well as many others—view language today. The theories of Noam Chomsky, Roman Jakobson, and Joseph Greenberg, for example, trace back in part to assumptions of de Saussure's.

   A. De Saussure was a specialist in Indo-European languages. He is best known for his *Cours de linguistique générale* (*Course in General Linguistics*), which was based on notes taken by his students from lectures he gave at the University of Geneva from 1907 to 1911.

   B. The *Cours* is the first statement of what is now known and practiced as modern linguistics. Much of what is taken as evident today even by many people outside of linguistics needed explicit statement in the very different intellectual climate of the late 19th century.

III. One of the prime concepts from de Saussure is a difference between the *signifier* and the *signified*.

    A. A primary concept in de Saussure's outline of how language works is that in any language the link between a concept and the word used to refer to it is arbitrary. There is nothing inherent to a dog that makes the sounds [dɔg] correspond to it, no more than there is between dogs and the French word *chien* or the Spanish word *perro*.

    B. Thus there is no inherent link between the signifier (the word or a sound within a word) and the signified.

    C. The subfield of *sound symbolism* studies the occasional corners of language where signifier and signified may have some inherent relation.

        1. Across languages we see a very strong tendency for high sounds in the mouth such as [i] and [u] to be associated with things that are small and cute.

        2. Words that begin with a stop [g] and liquid [l] and then sprout into a vowel might have something to do with why words such as *gleaming* and *glimmer* are related to light.

        3. However, such patterns are at best rare, and focusing on them tends to be very limiting.

    D. Specifying the distinction between signifier and signified was necessary in the wake of a long philosophical tradition in which some considered that there might be, either in a historical or a mystical sense, a connection between words and concepts, as in Plato's dialogue between Cratylus and Hermogenes.

IV. De Saussure also defined a fundamental role for *opposition* in the way a language works.

    A. Fundamental to the *Cours* is the idea that the very nature of a linguistic system is that each sound or morpheme has value in the fact that it has a meaning different from other sounds and morphemes; each unit's "meaning," therefore, is not-the-other-thing, "not *x*."

    B. In demonstrating this, de Saussure referred to the fact that languages differ in arbitrary ways in how they cut up the array of sounds or morphemes and designate them as meaning "not *x*."

1. For him, an example was the fact that in some languages, the difference between two sounds makes the difference in meaning between two words.

2. For example, [pul] and [pʰul] in English would be different ways of saying the one word, *pool*; in Korean they are two different words. In English *pat* and *bat* are different words, while in Korean the [p] and [b] sounds are just variations on one sound.

C. In this de Saussure was one of the first scholars to clarify the distinction between the phonemic and the allophonic, which writers had been unclear on before.

D. To de Saussure, a good illustration of how opposition is the core of meaning in language is how absence can signify an opposition.

1. In Russian, for example, the word for *newspaper* is *gazeta*.

2. It takes endings for case: *gazete* is "to the newspaper"; it takes endings for number: *gazety* is the plural.

3. However, in the genitive plural there is no ending at all. *Gazet* means *of the newspapers*.

4. That is, absence means *of the* in the plural.

5. What conveys that you're talking about the genitive plural is not even something: It happens to be nothing; nevertheless, the opposition is conveyed.

6. His idea was that opposition—that what something means is not-the-other-thing—is a basic organizing principle of grammars.

V. Another fundamental idea from de Saussure is the difference between *synchrony* and *diachrony*.

A. De Saussure was the first linguist to clearly suggest a field based on analyzing language as it is at the present time (or as it was at some past time), rather than analyzing how languages change over time. Before de Saussure, historical linguistics (diachrony) was considered the main task of linguists, rather than synchrony.

B. De Saussure specified that all languages are always in a process of gradually changing and that at no identifiable point does it become a new language, just as if you take pictures of yourself monthly from age 15 to 85 and line the photos up, at no point on the line do you become a new person.

C. As such, what is interesting about language is what it is like at any given time, rather than the fact that it is not at one point the way it was at another, because at all times a language is just a variation on the basic pattern of signifiers expressing thought via oppositional connotations.

D. He pointed out that written language does not change as quickly as spoken language does and that this obscures the eternally changing nature of language. He used as an example that the words *quatre* [katʁ] and *lettre* [lɛtʁ] in many parts of France were almost always pronounced, in casual speech, [kat] and [lɛt].

VI. Language is not "alive."

    A. De Saussure was also at great pains to show that a language is not a "thing," an "organism." He showed, for one, that there is no such thing as a language being "born," since French, as Latin morphed into it, did not arise on any particular day. All languages are variations on what was the first language.

    B. He also noted that it is difficult to draw distinct lines showing where one dialect of a language begins and another ends. For example, he shows that one could not identify where a unitary concept such as the Savoyard dialect of southern France was spoken.

        1. The final [a] in the Latin progenitor *femina* is preserved in the Savoyard word *fena* ("woman"), unlike in standard French *femme* ([fam]), but it is preserved in many speech varieties in southern France.

        2. More peculiar to Savoyard, the Latin accent shifts to the final syllable in words like *lná* (standard French *lune*, Spanish *luna*), but that's only in some Savoyard dialects.

    C. Thus in each location there is a variation on the de Saussurean template, differing from neighboring ones to various degrees for fortuitous reasons.

    D. De Saussure was writing in contrast to earlier linguists, who were focused on issues such as comparing related languages, making claims that some were "more advanced" than others, or supposing that languages emerge, thrive, and then die like organisms as described by Charles Darwin in the theory of natural selection—which, when de Saussure wrote, was still relatively new.

VII. Reflecting the idea that language is harder to pin down than we might think, de Saussure made a fundamental division between *langue* and *parole*.

    A. This was a distinction between a language as known and understood by all of its speakers in the sense of a social "agreement" (*langue*) and the actual production of speech by individuals (*parole*).

    B. De Saussure's main interest was *langue*, language as a kind of an abstract communal grammar. His intent was to distinguish his paradigm from the study of the way language actually comes out of people's mouths, including mistakes, switches between one dialect and another, and so on—real language, so to speak.

    C. That distinction was inherited by a more recent founding father of linguistics, Noam Chomsky, who also is interested in *langue* and expresses that interest in terms of *competence*.

        1. Under Chomsky's paradigm, the aspect of language of interest in the study of syntax is a general, idealized competence— what the language "is" in an abstract sense.

        2. By contrast, individual *performance*, how people actually produce language and how language interacts with social and sociological factors, is messier and is thought unable to lend itself any kind of scientific inquiry.

    D. Performance, however, is precisely what sociolinguists are interested in—how people's speech reflects the fact that they live in a world with different hierarchies and different classes and so forth. To sociolinguists, looking only at competence seems rather peculiar.

Essential Reading:

De Saussure, *Course in General Linguistics.*

Supplemental Reading:

De Saussure, *Writings in General Linguistics.*

Questions to Consider:

1. Clearly some signifiers have a nonarbitrary relationship to the signifieds—for example, onomatopoeic words like *pow* or *clink*. It has also been noted that sound symbolism plays a part in the link between signifieds and signifiers; for example, *glimmer*, *gleam*, and *glow* all

refer to phenomena having to do with reflection of light. In that vein, which vowel or vowels, for you, connotes cuteness? Think of how you may talk to babies or your pet, or what vowel you are likely to be producing when your voice goes up in referring to how adorable something or someone is.

2. The distinction between *langue* and *parole*, especially as adopted by Noam Chomsky under the competence-versus-performance distinction, has been criticized for lending an implication that the study of things like variation, conversation, speech acts, and other aspects of "how people actually use language" is not "real linguistics." Many consider the very idea of linguistics as the study of *langue* or competence as an arbitrary and intellectually flawed notion. To you, is studying language in the vein of *langue* or competence—which was much of what the first half of these lectures has consisted of—intellectually inappropriate, or do you feel that there may be a case for delimiting the purview of the study of language in certain ways toward certain ends?

Lecture Twenty-Five—Transcript
What Is This Thing Called Language?

Imagine what your cat, if you have one, perceives when he or she watches you speaking. Imagine what it looks like. I know this brings to mind for many the Gary Larson cartoon where all a dog can hear is their name and then just "blah blah blah blah." Imagine that from the animal's eyes. Clearly language has to do with, for one thing, calling people. Even an animal gets some sort of sense—probably rather abstract—that there's such a thing as a name, or at least when this sequence of sounds is uttered it means that I should come, which, if you think of it, is more or less the same thing. But what about the rest? What is all of that "blah blah blah blah" that we're doing? How does that allow us to do what we do and be what we be, which is not cats? What is that? This is a general perspective, which in terms of the formal goes under the designation of *philosophy of language*. We're now going to move into that module of the course.

We've seen how language is put together with phonemes and morphemes, and we've seen the basics of how syntax works. Then we have seen that language changes over time, and so the conglomeration of phonemes and morphemes and syntax and semantics changes over time. Then we've taken a look at how our rendition of those things varies according to sociological factors such as class, gender, and race. Now we're going to look at that whole conglomeration and how we use it to be human—or we're going to look at various schools of thought as to how we do that and why we do that and whether there is any advice on whether we should do that in a different way.

Our first lecture in this philosophy of language module is going to be about one of the foundational figures of linguistic science as it's practiced today, and that is Ferdinand de Saussure. The reason that we're going to take a quick look at de Saussure is because he was a philosopher of language in that he was the person who laid down the basic perspective on how linguists look at language and how, I think, when we get it across to laymen, it seems pretty intuitive to look at language but which would not have occurred to someone who lived much before de Saussure's time.

De Saussure lived from 1857 to 1913, and so he straddled the 19th and 20th centuries. He also was an Indo-Europeanist; he was one of the early scholars of Indo-European. He is most famous for his grand work, which is called *Cours de linguistique générale*, or *Course in General Linguistics*. What's interesting is that this is not actually a book that he sat down and wrote; it is actually a compilation of notes that two students of his took on his lectures. The work itself was actually kind of second generation. Nevertheless, it's there, and it's lectures that he gave from about 1907 to 1911.

The *Cours* is the first statement of what is recognizable as modern linguistics today. Much of what is taken as evident today was actually first enshrined in his work, which seemed less intuitive then than it does now because we do not live in the late 19th century and very early 20th century. In any case, one of the prime concepts that de Saussure got across was a difference between what he called the *signifier* and the *signified*. For example, we know that there is a canine animal, and we often own them. The best kinds are golden retrievers and black Labradors, and then there are these other kinds, but we all know what the best two kinds are. We call that a *dog*, and that sounds so much to an English speaker like what a dog is. You could swear that they know the word dog—and often they do—and maybe it sounds kind of shaggy; something like that. But actually, on another level, we know that a dog is called a dog in English for arbitrary reasons; there is nothing inherently canine about the sequence of sounds which is the word *dog*. Part of the reason that we know that is because in French they feel that *chien* is just as "doggy"; then in Spanish you've got *perro*; in German you've got *Hund*; in Hebrew you've got *kelev*; and in Russian you've got *собака*. All these things are very different words, which seem every bit as tongue-hanging-out and smells-bad-in–the-rain as *dog* does to us. It's completely arbitrary, this relationship between the signifier, which in English is the sequence of sounds that comes out as *dog*, and the signified, which is that creature that it refers to. There's no inherent link between the two.

Some link, of course, in some ways. For example, there is a subfield of linguistics called *sound symbolism*. It's been shown that across languages there is a very strong tendency for what you all will now know as high sounds in the mouth. I could say *i* and *u*, but that's not really very precise. The idea is that [i] and [u] tend to be associated with things that are small and cute. You'll say, "The cute little animal," or our diminutive ending is [i], like "little Billy." "Billo" doesn't sound as small and cute as "Billy," and there seems to be something universal about that. In English, notice that there's a bunch of words—*gleam, glitter, glow, glance*—all of them having to do with light bouncing off of things and with a little hint of the visual.

There might be some reason for that. It might be that because those words begin with [g], a stop, and the [l], a liquid, and then sprout into "voweliness" that it has something to do with *gleaming* and *glimmer*, etc. But notice that that only works for occasional corners of the language. What is unhappy about the word *despair*? There's no relationship. Take a *radish*. Is there anything radish-y about that word? It's just there. Really, sound symbolism is very limiting, and really there is no relationship between the signifier and the signified.

This is something that was less intuitive to people, especially before the late 19th century. For example, in one of the oddest Plato dialogues, actually one of them that—I think you're not supposed to say this, but it's not really one of the better ones; Plato did not always bat it out of the park—he has this bit with Socrates mediating this debate between Hermogenes and Cratylus. Hermogenes believes that the relationship between the signifier and the signified—of course, he doesn't put it that way—is arbitrary. Then there's this foil, Cratylus, who thinks that there is some relationship. Socrates mediates between the two, but he never really comes to any conclusion, and it just kind of trails off. What one takes from it—if one reads that one—is that there would seem to be a question about that. It was a much easier misimpression to fall under if you are an ancient Grecian person, because it wasn't apparent how very many other languages there were in the world, and it was easy to think—when you were wearing those glasses—that other languages were just kind of a babbling and that Greek was somehow real. But these days we know better, and de Saussure was one of the first people to put that forth in a serious way.

There was the relationship between the signifier and the signified, and then de Saussure also laid down a fundamental role for opposition in the way a language works. His idea was that the very nature of a linguistic system is that each sound or morpheme has value in the fact that it has a meaning other than other sounds or morphemes; therefore, each unit's meaning, in a way, is not-the-other-thing, or "not *x*." For example, he demonstrated that languages differ in the way that they cut up the field of sounds. We've seen this. For example, in English, if I say [pʰul] then that means something that you have to clean and that has a shallow end and a deep end. If I say [pul], then I just said "pool" funny; but there are two ways of saying /p/: [pʰ], [p] If in Korean I say [pʰul] and then I say [pul], those are words with completely different meanings: One of them means *fire*; one of them means *grass*. There is a difference there. In Korean, [pʰ] and [p] are in a kind of opposition that they are not in English. Whereas—as we saw a very long time ago now—in Korean [b] and [p] are not in the kind of opposition that they are in English, where [pæt] and [bæt] are different words. In Korean, [pæt] is one thing; saying [bæt] would just be a strange way of saying [pæt], if they said that at all. What we're seeing is the difference between the phonemic and the allophonic, and this is something that was first expressed in a clear and comprehensive way by de Saussure.

The essence of that whole idea is the nature of oppositions in a language and how much difference they make in terms of conveying meaning. The fact that this opposition is the core concept is something that de Saussure indicated by showing that in a language, absence might be what indicates the opposition. For example, in Russian, the word for *newspaper* is *gazeta*—I'm trying to do a Russian accent, probably badly—but if you want to do the genitive, and you want to say, "of the newspaper," then you have *gazete*; and so that's there. If you want to have two newspapers, then you have *gazety*. That little funny sound I'm making, that's not an accent; that's actually, as we saw in a much earlier lecture, a nice high central vowel. We don't have it in English; they do have it in Russian. Plural is *gazety*—like that. Now if you want to say, "of the newspapers," you'd think that it would be *gazetech* or *gazetooco* or something; there's some ending on there. But actually, it's just *gazet*; there is no ending there. If you want to say, "of the newspapers," then what you have to remember is to not put an ending. In the bare, vanilla nominative, it's *gazeta*, but "of the newspapers": *gazet*. What conveys that you're talking about the genitive plural is not even something; it happens to be nothing. Nevertheless, the opposition is conveyed. His idea was that there was this basic role of opposition: What something means is not-the-other-stuff. That's a basic organizing principle of grammars. That's another piece of de Saussure that came down through the ages, and most of it did.

Another part of de Saussure that is now fundamental is the difference between *synchrony* and *diachrony*. What I mean by that is that there is the way a language is right now—right here in the present tense, like what you would put in a grammatical description of the language—then there is how the language changes over time. Of course there are egghead terms for that: Synchrony is the language right now; diachrony is the language over time. De Saussure was the first linguist to clearly suggest that there could be a field where you analyzed language in the present tense just the way it is, rather than charting the way a language changed over time. It used to be— as we saw, for example, with Jacob Grimm—that if you were going to write a grammar of a language, then the assumption was that you were going to start way back in the mist of time with ancient documents, and then you were going to show how you got, for example, from Old High German to modern German, step by step. It's weird to read an old grammar and to find that they feel they have to do this, rather than just describing the present tense of the language. But de Saussure specified that all languages are always in a process of gradually changing.

At this point, it was certainly known that there were ancient languages that had changed into modern ones. But the idea that this is something that all languages are always doing—that this is inherent to what language is—was less clear, even to very smart people. De Saussure was showing that all languages are always changing and that therefore there might be value in looking at the way language changes. But really—technically—language changing is just language always in a certain state, being a conglomeration of oppositions and arbitrary relationships between signifiers and signifieds, and that these things are always changing; but you've always got a qualitatively equivalent system. It's not that the language gets better; it's not that the language gets worse.

For example, he gave the analogy—because by this time there was photography—he said imagine if you could have a photograph of somebody from when they were a teenager up to when they were 85, with a picture taken each year. At no point would you see a new person emerging; you'd just see the person, the various changes that happen as a person goes on through time, never any particular break. It's not like here on this day Marvin became old; it was just something that happened. In the same way, that's what a language is like. Language is always changing in that way, but in any given time it is still Marvin, and there's a Marvin-ness that always continues. Language, therefore, in terms of how it changes, can be analogized to—and I really mean this, despite the fact that it's a kitschy object now—it's like a lava lamp. It's like the globe—or globus, or whatever that stuff is in the lamp—it's always kind of squeezing and gwunching and changing; you imagine it's kind of like what happens to material being digested in your stomach. It's always a different shape, but really it's always that same ball of stuff; it's always the same lamp.

He pointed out that this was a process that not only happened to languages that happened to be captured in writing and now were written, but that this was something that you could see happening in any language nowadays, including varieties that are only spoken. He pointed out that in French the word for *four* is—in writing, in standard French—*quatre*, and so you have this [ʁ] sound on the end. But he said that in a great many parts of France, the way it's actually said most of the time is just [kat], which is true. If you find yourself learning to speak French, you notice that you have to get used to hearing just [kat] for *four*, not [katʁ] like on a language tape or something like that. Or letter: *lettre*, which is very intuitive for English speakers because we have *letter*, but really, especially in rapid speech, it's just [lɛt]. De Saussure was quick enough to realize that this was a sign of how the language was changing. You can listen to that and you can think, "Well, this person is leaving off a letter," but really that's how languages change. Letters being left off, or actually sounds, is how one got from, for example, Latin to French.

He noted that actually written language tends not to change as quickly as spoken language does, but that if you look at things like this, what you're seeing is a language that is maintaining the same qualitative state over time. The system marches on; it's just changing its oppositions. It's just changing what signifiers are related to signifieds, etc. He made a further point related to this, which is that a language is not … I guess the best way to put it is that a language is not a thing that, in a sense, there is no such thing as a language under the label that we often conceive it. For example, he lived in a time when the ideas of Darwin were still new, so there's this idea that creatures evolve. We have a sense, when we think about the evolution of creatures, that a giraffe evolved. First there was nothing like a giraffe, and then there was. The technical fact is that if we really understand Darwin, we realize that really there was something that I presume was kind of like an antelope, and then there's one with a slightly longer neck, and there's really no point at which you could say that there was a giraffe. Still, we have that artificial template in our head that a giraffe evolved, and of course that is a convenience. Actually, you can see in a zoo something that's sort of like an intermediate between that antelope thing and the giraffe—I recommend this animal—it's called the okapi. They are the most beautiful creatures. Imagine a giraffe with a much, much shorter neck. It's brown. It's got stripes on the back. It's got huge brown eyes and a long lavender tongue. It's the size of a giraffe, but it's more approachable because its neck is shorter. I find the okapis in every zoo I go to; they seem to like me, too. I don't know why, but they come up and they stick out their tongues and I've fed them branches. Okapis were not known until only about 100 years ago and change. They were found in the rainforest. OK, I'll stop.

We have this notion in our head that a giraffe came. In the same way, we have that idea about languages often, but really it doesn't make sense when you try to grab a hold of it. For example, what's English? I think in my head, certainly my folk sense of it, is that it's what I'm speaking, roughly. It's this thing. It's American; it's got my vowels, and I'm trying to speak standardly. I'm sure I'm making some mistakes, but this is reasonable standard English. But then again, that's not how some Brit would feel. I'll bet I shouldn't have put it that way in case anybody who buys this is from Great Britain, but I'm sure you take my point. Somebody in Great Britain would think that English is something else and I'm using an accent. They would think, well, this dialect arose after theirs, in a sense. So what's English?

Or I remember one time it was the last day of college and I had moved all of my stuff out. I don't know who it was who they had moving into the dorm for the summer, but there were these two guys and they were standing on the steps and they were speaking something. I could understand the words—"television," "about," "come," "do"—but I could not follow what they were talking about. I had to ask them, "What are you speaking?" They looked at me kind of strangely, and they said, "We're speaking Jamaican Creole." I had never heard that. I had never listened to my own language spoken in a way that I couldn't understand. Since then, I actually ended up studying creoles. I can't say that was really the beginning, but the point is they were really speaking something. They were clear, they were animated, they were articulate, and they were crisply annunciating this thing, which is part of what really threw me. "Television." How come I can't understand how it's being used in the sentence? To them, what they were speaking, that was a form of English, and that's very much a thing as well. The fact of the matter is that, first of all, all languages—when you look at them up close—are bundles of dialects, and really all languages can trace back to the first language or few languages.

What this means is that obviously because there's such a thing as France, we will think that there is something called French. Really, the fact is French is Latin, because there was never any break between Latin and French. Nobody woke up one day saying, "Hey, you know, today we are speaking French." No one knew. There was a time when everybody was speaking Latin. There was a time when people felt they were speaking the Latin of the streets. Then there was a time when people were thinking of themselves as speaking Latin the way we speak it here in France, and pretty soon it was French. All of that was a very gradual process.

Or, in the same way, I'm speaking Anglo-Saxon. That's what I'm doing right now, because there was no break between Old English or Anglo-Saxon, Middle English, and modern English. There was a lot of change, and so there were a lot of changes between what signifiers are linked to what signifieds. There were a lot of changes in terms of how oppositions work, in terms of for example the morphology of the language. But all of this was very gradual; each generation could understand the other one. In the same way, birds are dinosaurs. We know that they're things that fly and make messes on our patios and things, and we think of them as birds because we're familiar with them. Dinosaurs aren't around, but it's been established that actually birds developed from the kind of dinosaur that's related to *Tyrannosaurus rex*, broadly. It never stopped; there was never any break between the dinosaur and what gradually got feathers and took to the air and became a bird.

It's the same thing with languages. It's not that a language arises at a particular time; that language always existed as long as there were people speaking in something that ended up producing it. De Saussure also gave one the first useful demonstrations of how hard it is to even determine what a dialect might be, where one dialect begins and the other dialect leaves off. For example, in France we say that French is spoken. But technically, in the south of France, there is something else spoken that a French person cannot understand. If a person is raised only speaking these southern French varieties—which is increasingly rare these days, if not nonexistent—then they can't understand French. Really, what's spoken down in the South is called Occitan, and one of the dialects of Occitan—Provençal—was the one that was used by the troubadours back in the Middle Ages. More to the point, there's even finer detail than that. A lot of people know about that split between the French of the north and then that other thing in the south. Really, if you look in the middle region—especially over in the east—there are varieties which roughly are called Franco-Provençal, which are neither of those languages. Of course, there are many dialects of French and many dialects of Occitan.

There's this other region where it's really something completely different. One of the varieties there is called Savoyard. One refers to Savoyard— Savoyard-speaking people refer to it—but when you really try to identify what is Savoyard, you find that actually there is no one thing. It's like trying to pick up a tomato seed or something. For example, in Savoyard, you could say that this is a language where in the word for *woman*, the final *a* in the Latin progenitor *femina* is preserved and similar final *a*'s in Latin. The word for *woman* is *fena* in Savoyard, as opposed to—for example—in French, where the word is *femme*. Even though there's that *e* in the spelling, it's not pronounced in the spoken language at all. The fact is there are a lot of southern French varieties that preserve that [a], so that's not unique to Savoyard. Then there's something about Savoyard that's kind of peculiar: Latin stress—remember accent stress—is switched to the final syllable in words like what is *lune* in standard French. For example, *moon* is *lune*; in Spanish—a kind of normal outcome—you have *luna*; but then in Savoyard it's *lná*. The accent—the stress—has shifted to the final syllable, but not all Savoyard dialects do that. Trying to actually figure out what you would put in a grammatical description of Savoyard would be very hard. It's actually that bundles of features kind of shade one into the other, and to actually decide that there is a one thing is difficult.

There's me, there's those Jamaicans, and then there's Alistair Cooke; what is the real English? It's actually a rather abstract concept. This is something that was especially useful when de Saussure wrote, because there was the idea that some languages were more advanced than others. There was an idea that languages emerged and died like organisms. Just today, a kindly gentleman asked, "Can you tell me about the emergence of Sardinian?" I get the question; I understand there's an island—Sardinia—and there are many Romance languages, and Sardinian is one of them. It's actually the one that's closest to Latin. What's the emergence? The truth is that the emergence of Sardinian is that Latin spread all over the place; one of the places it splattered was Sardinia, and now the Latin that's spoken in Sardinia is Sardinian. What he was waiting for, I think, was "Well, the Sardinian somethings and then these other people came together, and there was a ceremony, and then somebody wrote a big book and [makes sounds] that's Sardinian." That's not how languages emerge. It's that kind of question that de Saussure kind of steers us around.

Finally, reflecting this idea that a language is actually harder to pin down than we might think, de Saussure established a division between what he called *langue* and *parole* in French. His idea is that there's a difference between *langue*, which is language as we think of it in our heads, language that is agreed upon by all of its speakers to be the language, a kind of an abstract communal grammar, and then *parole*, which is the way that an individual will actually produce language. It is the way language actually comes out of people's mouths, including with mistakes—that's one thing—and including with switches between one dialect and another—and so real language, so to speak.

That distinction has actually come down into a bifurcation in modern linguistics between Noam Chomsky and sociolinguists. Noam Chomsky and his gang are interested in the *langue* part, and what he calls that is *competence.* There's the idea that there's this language as it's conceived by all of us despite how we might all render it in individually different ways, and that abstract communal conception of language—the competence as Chomsky calls it, the *langue* as de Saussure would have called it—that is what we should be analyzing; that is what syntax is supposed to be all about. Performance—all of that—is individual. It's kind of messy. It presumably won't lend itself to any kind of scientific inquiry. On the other hand, sociolinguists find *performance* particularly interesting. For them, how people actually speak—or how people's speech reflects also the fact that they live in a world with different hierarchies and different classes, etc., all of that—the performance is considered the object of interest. The idea of analyzing language in as abstract a way as only looking at the competence, to sociolinguists, seems rather peculiar. There's always been a kind of battle along those lines.

De Saussure could not have anticipated any of that, but his idea was that language and the study of language, in terms of linguistics, should be different from the study of phonetics and the production of sound. For him, he wanted to stress that those things—that aspect of performance, or what he would call *parole*—were different from looking at the grammar that those sounds—that all of that articulation—actually produces. He was trying to delineate what the field should be. His interest was in *langue*, and nowadays that's reflected in syntacticians' interest in competence. For him, *parole* was something different; to him, *parole* was, say, Henry Higgins studying people's sounds. To him, Henry Higgins was not doing what he considered *linguistique*—linguistics. Today, people who are most interested in *parole* are, for one thing, still phoneticians, and a great many of them doing incredible work; then there are also sociolinguists, who are interested in what today is less often called *parole* than performance.

What I've tried to give you is the basic ideas of Ferdinand de Saussure and to show you that this is the beginning of a lot of the ideas that have undergirded, for example, this course. I will see you next time, when we discuss speech acts. If you wonder what that is, then tune back in and find out.

Lecture Twenty-Six
Speech as Action

Scope: Language is not just about making statements, communication, and truth. As often as not, the words do not convey information but serve a social function. In other words, much of what we say is less saying something than doing something. This is the concept termed the speech act, and this lecture explores how they have been explained and classified.

Outline

I. In this and the next lecture, we will address the thoroughly understandable misimpression we have that language is mostly a matter of exchanging information—partly because we most immediately think of language as composed of words, and words correspond to objects and concepts.

   A. A great deal of the use of language, despite being composed of words, entails performing an action, changing the world around us in various ways.

   B. Importantly, the way that we do this according to social convention involves formulaic disjunctions, understood by all speakers of a language, between the formal content of a sentence and its intent.

II. The term *speech act* was first used by philosopher John Austin (1911–1960), in the William James lectures at Harvard in 1955.

   A. Austin identified four utterance types:
   1. *Locutionary*—saying something and meaning it: "I had a busy day today."
   2. *Phatic*—indicator of sociality: "Nice day!" "How do you do?"
   3. *Perlocutionary*—produces an effect: telling a joke, saying, "The teacher's coming!"
   4. *Illocutionary* (or *performative*)—in itself an action: "I promise you I'll go." "I sentence you to five years in jail."

   B. Performatives are what he called speech acts. The insertion of *hereby* distinguishes a speech act. Thus if a wife asks her husband, "What do you do to make up with me when I'm mad at you?" and he answers "I promise you that I'll go to the bank" (the idea being that this is something done on a regular basis), this is not a performative because *hereby* would not work.

III. Performatives get a lot of attention in part because of the *Gricean maxims*.

    A. Philosopher of language H. Paul Grice (1913–1988) proposed that human exchanges are governed by four maxims tacitly agreed upon, constituting the *cooperative principle*: you must act in conversation in accord with the general principle that you are mutually engaged with the listeners in an effort at mutual understanding.

    B. The cooperative principle is constituted by the four Gricean maxims:

        1. *Quantity*—be informative.
        2. *Quality*—be truthful.
        3. *Relation*—be relevant.
        4. *Manner*—be clear and concise.

    C. Grice proposed that the convention of *conversational implicatures* allows speakers to flout these maxims regularly.

        1. Flouting the maxim of quality conveys that there is something wrong without being brusque, as in a letter of recommendation that doesn't mention the qualifications in question.
        2. The maxim of quality is often flouted in sarcasm; for example: "Fine friend you are!"
        3. The maxim of relation must be flouted if one is a civilized human being: A says, "I'm out of gas." B says, "There's a station around the corner" (rather than answering "Indeed, you are!" and moving on).
        4. Flouting the maxim of manner can be a way of being polite or sarcastic: "Miss X produced a series of sounds that corresponded closely with the score of 'Home Sweet Home.'"

IV. Philosopher John Searle (1932–) from the University of California, Berkeley has continued in Austin's vein, showing how the way we use performatives is influenced by floutings of Gricean maxims. He has proposed that performative utterances entail four *felicity conditions*.

    A. For example, "I apologize" entails these conditions:

        1. *Propositional content condition*: The utterance concerns the hearer forgiving the speaker.

2. *Preparatory condition* (all conditions are acknowledged): The speaker was responsible, and thus apology would not happen otherwise; the hearer was hurt; and the speaker wants to make the hearer feel better.
3. *Sincerity condition*: The speaker does regret the act.
4. *Essential condition*: The uttering of the words commits the speaker to apologizing and accomplishes it, and both speaker and hearer understand this.

B. *Indirect performatives* arise when convention allows wording to drift from literal correspondence with these conditions for the speech act.

C. Thus to apologize by uttering *I'm sorry* technically fulfills only the sincerity condition and flouts the others, but we agree that it stands for an apology.
1. This abbreviation is more likely, with apologies, of the sincerity condition than, for example, the preparatory one ("Your foot hurts").
2. "I'm sorry" is received as an apology via a conversational implicature in the Gricean sense: We readily understand the gap when the other three conditions are abbreviated.

D. "I'm sorry" has become so conventionalized as an apology that when used in its literal connotation of regret that it is often misunderstood. (A: My aunt died. B: I'm so sorry. A: It wasn't your fault.)

V. Politeness adds another layer to the study of speech acts.

A. In 1978, psycholinguist Penelope Brown and philosopher of language Stephen Levinson supplemented Grice's maxims with a proposal that communication also depends upon politeness.

B. They proposed that making a request constitutes, inherently, a *face-threatening act* (FTA).

C. There are various ways of wielding an FTA:
1. *On-record FTA without redress* is pure imperative.
2. *On-record FTA with redress* shows concern for the hearer's right not to be imposed on: "I hate to impose …" Plural *you* used as singular in many European languages such as French *vous* instead of *tu* does this in a formal way, just as in Spanish *usted*, which was originally "your mercy," is used instead of *tú*.

3. *Off-record FTA* is dropping a hint while leaving open the possibility of not having intended it at all.

D. Thus the same request can be expressed in various forms depending on what kind of performative is used:

   1. Performative:
     a. I request of you that you give me some help.
     b. I want you to give me some help.
     c. Help me.

   2. Indirect performative:
     a. Can you give me some help?
     b. Will you give me some help?
     c. Could you give me some help?
     d. Would you give me some help?

   3. FTA on-record with redress:
     a. May I ask you to give me some help?
     b. I'd like to ask you to give me some help.
     c. I must ask you to give me some help.
     d. I could use some help.

   4. FTA off-record:
     a. This sure is hard to do alone.
     b. I've been running around like crazy all day and now there are all these dirty dishes!
     c. Whew!

Essential Reading:

Brown and Levinson, *Politeness*.

Supplemental Reading:

Watts, Ide, and Ehlich, eds., *Politeness in Language*.

Questions to Consider:

1. Brown and Levinson's conception of politeness and language has been criticized for assuming that politeness is expressed in the same ways worldwide, when in fact many languages convey politeness in forms different from those in English. If you speak a second language, think about whether requests are given in the ways they are in English. For example, in your second language, does one soften requests by using words like *can*, *may*, and *would* or in some other way?

2. One person asks, "Do you have the time?" He gets the answer "Half-past two." What is the utterance type of "Do you have the time?" under John Austin's conception? What Gricean maxim is flouted in the answer "Half-past two"?

Lecture Twenty-Six—Transcript
Speech as Action

You know how when you're taught a language in school, or when you try to teach one to yourself, you often have these kind of bland sentences that don't really come much in handy once you actually try to be a person in the language? If you're learning French or Spanish, all these sentences like "My uncle is a lawyer, but my aunt has a spoon," and kind of recite that? You realize that that has nothing to do with actually communicating in the language. There are all sorts of things that you don't really get taught, that you just kind of have to pick up. A lot of that is because even on the level of second-language teaching there is often a thoroughly understandable misimpression that what language is about mostly is exchanging information or running around telling each other things. We've got words, and the words refer to things—signifiers and signifieds—and so we're expressing meaning. That's what a lot of those textbook sentences are about, but actually, in terms of how language is used on a daily basis, there is a great deal more than that.

A whole lot of the way we string words together is about performing an action rather than making a remark. How many remarks are there to make? Really, we're trying to do things. We've seen how there is grammar, but there's also an aspect of philosophy of language—the module we're in—which looks at the fact that when we speak we're often not remarking, but we're acting. In other words, we are committing *speech acts*, as it's put. So we're performing actions, and in addition, a whole lot of being a linguistically competent—and I mean on a very basic level—human being is an understanding that there are formulaic disjunctions between how we compose our sentence (what we say) and what we actually intend in the utterance of that sentence. This is the study of speech acts. It's a large subject and I, of course, can only get across so much of it in this tidy half hour. But let's take a look at the study of what is called speech acts.

The term was first used by John Austin, the philosopher. He was giving the William James lectures at Harvard in 1955. Austin noticed that, in terms of utterance types, there are four, as opposed to what one might think. There are four utterance types, according to his classification. One of them—the first one—is *locutionary*; locutionary is the vanilla, "My uncle is a lawyer and my aunt has a spoon" kind of utterance. That's the one where you say something, and you mean it: "I had a busy day today." You're remarking upon the fact that you did, and presumably you did. "Sardinia is a smallish island with its own Romance language." That is definitely true, and I just said it. "Sardinia has people who are unusually short." That is also true— not pathologically, but they are not a tall people. That is true. That's locutionary, and that's only one of four kinds of utterances.

There's also what's called *phatic* utterances. If I say it quickly—"Phatic"— I'm not saying like a fad, *f-a-d*. Phatic; it's phatic utterances. Those are just indicators of sociality. For example, "How are you?" "Fine." That exchange did not really mean *What is your emotional state? Please burden me with telling me.* That's not what "How are you?" really means, or if it does, you have to say, "So how are you, Susan?" Then you might really want it. But "How are you?" really just means *I acknowledged that you were there because to not do so would be rude.* In other words, there's kind of an opposition between the acknowledging and the not acknowledging. To not say anything is one thing, but life is short; we can't have a conversation every time we see each other for the first time. And so "How are you?"— that's really all it means. Or think about "good night." What is that? Think of all the people that you say, "Good night!" to. Theoretically, it means *I hope that it will be that the rest of your evening is pleasant to you.* Is that really what you mean? Because presumably the person's going to have a good enough night and so are you; it's just that you can't not say anything. When you say, "'Night," you really are just basically saying, "We have had a social occasion and now it's ending," and I once again acknowledge you in what is, if you think about it, a very tribal and arbitrary kind of thing. You can't say "good night" in all languages. Why would you? In some tribal community it might not be that you're always telling people that you hope that the second half of their day will be pleasant to them; that's rather arbitrary. It's just phatic communication.

Then the third kind is called *perlocutionary*. Perlocutionary speech acts are ones that are designed to produce an effect. For example, you can imagine a bunch of kids are cutting up in a classroom, and one of them says, "The teacher's coming." That person is not remarking the teacher is coming; there would be no real reason for that. Everybody can presumably see. Really you're saying, "The teacher's coming," in order to make everybody put away their slingshots or whatever everybody is doing or to get up off the top of the desks or something. Or a perlocutionary act is a joke. What a joke is, is not that you're making a remark; the idea is to make people's diaphragms titter so they'll make this kind of jerkety-jerkety sound, which is one of the oddest things that human beings do. If you think about it, no matter how human you think your dog is, or your guinea pig or your cat or even a chimpanzee, laughing—"ha ha ha"—what is that? That's something that we do, and we like hearing other people do it. For example, if I say—I would never say this—but if somebody said, "I'd rather have a bottle in front of me than a frontal lobotomy, ha ha ha ha," the reason that he's saying that is not because he would like to have his brain sliced into or something like that; he's saying that because the idea is that he will get people to have the diaphragm-tittering experience, and so it's a perlocutionary act.

Those are the first three, but the one that a lot of speech-act study focuses on is called the *illocutionary* kind of speech act. These are the ones that constitute, in themselves, an action. For example, if you say, "I promise you I'll go"—now you could technically think of yourself as saying, "I am in the state of promising you that in the future I will go," but that's not really the purpose of saying that. When you promise somebody that you'll go, what you're doing is committing an action; it's something that you are doing. Or "I apologize for stepping on your foot." You're not saying that you apologize; you are doing the apologizing. "I sentence you to five years in jail." You're not describing yourself doing it, like you're saying, "I rake the leaves after they start stacking a little high"; you are committing that person, so to speak, to imprisonment. That is the illocutionary kind of speech act, and that's the one that has evoked a special amount of interest among people who study speech acts.

Another term for illocutionary speech acts is *performatives*; these are our performatives. Performatives are distinguished by the fact that you can insert *hereby* into them. For example, if you say, "I hereby promise you that I will stop taking money from the checking account without telling you," then you have made the promise—in a rather wordy way—but the *hereby* makes sense. Whereas if you say something in answer to a question like, "What do you do to make it up to me when I'm mad at you?" Then your answer is, "I promise you I'll go to the bank"—the idea being that this is something you do on a regular basis—that is not a matter of a performative; you can't put *hereby* in that sentence. You can't say, "What I do to make you feel better after I've made you angry is that I hereby promise to go to the bank." That's a different kind of sentence. But performatives are what get a lot of attention.

The reason will become clearer when we take a look at another subschool of thought within the speech-act school. This is what is called the *Gricean maxims*. They're called that partly because they're maxims, and partly because they were developed by the philosopher H. Paul Grice. His idea was that human exchanges are governed by four maxims that are tacitly agreed upon, and they constitute the *cooperative principle*. The cooperative principle is that in a conversation, you are going to engage in the activity based on an idea that everybody is mutually engaged in the effort towards mutual understanding. What I mean by that is that the four maxims—and bear with me because the four alone are not important; it's what happens with them—but the four alone are (a) the maxim of quantity, and that is "be informative"; don't hold back information. Then there's (b) the maxim of quality, which is to be truthful, so you're not supposed to lie. Then there's (c), which is the maxim of relation, and that is to be relevant. If someone says to you, "What time are we going to eat?" then your answer presumably will not be "In Poland they usually hire bald cooks in autumn." That doesn't really pertain; that's not relevant. What you're going to say is going to relate to what the other person said in some way. Then there's the maxim of manner, which is that one is to be clear and concise.

In itself, those four things seem rather obvious; it almost seems like some sort of lesson in politeness. But what's interesting is that what we do regularly when we speak is that we allow what are called *conversational implicatures*, which allow speakers to flout these maxims. The idea is that we flout these maxims—we break these rules—all the time, and yet social convention is such that we understand one another anyway. One has to know how to break these maxims in order to actually speak.

For example, the maxim of quantity: Be informative. You can be asked for a recommendation for a student—I remember having this experience when I was a professor—and sometimes you find yourself in a position where you don't really have anything positive to say, but you don't want to condemn the person. You need to be polite, and so there is a kind of recommendation that's pretty standard in the industry, which is a very civil way of indicating that a person is really not quite up to snuff for whatever that recommendation is supposed to be for. You don't write letters saying, "This person would be a terrible addition to your department." That's simply not done. But you write things along the lines of, "This person was a wonderful citizen in the department. They made good coffee. We often had parties at this person's house. They were gracious. They were kind. They had a cute child," or something like that. Then you sign it. But you never really say anything about their academic work or whether they seemed like they were going to be very promising. That is the way you do it. You are flouting the maxim of quantity, and in our society it's understood that when you flout that maxim, you are conveying that there is something wrong without being so brusque as to call it right out.

I was at a conference a little while ago where this French guy had no idea what he was supposed to be delivering on. It was a conference about a particular topic, and then this perfectly charming person gave this talk that was like way off on a slant. If this conference has been about Thai cuisine, he came in talking about how to sharpen knives. It was like, "Why … ? You didn't really know what this conference was about." We were all kind of standing around afterward. If it had been the '50s, we would have all been smoking, but you don't do that, so we kind of had our hands at our sides. One witty Finn said, in that kind of British accent that they often have, "Talks differ." That's all he said. We all just fell out laughing. What he meant was talks differ in that some are quite bad, but one doesn't say that. He just said, "Talks differ." That was flouting the maxim of quantity, because he didn't say how they differ, but we could all fill it in, and that was all anybody needed to say. That was his way of kind of soliciting general agreement among us that that French guy had kind of missed the ball. Then we kind of moved on.

The maxim of quality is something that you often break when you're being sarcastic. For example, the standard example that you give in the literature is when somebody says, "Fine friend you are!" OK, the idea is that you're not really a fine friend. I'm finding myself, when saying that now in this year, feeling that that's a little archaic; that's not a very current expression. A better example of that would actually be, for example, there's a tendency among a certain subset of men to call each other things like, say, "bastard" in affection. This is mentioned in one episode of *Seinfeld* when George Costanza falls in with a bunch of guys: "Hey, ya bastard. Hey, you gonna drink some beer with us? I'll do that, you bastard." That sort of thing. Or Russian men call each other *muzhik*, which means *peasant*. That's considered a good thing. Boris Yeltsin drinking his way through his presidency: That was considered being a good *muzhik*. He seemed like somebody who would be nice to have a beer with, or in his case a case of vodka with. That is standard; it breaks the maxim of quality because you like this person. If you didn't like this person, you wouldn't be calling them a bastard, for example. That's the odd thing: If you didn't like this person, you'd call them "sir." A lot of humor and a lot of affection is based on breaking the maxim of quality; flouting the maxim of quality.

Flouting the maxim of relation—be relevant—is what makes the difference between a person who's using a language in context and a Martian, really.

For example, let's say that you're walking down the street, and you see somebody who is standing there next to their car. That person says, "I'm out of gas." You look at the person and say, "Yes, you are," and you keep going. You're supposed to know when the person says, "I'm out of gas," that they're saying it meaning that they would like to know where they could get some gas. The proper answer to, "I'm out of gas," is, "Oh, well a mile down there is a gas station." Or "Oh, well let me siphon some gas from my tank and give it to you." In the same way, "Have you got the time?" The answer is not, "Yes." "Have you got the time?" and then you're supposed to tell them the time. Theoretically, all they uttered was, "Do you have the time?" If we were really going to take that as just an ordinary kind of locutionary utterance, then we would say, "Yes, I do have the time, thank you for asking," and then you keep going. They're asking you that because then you're supposed to give them the time. That is a matter of the maxim of relation. You must flout the maxim of relation to be a civilized human being.

Flouting the maxim of manner, and not being clear and concise, can also be a way of being polite or even sarcastic. You could say, "She sang *Home Sweet Home.*" Or you could say, "She uttered a sequence of notes, which approximated that in the song *Home Sweet Home.*" That would be one way of saying that she doesn't happen to have a gift of singing. Another flouting of manner—being clear and concise—that is considered understood is in some compartments of academia where it's considered the height of intelligence and fashion to use 10-dollar words and to string them together in very dense ways—tapeworm sentences, sentences that last longer than some people's lives. Only the people who are within this world of academia—and particularly the world of literary criticism—are really capable of understanding this language, where the essence of it is really flouting the maxim of manner. You are not supposed to be clear and concise. I've seen some of those people—some of the nicest people you want to meet—at the conference, and then the minute they get behind the podium all of a sudden they're speaking this elaborate, fearsome sludge. For them, that's what they have to do. You can't be clear; you can't be concise. Books have been written about why they do that, but they certainly do. The flouting of these maxims is central to communication.

Going on with that, it's interesting how flouting works when it comes to our performatives. There is at the University of California at Berkley the philosopher John Searle. Searle continued in Austin's vein by showing that the way that we use performatives is influenced by floutings of the Gricean maxims. His idea is that, for example, when you do a performative there are four *felicity conditions*. For example, let's say that you are apologizing. There are four things, and of course all these people have their taxonomies, and the jargon is less important than what all of these things are just meant to say. Clear and concise. So, (a) *propositional content condition*, and that is that what is to be said, this apology, will concern the hearer forgiving the speaker, and so just establishing that's what our content is going to be in terms of the proposition. (b) The *preparatory condition*. The preparatory condition means that, within this context of an apology happening, all of the conditions are acknowledged. The speaker was responsible, and therefore the apology wouldn't happen otherwise. The hearer was hurt and the speaker wants to make the hearer feel better, so that's the preparatory condition. Another condition within a performative, according to Searle's taxonomy, is that there's the *sincerity condition*, which is that the speaker does regret the act. Finally, there is the *essential condition*, which is that the utterance of the words commits the speaker to apologizing and accomplishes it, and both the speaker and the hearer understand that. The idea is that once this is done then, yes, the air will be cleared; we are engaged in this activity. You have those four conditions.

Searle noted that you can have what is called an *indirect performative* when convention means that the wording that you use when doing a performative, such as apologizing, drifts from literal correspondence with these conditions. What I mean by that is how we use to apologize the words "I'm sorry." We don't usually say, "I hereby apologize to you for stealing your spouse," or something like that. What you say is, "I'm sorry." If you think about it, if you look at all of the conditions, "I'm sorry" only fulfills the sincerity condition. "I'm sorry"—meaning that you feel this regret that leads to the apology—is really just one part of the entire act that apologizing consists of. But we all agree; we understand that flouting of some of the other felicity conditions as a legitimate apology. In fact, it would be flouting the Gricean maxim of manner to express all of the conditions of apologizing: "I hereby understand that you were hurt, etc., etc., etc." However, the sincerity condition is probably the one that you would most likely use as the abbreviation, because, for example, if you abbreviated it to the preparatory condition—this is the one about acknowledgment—then what you would say for an apology is something like, "Your foot hurts." If you stepped on somebody's foot and you're going to apologize, and then you walk up to them: "Your foot hurts." That's the Martian. The sincerity is the one that seems to abbreviate the best.

But "I'm sorry" is received as an apology via a conversational implicature; there's a gap, which we understand readily. What's interesting about "I'm sorry" is that it's so conventionalized as an apology. If you really think about it, that's not an apology: "I'm sorry." That's really only part of it. We're so used to thinking of it as an apology that when we use it in its literal meaning—which is just to say that, "I regret; I am in a state of regret"—often it's misunderstood. If somebody says, "My aunt died," and you say, "Oh, I'm sorry," notice how sometimes people say, "Well, it's not your fault." No, no, because you're actually using the words literally. "It pains me to see that your aunt died, and you loved your aunt, and so I am reaching out to you and empathizing." "I'm sorry"—that's when they say, "Oh, well it wasn't your fault." You say, "No, no." You know that little eddy of misunderstanding on "I'm sorry." That's because it's been so conventionalized as meaning that my "sorryness" is related to the larger structure of the fact that I hereby tried to exonerate myself from stepping on your foot, and you understand that I'm doing it sincerely, etc.

What Searle has shown is that a performative actually involves all kinds of background assumptions that you don't think about consciously. In terms of our utterance, really we're only going to give voice to one part of it, with the rest of it understood. It's kind of like—and Searle never said this, but in terms of putting this in your head—it's kind of like we saw that there are unfilled nodes on a syntactic tree. For example, there's a comp node at the beginning of just about any sentence—even if we start with an NP—there's this unfilled node that's already up there. As trees get more elaborate, we can actually see—I haven't burdened you with this—but one actually sees in hardcore study of syntax that really there are often more unfilled nodes than filled ones. The whole tree is kind of like boom boom boom boom boom boom boom boom boom boom, and you just say, "boom, boom, boom," like that; that's how it goes. It's the same thing with these.

Another example of drifting from the felicity conditions would be something along the lines of, "Can you get me some water?" That's one way that you would ask somebody softly about water. But if you think about it, the actual propositional content of that doesn't correspond to what you're doing. "Can you get me some water?" Technically that means *Are you capable of getting me some water?* The fact is that you both know that the person is capable; this is something that is acknowledged by both of you. It has to be, because you're normal human beings; that's your preparatory condition. Really we're drifting somewhat from the meaning. There's a conventionalized implicature there. There's an implicature—a gap—between the actual way that the sentence is put together and what you're doing with it. When you ask somebody, "Can you get me some water?" that's a way, really, of saying, "Get me some water." You're kind of softening it; that's what we do as people. You're saying, "Get me some water … I don't mean to bother you with that." That's something that happens. This is where the study of politeness comes in, to add one more layer onto all of this.

In 1978, Penelope Brown, who is a psycholinguist, and Stephen Levinson, who is actually a philosopher of language, supplemented Grice's maxims with a proposal that politeness also factors into these things. They posited that making a request is what they called a *face-threatening act*, inherently. There are various ways of wielding a face-threatening act. It is delicate to make a request of somebody; you are requiring something of them. One thing you can do is an *on-record* face-threatening act, as they call it; that's a pure imperative. For example, "Wash my clothes." That's not usually what you do, especially if it's not a child or your spouse or your pet. Usually you'll do something softer, like for example what's called an on-the-record face-threatening act *with redress*. What that is, is that you are demonstrating in some way that you are imposing upon a person in some way. You could say, "I hate to impose, but could you open the window?" Or for example the way in many European languages the word for *you* is plural in the formal as a way of doing that. For example, you refer to this person in a way that implies that they are just so protean and so spectacular that they are actually two souls. Instead of *tu* in French, it's *vous*; or instead of *tú* in Spanish then you have *usted*, which is originally "your mercy." In any European language that you happen to know, that is a matter of softening for when you address a person such as when you might make a request.

Then there is what Brown and Levinson called the *off-record* face-threatening act. That's where you drop a hint that you might want something, but it always leaves open the possibility that you didn't make a request at all. For example, I could sit on the couch and say, "Boy, I sure am hungry." That could mean that whoever was in the room with me—I do not treat my wife that way—is supposed to make me a meal and hopefully clean up afterward. If the person said, "Make your own darn food," then I could say, "All I just said, I just said I was hungry." It was just a locutionary statement: "I have skin, I breathe air, and I am hungry." Or somebody might kind of go, "Ahem," and what they really mean is they want the person to go away. Then the person says, "Why do you want me to go away?" and you can just say, "I was just clearing my throat."

What this means—and you can look at these sentences here—is that there are all sorts of ways of making a request, all sorts of ways of wielding a performative. You can see that you can say, "I request of you that you give me some help." That's highly polite, but it's certainly a sentence of English. Or "I want you to give me some help." These are our nice ordinary performatives. You could say, "Help me," a just kind of straight-out imperative. That would be an on-the-record face-threatening act, and it's not something that usually happens. More often we have indirect performatives, and so, "Can you give me some help?" "Will you give me some help?"—as if you're actually asking about whether this will happen in the future. It's another way of softening, despite the actual propositional content. "Could you give me some help?" "Would you give me some help?" Those things, if you're kind of in the shower and you just think about what "Would you give me some help?" means strictly, it's a very a peculiar sentence. Would you? If when? What? It's just our conventionalized way of asking softly. Then you can have a face-threatening act with redress, and so, "May I ask you to give me some help?" The presumption is that the help will be given. "I'd like to ask you to give me some help." "I must ask you to give me some help." "I could use some help." That doesn't presume that you're going to get it. You're just stating that you could use some help.

Or then you could resort to the off-record face-threatening act where you don't really say it, and you leave yourself room for denial. "This sure is hard to do alone." You just kind of leave it there. Now if the person … you could say you're just saying that, but you're hoping that you'll get it. Or, somebody will say, "I've been running around like crazy all day and now there are all these dirty dishes." That does happen in my house. You're inviting something. Or you might just go, "Whew." That's one I use. What that really means is, "I am tired and therefore I expect you to sweep this stuff up today," or something like that. These are all of the ways that we can phrase our requests; we can phrase our performatives in various ways. The essence, though, is that these things are not remarks, they are performatives. They are speech acts.

Lecture Twenty-Seven
Uses of Talk from Culture to Culture

Scope: Cultures differ in how they use language in particular situations. In some, direct questions are processed as rude; in others, spending time together in silence is ordinary, etc. These differences constitute alternate renditions of several components of speech that apply across cultures, which have been analyzed within the paradigm of the ethnography of communication.

Outline

I. Ability in one's native language is not only a matter of having a command of the grammar but also of having a spontaneous understanding of certain social norms. Speech acts took us part of the way, but there is also a broader point to be made in terms of cultures.

   A. Anthropologist Dell Hymes urged that we study the patterns and functions of speaking as an activity in its own right, in contrast to linguists' emphasis upon linguistic structure and anthropologists' emphasis upon kinship systems and medicinal systems.

   B. He urged that there be comparative studies of speaking on what he termed the *ethnography of communication.*

   C. The basic insight is that grammar is only part of communicative competence, that knowledge of the forms appropriate to social norms are equally essential to control of a language.

   D. Ethnography of communication addresses questions about cultural variations in the use of language.

II. The uses of speech are vastly different across cultures.

   A. The !Kung (pronounced [!xū]) of the Kalahari have a harsh lifestyle that conditions certain traits.
   1. A set type of talk is used to resolve disputes.
   2. A repetitive trance-like speech indicates hunger.
   3. Set stories are told that reinforce various cultural traits and assumptions and hopes, but language is not used to make up stories.

B. Cultures differ in terms of talkativeness.
  1. The Roti of Timor interpret silence as an indication of distress.
  2. The Western Apache are silent upon meeting new people, upon re-encountering one another, and after the emergence of conflict.
  3. Danes, it is said, are not inclined to "small talk" and can be in one another's company without talking for long periods of time.

C. Use of questions and requests also varies: Among rural speakers of Malagasy, an Austronesian language spoken on Madagascar, the simple imperative *Wash the clothes* (*Manasa lamba*) is rude:
  1. A passive construction is possible: *Let the clothes be washed by you.*

Sasao-nao	*ny*	*lamba*
wash-by you	the	clothes

  2. Most likely is a passive construction in which the person being requested to perform the action is not even indicated: *This soap is to be used to wash the clothes.*

Anasao	*ny*	*lamba*	*ity*	*savony*	*ity*
be washed	the	clothes	this	soap	this

III. In the ethnography of communication paradigm, Hymes applied a basic schema to occasions where speaking happens in any culture, a schema with three components nested within one another.

A. The basic unit of interest is a *situation*, whether marked by speech or by the absence of speech.
  1. Situations include ceremonies, fights, hunts, courtship, parties, etc.
  2. Situations are not purely communicative but may consist of speech and other things.

B. Within a situation, there is the *event*—the communicative part of a situation. Events include prayer, conversation, etc.

C. Within the event, there is a *speech act*, a minimal unit during an event, mediating between grammar and the event in implicating both linguistic and social norms.
  1. One example might be a joke told during a conversation at a party.

2. Note, this speech act is different from the Austin/Searle conception, in that it is not identified with a unit of grammar such as a single utterance.

IV. Hymes constructed an analytical framework to serve as a guide for analysis with minimum cultural bias.

    A. The components of speech were named in order to form the acronym SPEAKING: situation, participants, ends, act sequence, key, instrumentalities, norms, and genres.

    B. *Situation* is the setting (physical place, time) and scene (specific activity, e.g., a card game, a poetry recital, bargaining).

    C. *Participants* are not only speaker and addressee but also audience and intermediaries (e.g., a chief may speak through an addressor, an official may speak through a lawyer, or a dignitary may speak through a press agent).

    D. *Ends* are the goals and outcomes (e.g., in bargaining, an exchange; in a breakup dinner, the end of a relationship).

    E. *Act sequence* is what form the speech act is couched in, in terms of set phrases and grammar (e.g., direct versus indirect quotation).

    F. *Key* is the manner (jovial in a clown, solemn at a funeral, etc.).

    G. *Instrumentalities* are channels of communication (oral, written, phone, drums, etc.) and forms of speech (dialect, formal versus informal, etc.).

    H. *Norms* include conversational styles (gaps or no gaps) and meanings of intonational patterns.

    I. *Genres* include proverbs, myths, commercial messages, casual speech, etc.

V. Hymes intended each of these components as universal aspects of speaking, handled different ways by each culture, in a relationship equivalent to that between a phoneme and an allophone.

    A. He terms the different ways cultures handle these components *etic* distinctions, as opposed to the *emic* nature of the components themselves, which all cultures deal with in one way or another.

    B. For example, in couching requests without reference to the hearer, Malagasy requests differ in act sequence from those in English.

C. In rural Antigua, where West Indian Creole English is spoken, overlap and repetition during informal debate is treated as a constructive rhetorical strategy more than in standard English.

D. The Cuna of Panama listen every second day to a two-hour speech by their chief in which he discusses politics, religion, or history.

    1. There must be a responder (*apinsuet*) who says, "*Teki*" ("it is so") after each "verse" of the speech, and "policemen" who periodically shout "*Kapita marye!*" ("don't sleep"). Participants are set in a certain way here.

    2. The speech is couched in highly allusive fashion, such that for an hour afterward, a spokesman (*arkar*) interprets the speech in clearer terms for the audience. The act sequence is one that is different from what we expect of a public presentation.

    3. The language style of the speech (*sakla kaya*, "chief's talk") is highly elaborated, with fuller renditions of underlying sounds and special affixes used almost only in this way of speaking.

    4. Formulaic connecting material (a particular instrumentality) is common; for example, the chief signals that his speech is over by abruptly lowering his voice.

    5. As peculiar and formulaic as this may seem to us, the essence is simply a different setting of the SPEAKING paradigm.

E. In terms of ethnography of communication, American conventions such as stand-up comedy and television commentary directly after political debates or speeches are, in their way, just as arbitrary.

F. The maintenance of significant interpersonal relationships via e-mail today relies on an instrumentality that would be quite alien to less print-bound cultures.

Essential Reading:

Saville-Troike, *The Ethnography of Communication.*

Supplemental Reading:

Bauman and Sherzer, *Explorations in the Ethnography of Speaking.*

Hill and Hill, *Speaking Mexicano.*

Questions to Consider:

1. A child comes up to you and says, "Knock knock." What are the components of speech of what the child said, your response, and what the rest of the exchange will consist of?

2. Some people are more comfortable with silence than others. During a lull in a conversation, are you more inclined to fill it with some kind of verbiage or let it ride? In this, would you consider yourself a product of your upbringing or current environment, or is it an individual trait (i.e., is it, in you, an *etic* trait)?

Lecture Twenty-Seven—Transcript
Uses of Talk from Culture to Culture

We've seen how having a true ability in one's native language is not only a matter of having a command of the grammar but having a spontaneous understanding of certain social norms. In this lecture, I want to examine that basic notion further. Speech acts takes us part of the way in that, but it's been looked at from other perspectives, and there is a broader point to be made. It was made in a foundational way by Dell Hymes, an anthropologist. Hymes's idea was that a linguistics that only analyzed grammatical patternings (our phonemes and morphemes, etc.) was interesting but incomplete, because he observed that the way people use language—what people use speaking for—differs from culture to culture. For him, he felt that linguistics ought to be about language use as much as about the grammatical essence of language.

This ended up being a formal paradigm that has been studied a great deal since. Its technical term is the *ethnography of communication*. The idea is to study what it is to use language from culture to culture because the ways that we happen to use language in our American culture, for example, or in general the way languages are used in many Western cultures are very different from very basic ways that language is used in other places. The amount of variety is much more than one might think. Grammar is only part of competence in a language; there's also the issue of how you be a person in that language.

In the general sense, what Hymes was getting at was that the way people use language is vastly different from place to place. Take, for example, the !Kung; these are the people who live in the Kalahari Desert. Actually, for the record, you guys and gals, you people, are in a position to not have to rely on things like "!Kung," *k-u-n-g*. Actually, that is the closest you can get—or the closest it's been decided that you can get—in English spelling to what is actually a click sound ([!]), and then a nice velar fricative, [x], and then an [u] that's nasalized. Actually, we can say [kuŋ], but really it's something like [!xũ]; that's what it is. This idea of it being a *k* is inaccurate; it would be more like a *kh*, so it's a [x]; it's that "Bach" sound in German. Then it's not [uŋ]—that's not the way it's pronounced in the language—it's [ũ]; and so you can say, "bonk," and you can have this [ɔ̃] nasalized as in French *bon*; then [ũ], and so that's what "!Kung" is. I don't feel like saying

[!xũ] any more times than I just have, because I don't do it well. That's just to let you know that !Kung is an approximation that you, armed with how sounds really work, are now able to step beyond.

Anyway, they're in the Kalahari, these people. They have a harsh lifestyle, and it conditions certain traits. For example, among them you do not just have arguments in an open way. That kind of escalation—allowing things to kind of boil over—is not something that happens very often. Once there seems to be a kind of disagreement brewing, there's a very set kind of speech and a very set kind of exchange that is used to resolve disputes. Everybody knows to go right into it. There isn't much equivalent to that in our culture, except, actually, if you have a kind of couple's therapy, you can learn a certain way of speaking: "What I'm hearing and what you're saying is that you think I hear anger in your voice." That sort of thing. Among these people, that sort of thing—except not in those anodyne terms—is standard.

Something else about them is that when they are hungry—and that happens when you are reliant on spearing something to eat. Really imagine what that would be like; sometimes you're just not going to be able to find an okapi (actually, they don't live that far down). But there is a kind of a trancelike speech that they go into to indicate that they're hungry. There's no such thing as running around saying, "I'm hungry, I'm hungry," because that happens a lot and would be kind of annoying. There's just this sort of trancelike speech that you go into, and it's repetitive; you kind of vent it by sort of singing in a way. That's what one does. Not just that weird guy over there; that's what one does as a member of the culture.

These are people—notice how I'm avoiding saying their name—who do not make up stories. We think, "I'm going to make up a story about a princess who kisses something," etc. There are many stories made up in this society—people sell them for money—whereas among these people, you tell set stories, and the stories have certain characters and they serve to reinforce various cultural traits, assumptions, and hopes that the people have. That's what it's for; they wouldn't put it that way, but that's what it's for. But the idea that now I'm going to make up a story where Mr. Rabbit tries to build a fence and it rains or something like that, that makes no sense to them. They're not interested in making up stories for no particular reason. That's just not in their chords, so to speak. Language for them is very different than it is for us; they use it in different ways. Talk about the grammar of this language, that's one thing—including the marvelous clicks that I can't do properly—but then there's just what you use language for.

Talkativeness varies massively between cultures. The island of Timor—which we've seen—is quite small and has many languages. On one end of it is a language called Roti, and the Roti are very talkative people. For them, silence is a little bit disturbing. If things get quiet, then something is wrong. Or the friend I mentioned in one lecture who came back talking about the "mongeese" in India: Another thing that he mentioned—other than these "mongeese"—were that, at least his impression was, people in India talked a great deal more than Americans to fill in space. He said that he had the guilty feeling after awhile that the Indians "wouldn't shut up." Now I'm sure that this varies massively according to various cultures within India, but this was an impression that he had, that one had to talk to fill space. That is a trait that some Americans have as individuals—I've known people who, "Just will you stop it?"—but it's a cultural trait with some other peoples.

The Western Apache are silent when they meet new people. There's none of this business of "Good to meet you" or "Good to know ya"—that seems to be an older expression; Fred Mertz on *I Love Lucy* always says, "Good to know ya," which I only ever heard on *Lucy*—but "good to meet"—something like that. You are quiet. If you come upon someone again, then you are quiet; you don't talk. Also, for them, when a conflict comes up, what you do is you get quiet. The idea, again, is to avoid it. You have your set speech among the fill-in-the-blank, and then with the Western Apache you get quiet. Or it's said—I frankly have never seen it, but maybe it's because I've only met maybe eight and a half Danes—but it's always said that Danes are very comfortable with silence and that they can just sit around in the living room and not speak for long periods of time and that's OK. I suspect my sister's about to marry a Dane, and so I'll let you know one day whether he's comfortable with silence. But that is said about them.

What's interesting is that if we look at all these people—the Roti, the Western Apache, and the Danes—probably, if we are American, then the system that makes the most sense to us is the Roti and their discomfort with silence. I don't know how many times I have stuck my foot in my mouth—and I mean deep down, tasting the leather—because of being afraid of silence. I'll just say the dumbest thing. I think a lot of us do that because you're not supposed to be quiet, but actually all the systems make sense. It makes complete sense to me, for example, to be a Dane and to not talk when there's nothing to be said. Because, for example, remember when I talked about the frat boys and the "Woo! Yeah! Let's do kegs! Woo!

Yeah!" There was nothing to say; they could have shut up. That would have made perfect sense to me. But these things vary from culture to culture.

Something else that varies is questions and requests. For example, think about Madagascar, which is off the coast of Africa. The language that's spoken in Madagascar is called Malagasy. Interestingly enough, Malagasy is Austronesian language. The home of Austronesian is actually Southeast Asia, the Philippines, Indonesia, and then a bunch of languages spoken eastward of Australia. It's a huge family, about 1,000. That's Austronesian. Then way down across the Indian Ocean there's just this one Austronesian language—and just one—and it's spoken on Madagascar. You'd think that some African language would be spoken on Madagascar because it's kind of in Africa—Africa's right across the sea—but for some reason what they speak on Madagascar is not a language related to Swahili. They speak a language which is very closely related to languages way over in Indonesia. It's one of those things where people, long before what we call technology, were capable of a lot more than we think because clearly they weren't put there, and it's not that Madagascar drifted across the Indian Ocean so quickly; it wasn't a matter of continental drift. Clearly those people sailed there, and they must have done it in tiny little boats, and a giant squid did not catch them. They did not dehydrate. They actually got to Madagascar healthy enough to then procreate, and now they're there. It's one of the linguistic puzzles of the world: How did those Austronesian speakers get to that island? But they're there now, and they speak a language, and it's called Malagasy.

In that language, you don't make direct requests. Or if you do, it's kind of fighting words or you're known as a kind of a scrappy, kind of a Snuffy Smith, crude sort of person. You don't do it. For example, let's say that you were asking someone to wash the clothes. You might say, "Wash the clothes." That's grammatical. If you look in a grammar of Malagasy and you look up imperative, then you will find that that is the form, as you can see on the screen ("*Manasa lamba*"). But actually you can soften it. Much more likely than this just "Wash the clothes!" is that you use a passive construction and you say, "Clothes are to be washed" ("*Anasao ny lamba*"), and you just leave it there. But what's interesting is there you'll say, "The clothes are to be washed by you" ("*Sasao-nao ny lamba*"). That's specifying who's going to do it. But really, even more, this is a place where performatives get really hyper-indirect. The proper way to tell someone to wash clothes is to say what translates into English as, "The clothes are to be washed by soap" ("*Anasao ny lamba ity savony ity*"). You don't even mention the person; that's considered rather rude. It's much too direct. "The clothes are to be washed by soap," and then you watch that happen. That's very natural in Malagasy. This is something that one only notices … this was actually only noticed in a classic study by someone who actually took the time to live in a Malagasy village. All of those things are Malagasy sentences, but they have a very different cultural meaning within the Malagasy context than they would within our context, where you could say, "The clothes are to be washed with soap" to someone. That's a sentence, but it also makes you someone who would very discreetly be taken to a room that you could not escape, and that would be that; you would be insane.

Hymes, noticing these sorts of things, had an idea. His first idea was that you could take speakings—occasions where speaking happens—in any culture, and you could apply a certain basic schema to it. The schema's just the beginning, but his idea was that the first thing we might look at—if we're trying to come up with a culture-neutral analysis of what speaking is and how it varies from culture to culture—then first of all you might say that our basic unit of interest is a *situation*. There are various kinds of situations: There are situations that are marked by speech; there are situations that are marked by the absence of speech. For example, let's say that a situation is a ceremony or a hunt or a party, something like that. The question is, what kind of talking happens during this situation? For example, a reunion; for us, in that situation, there's going to be all sorts of jabber, etc., etc. All very pleasant for us, whereas among the Western Apache, in that situation, the first thing that we know about talk is that there's not supposed to be any. That makes a certain sense. I remember once a very early lady friend of mine had come back from a vacation, and I remember the whole mise-en-scène of this. I was standing facing this way, and I was talking to somebody within a room; it was a dormitory (God, I do not miss dorms). She came from behind me, silently, and put her arms around my waist; just silent. I was still talking, and she just kind of went, "Mmm …" *vlump*, and she just kind of rested back there. That was a very sweet kind of reunion. That relationship, in fact, was doomed, but that little vignette alone was very sweet.

There is a situation; then, within a situation, there is the *event*. Here is—if there are any within it—the communicative part of a situation. For example, a conversation is an event; a prayer is an event. As we've seen in the previous lecture, conversations vary very much. There are people for whom overlapping conversation is perfectly normal; there are people whose conversations are what we might call tidier. But that is the event. Then—and you can see in Hymes's schematic—within the event, there is what Hymes called a *speech act*. The speech act for Hymes is a minimal unit during an event, and that mediates between grammar and the event. For example, if we were at the party, the event would be a joke. Terminology is often messy, and what Hymes meant by speech act was slightly different than what was meant by speech act in the work of Austin, etc.; but you understand the basic intention here. We're not talking about a unit of grammar or a sentence, but we're talking about an actual kind of occasion; and so you have this schematic.

Beyond this, Hymes came up with an analysis of what he called *components of speech*. The idea was to look without cultural bias at the way people talk and to come up with, as it were, some phonemes, and then to note that there were allophones of these phonemes in different cultures. Except that we're not talking about sound; we're talking about how speech is used.

We'll start with the acronym: The acronym happened to spell SPEAKING. It was rather contrived but kind of elegant, and it's good for the memory. Each one of the basic elements—each one of the "-emes" so to speak—that he proposed ended up lining up to spell SPEAKING if you looked at their first letters.

S was for situation. Situation involved the setting—and so whatever the physical place is and the time and then the scene—the specific activity. Is it a card game, or is it a poetry recital, or is it bargaining? Situation is one thing. When you're analyzing an episode of talking or nontalking in a culture, the first thing to note is, what is the situation?

Then the second thing to note is the *participants*. The participants is not always as simple as someone is talking and someone is being addressed; it's not like that at all always, because of course there are intermediaries. A chief, in many cultures, will only speak to his or her flock through some kind of addressor, somebody who he speaks through. As formulaic as that can seem to us, notice that—for example—if the governor of a state is found to have committed some heinous kind of act that you would not have expected, he might speak to the public only through a lawyer. Suddenly that governor becomes silent. Or, for example, a star will talk only through their press agent if something untoward has happened. Participants can be more layered than just I'm talking to her. It can be a matter of intermediations. When we're looking at an occasion of speaking in a culture, then another thing to account for—another thing to describe—is the participants.

Then there is *ends*—pretty soon we'll have spelled SPEAKING, and so ends. Ends is the goals and the outcomes that are desired. For example, in bargaining, what are they trying to do? In many occasions, there are ends. It could be just to have a good time, but is it a bargaining, where people are doing that? Is it some kind of exchange? Is it a breakup dinner? Those have certain patterns, if somebody is sitting there. Maybe the end of this, i.e., the goal, is that the people are no longer romantically involved when the dinner ends.

Then there is, for *A*, *act sequence*. I suspect that's one of the ones where for Hymes it was kind of like I remember in … I used to have this old book, and I think it was more than one, with the ABCs of the animals. *V* would be for vole and then *w* would be walrus—that's easy—but then *x* was something called a xerus. You can tell they just kind of got stuck and they found this animal. I seem to recall it being kind of like a weasel. I think act sequence was that moment for Hymes. But what he meant was what form that the speech act is couched in, in terms of whether there are set phrases that are used within this act. For example, if you are having the breakup dinner, then it's "It's not you, it's me." There's going to be something like that. You can expect it. Or, for example, how the grammar is going to work, for example direct quotation or indirect quotation. Let's say you're doing a sermon. If somebody is doing a sermon, they might say, "Jesus said, 'Let he who is without sin cast the first stone.'" That's the way you would say it. If you think about it, in the sermon you wouldn't say, "Jesus said that you should not cast the first stone if you are without sin." In other words, you quote him directly—"Jesus said"—and then you imitate him (I'm not going to do a Jesus imitation). But you don't say, "Jesus said that you should …"—no, you don't think about that, but that is part of the act sequence of the act of speaking that is known as a sermon.

K is for *key*, and that is, what is the manner? Is it jovial, as in a comedy routine or a clown? (I hate clowns.) Or is it something solemn, such as at a funeral where you don't laugh, you do not bring a tuba? These are things that are important in describing things.

I is *instrumentalities*, and what that means is, what is the channel of communication? You could be just talking—that's fine—but you could be just writing; you could be talking on the phone; you could be banging the drums. Then there's the issue of dialect. Are you using the standard, or are you using the nonstandard? These things change. Even in American culture, these things change. In a pop song today, it is assumed in modern popular music that you will use informal, colloquial, nonstandard dialect; that's the expectation. The whitest, most middle-class, buttoned-up singer will pick up a guitar and suddenly be "tellin'" instead of "telling"; "eyu" instead of "you." It's just expected; one doesn't even think about it. This was not true, say, 100 years ago, even 75 years ago—much more uptight. There was a time when there was a song, "Ain't She Sweet, Do You See Her Walking Down the Street?" I'll bet I can't sing it because we have to get the rights to it, but it's a song that's from I think the teens, early '20s at the latest. That was considered a big deal then, to have a pop song that used "ain't" in it. That was part of the selling power of the song. These things change; our instrumentalities in terms of pop music have changed.

Then there are *norms*, so that gets into the conversational styles. Do you have gaps? Do you not? Are you a Dane, or are you what we saw was one Jewish New York style of conversing? Or even intonational patterns. For example, when you're doing this: "And then I went to 7-Eleven?" That thing that young people—and frankly I've heard people who were 40 doing it; I don't know how young that it is, although since I'm 42 I'll pretend that it is—but something that has happened over the past few decades in this country, that is now a norm. Whether you like it or not, that is the way a certain set talk, and if you didn't talk that way you'd seem a little forceful. Interesting: If you are clinically insane, you collect old radio shows the way I do, and you even get down to the bad ones. If you listen to *Quiz Kids* back then, you actually get kids speaking spontaneously, and not one of them that I've ever heard talks like this. That hadn't started in the 1930s and '40s. They talk like this. Boring little kids they were, but they did not talk like this. Nowadays it's standard; that is a new norm.

Finally, for *g* we have *genres*. Are we talking about proverbs? Are we dealing with myths? Is it a commercial message, or are people just talking?

That's our acronym: SPEAKING. His idea is that each one of these components is something that you could consider equivalent to the phoneme. All cultures are dealing with those components in one way or another. The issue is what the variations are between them—and so what the allophones are, in a way. Actually, Hymes put it that way. His idea was that there are *emic* distinctions—i.e., the situation as differentiated from the participants as differentiated instrumentalities—then there are the *etic* distinctions. The Danes don't talk, and the Rotinese talk too much—that sort of thing. His idea would be that in Malagasy, the way that requests are couched differs in act sequence from the ones in English. To say, "May the clothes be washed by the soap?" is different in terms of grammatically how you convey the request, just as cultures will differ in terms of within a sermon whether you direct quote or indirect quote.

In Antigua, the Caribbean island—rural Antigua—when people do informal debating, people just overlap all over one another and do a whole lot of repetition. That is considered perfectly normal. It's not chaotic—all sorts of business gets done—but our notion of what an interruption is, in that kind of setting (kind of barber-shoppy setting, except among people of either gender) in Antigua, all of that is quite different. Their norms are different. That doesn't mean that they're not normal; it's just that the norms of how one uses languages in that particular emic department differ in that etic way.

Or, for example, in Panama there is a Native American culture called the Cuna. Every couple of days they listen to a good two-hour speech by their chief, and he discusses politics, history, or religion. After he does this, for one thing, there has to be a responder, and the responder keeps saying, "It is so." "*Teki*" is what he says—it means *It is so*—after each kind of verse of the speech. That has to be there. The chief can't give the speech if there isn't somebody to sit there and do that along the way. Then there are what you can kind of translate as policemen who are continually shouting things along the lines of "Don't sleep! Wake up!" Those people are there, and they have to be there to kind of keep the congregation going. You can wrap your head around the sense in this, although it's very different from anything that we're used to. But what it really just means according to the Hymesian paradigm is that the notion of participants and where they fit in within that situation is different than what it would be for us. The chief's speech is couched in this very metaphorical, elusive way; that's the only way that he could make it. The idea of giving a policy paper would be quite impossible; you almost sing it. It's so arcane, really, that the custom is that afterward there's a spokesman and he interprets the speech. He actually tells people what it meant. The act sequence is different—what kind of grammar you use. The language style that the chief uses is a special kind of style—as a matter of fact, highly elaborated. There are underlying sounds, which in ordinary speech are lost on the surface, but which the chief will actually use.

You can look at, as a matter of fact, this sentence from one of his speeches. What he happened to be saying was, "God left wild boar strongholds for us" (*Papa yannu kalukana urpisa-ye*) and "we came in order to care for them" (*an soke aal akk^wekan nonimar an soke*) That's just one sentence. You can see in this sentence that for one thing, you'll see lighting up here sounds that would not be used in casual speech (*Papa yannu kalukana urpisa-ye*

...). Then there are affixes that are used, which you only use in this variety and never when you're actually talking; and so you see that *-ye* just lighting up. Then there are all these little set phrases that you use. You sprinkle this speech with all of these locutions that have nothing to do with casual speech but are the way that you put things when you're using this chief's language. It has a name; it's called "chief's talk": *sakla kaya*. Here you see those lighting up (**an soke aal** *akkʷekan nonimar* **an soke**). The casual sentence would be much less busy than this language that the chief uses. What this means is that he's using a very different instrumentality than anybody in any kind of equivalent American setting would. Then the chief signals that the speech is over by abruptly lowering his voice, not raising it. We're used to things like, "And that's how America's going to be great!" Then everybody goes, "Yay!" You wouldn't end it, "And that's how America's going to be great ..." That's no way to end a speech. That's pretty much the way it happens among the Cuna. In that, there is a different norm than something that we would expect.

If we were going to be looking at the Cuna, the idea would be to do an ethnography of communication analysis and look at how language is used in various situations. That has been done, for one, in terms of these chief's speeches and looking at in terms of this speaking paradigm. Then you can classify what allophones this culture uses in terms of ethnography of communication. It can make things look exotic, but it's interesting how exotic we are in some ways. For example, imagine how odd it is that we have a tradition where someone gets up in front of an audience, and the idea is that for 20 minutes that person is going to repeatedly make the audience laugh. That would seem very peculiar to many people in the world: stand-up comedy. You're going to laugh over and over, and I haven't done this right if you don't laugh. You're not going to laugh for any reason; I've actually sat down and concocted jokes for you to laugh at, and then I'm going to walk off with a wave. I am quite sure that to the people whose names shall not be spoken that would look absolutely ridiculous. If you think about it, it kind of is.

Imagine watching a political debate; and so "How'd she do? How'd he do?" You watch it, and everything made perfect sense; they're speaking English; you've got a brain. But then more shows have to be preempted because then you've got to have not just one person but probably two or three tell you what they said and comment. What did they think about the debate? That's considered perfectly ordinary: "And now David Brinkley will tell you what you just heard." That's really rather like what goes on among the Cuna; it's just that we are used to it.

Or I write an occasional inconsequential piece for a magazine, and I was first asked to do it over e-mail. The years have gone by, and I've written countless articles for this publication. I've had all sorts of very pleasant exchanges with the editor. We have only ever met through e-mail. Once he was about to call me, because it had been like seven years; I said, "John, let's just enjoy this. Let's see how long we can go without ever hearing one another's voices." Now it's just a joke between us. That's a weird instrumentality in terms of the speaking paradigm, that we're doing it all through sending symbols over wires. That would be something very interesting to an ethnographer of communication from among the people who shall not be named.

In any case, I hope that this has been somewhat enlightening. In the next lecture, we will look at a new aspect of philosophy of language: namely, to what extent is language about thought?

Lecture Twenty-Eight
Does Language Channel Thought? The Evidence

Scope: In the 1930s, Benjamin Lee Whorf popularized a hypothesis that the particularities of languages' vocabularies and grammars determine the way their speakers process the world. This lecture examines Whorf's case and also explores difficulties with the concept as applied to various languages, including English.

Outline

I. After looking at the ethnography of communication, in all its variety, one might naturally wonder about the relationship between language and thought.

   A. Linguist and anthropologist Edward Sapir (1884–1939) seemed to assume that a language had a kind of mentality or brain—that the language had a certain inner tendency that another language might not have.

   B. Sapir's idea was developed and most influentially promulgated by Sapir's student Benjamin Lee Whorf (1897–1941) in the 1930s.

      1. The hypothesis—that people's thoughts are channeled by aspects of their vocabulary and grammar—is known, therefore, as the *Sapir-Whorf hypothesis*.

      2. That is, one school of philosophy of language entails examining the extent to which grammar and vocabulary channel thought itself.

   C. The Sapir-Whorf hypothesis has been highly influential.

      1. In 2004 a *New York Times* writer supposed that the language of the Kawésqar tribe in Chile has no future-tense marking because, having been nomads travelling often in canoes in the past, they would usually have been so unclear on what was going to happen in the future that there was no need to ever talk about it.

      2. However, the Japanese language is one that lacks an explicit future, while there are also many tribal languages that do have future marking.

D. The version of the hypothesis that Whorf put forth has never been proven. In this and the following lecture, I will cover work on the Sapir-Whorf hypothesis, including a new strain of scholarship demonstrating that language can channel thought in less dramatic ways than Whorf supposed.

II. Whorf's analysis of the Hopi language included his most interesting, and most notorious, claim.

A. Whorf claimed that Hopi does not mark time in any way. He argued that this made Hopi speakers think in a way different from Westerners, less concerned with past, present, and future and more concerned with cyclicity.

B. Whorf drew some stimulating conclusions.

1. He said that "Users of markedly different grammars ... are not equivalent as observers but must arrive at somewhat different views of the world."

2. He suggested that Isaac Newton developed his ideas of space and time because he spoke a European language, where it is more important to mark tense in terms of past, present, or future than in some other languages.

3. He also said, "We cut nature up, organize it into concepts, and ascribe significances as we do largely because we are parties to an agreement to organize it in this way."

C. However, his description of Hopi was simply wrong.

1. Here is a sentence in Hopi (from a 1983 study by Ekkehart Malotki). The sentence means *Start sharpening your arrows; we're going hunting*:

Um	**angwu**	**pay**
you	**beforehand**	**already**

ùuhoy	tsuku-toyna-**ni**;
your arrow	make-a-point-**will**;

itam	maq-to-**ni**.
we	hunt-go-**will**

2. There are ample indications of time. Yet Whorf explicitly claimed that Hopi has "no words, grammatical forms, constructions, or expressions that refer directly to what we call 'time,' or to past, or future, or to enduring or lasting."

D. Nevertheless, the Sapir-Whorf hypothesis, based initially upon this characterization of Hopi, is still presented to undergraduates and is still addressed in books written for the public as if it were a going concern.

III. Looking at a lot of languages, rather than just one, shows that the idea that language channels thought in the almost magical and determinative way that Whorf was talking about is difficult to support.

  A. In Turkish, there are two past tenses.

    1. One is "normal": *I saw* would be "*gördüm*," while you use the other one (*görmüşüm*) to indicate that you heard about something but didn't actually see it.

    2. Some attribute this trait to something about Turkish culture. However, *evidential markers* of this kind occur randomly in languages all over the world.

  B. Russian is a language where future tense is indicated largely via context.

    1. Literary critic Edmund Wilson thought this was why Russians seemed unable to keep to a schedule.

    2. Again, the Japanese have that same grammatical feature without being regarded as laggards.

  C. Interesting differences between French and English can be exaggerated.

    1. In French there are two words for *to know*: *savoir* means to know a fact; *connaître* means to know a person or to be familiar with something.

      a. Journalist Mark Abley has written that "to a French speaker that distinction is central to how the mind interacts with the world."

      b. We can examine what the implications of that would be by making it go the other way.

    2. In French the word *sortir* and means a variety of things covered by different words in English.

      a. It literally means *go out*, but it also covers what English would express with *come out* (during the earthquake, *le tiroir est sorti de la commode*—"the drawer came out of the dresser"); *get out* (someone is in a hole and says, "*Sors-moi d'ici!*" "Get me out of here!"); and *stick out* as in one's tongue (*Sors la langue*, "Stick out your tongue").

      b. Yet obviously English speakers are not more attuned to the difference between these experiences than French speakers.

D. Comparisons often overlook the difference between general meaning and a more specific meaning of the same word that has been conventionalized.

    1. Abley also discusses how the Boro of India have words with intriguingly specific meanings, which presumably reflect their culture.

      a. *Egthu*—to create a pinching sensation in the armpit.

      b. *Khonsay*—to pick an object up with care because it is rare or scarce.

      c. *Onsay*—to pretend to love.

      d. *Goblo*—to be fat (as a child or infant).

      e. *Asusu*—to feel unknown and uneasy in a new place.

    2. However, English has words such as:

      a. *Bonding*—when people getting to know one another start to establish a sense of connection.

      b. *Reconciliation*—when a romantic pair have been estranged for a long period and decide to be together again.

      c. *Hover*—when one member of a couple stays always a vigilant foot or so away from the other member of the couple at a social occasion.

    3. Few would consider these words evidence of something unique about Anglophone culture.

    4. In addition, these are specific meanings amidst more general ones of the words.

      a. The specific meanings happen to come to mind most readily, just as is likely to be the case for the Boro words.

      b. English has ways of expressing most of the Boro concepts.

E. English could be viewed as extremely exotic. For example, consider that ordinal numbers are marked with *-th*, except the first three: *first, second,* and *third.*

    1. Most of the world's languages, like Hebrew and French, have a special word for *first* only.

    2. This might be taken to mean that English speakers have a heightened awareness of secondness and thirdness.

3. Estonian speakers would then be seen as having a heightened awareness of secondness, since their language has a special word for *second*.

IV. The idea that people speaking the 6,000 languages around the world are all channeled by their grammar into seeing the world in charmingly different ways has wide appeal.

   A. However, if you think about the languages of the world, not to mention look at a great deal of the experimentation on that topic, you see that the idea just doesn't hold up.

   B. Much of how languages are different is a matter of chance.

Essential Reading:
Lucy, *Language Diversity and Thought*.

Supplemental Reading:
Gentner and Goldin-Meadow, eds., *Language in Mind*.

Questions to Consider:
1. If you speak a second language, do you feel that you are "a different person" when you speak it? If so, would you say that this has to do with vocabulary and grammar, with cultural factors, or with both?

2. Would you be more interested in theories demonstrating that all humans' thought patterns are basically the same or theories demonstrating that human thought patterns differ fundamentally according to language and/or culture? Why?

Lecture Twenty-Eight—Transcript
Does Language Channel Thought? The Evidence

In the last lecture, when we looked at ethnography of communication, when we saw things like how the people who shall not be named mediate disputes or use language in a state of hunger, or where we saw how the Western Apache use silence and so on, a natural thought may have been, does language track thought, as it were? Is it that the language that we use is in some way reflective—in terms of how we use it—of our thought patterns—or more specifically our cultural patterns? That is a natural thought that many people have had.

In fact, one of them was Edward Sapir, who we have met before as one of the anthropologist linguists who were interested in showing that all languages are equal, which they are. In Sapir's work there is a strain where he seems to assume that a language had a kind of mentality or brain, that the language had a certain inner tendency that another language might not have. For example, in earlier English, we would say, "come hither" instead of "come here"; we would say "go thither" instead of "go there"; and we would ask someone not, "Where are you going to?" ("Where are you going to?" like the song); we would say, "Whither are you going?" Those words have dropped out of the language. Other Germanic languages keep them; English happens to have let them drop. Sapir had an idea that English was "impatient with nuance." He once said, "That we add to 'where' an important nuance of direction irritates rather than satisfies." His idea is that to be an English speaker is to have a certain mentality about language and grammar, a mentality in this case of having a certain irritation with nuance.

That was the seed of an idea that was taken and run with, so to speak, by a student of Sapir's. That student was Benjamin Lee Whorf, and he lived during roughly the first half of the previous century. He died young: He was born in 1897, and he died in 1941. But in the 1930s, Whorf promulgated a hypothesis. That hypothesis was that people's thoughts are channeled by aspects of first of all their vocabulary but also their grammar. The idea is that our grammars channel how we see the world. That has become known as the *Sapir-Whorf hypothesis*. It's been highly influential; it is a philosophy of language that commands considerable attention. It has been being researched from various perspectives for the better part, technically, of 100 years at this point. It is extremely influential; you find it everywhere in intelligent discussion.

In 2004 there was an article in *The New York Times* about a tribe in Chile called the Kawésqar. The Kawésqar tribe in Chile does not happen to have explicit future-tense marking. The writer very casually assumed that the reason the Kawésqar doesn't have future-tense marking is because they used to be nomads and they used to travel in canoes, and because they were nomads, they would have had so little idea of where they were going to go that there wasn't any reason to discuss the future. The problem with that is, first of all, that another language where you don't have an explicit future in that way is Japanese, and I think that the Japanese seem to have pretty much always known where they were going. Then of course there are many tribal languages with future marking just spilling out all over the place. But nevertheless, there was this idea. I remember talking to one person who was doing research on a small group in a very far away part of the world, and it happened to be a language where there were many different words for *going*. She said, "I can understand why, because they're always going; they're always going somewhere; they're always walking." But who isn't?

Nevertheless, there's always this notion in the air. The fact is that as interesting a philosophy of language as the Sapir-Whorf hypothesis is, it's never been proven in the way that it has gotten out there into the conversation. It is tantalizing, but in fact it's been highly elusive to researchers. So what I want to do in this lecture and the next lecture is to show what research on the Sapir-Whorf hypothesis has yielded, to show that there are pitfalls in taking at his word Whorf's ideas—although they were very seductively worded—but also to show that as this hypothesis has been examined further, there have also been shown to be things that support to it to a certain extent. But I think that in this course you, as now highly informed laypeople about linguistics, will be in a position to command a kind of Whorfianism that actually fits the facts.

Whorf gave talks on this idea—apparently, he was very good at doing that—and he wrote various articles on this idea, and what really socked it home was his analysis of the language of the Hopi Indians. His claim, the most notorious claim, was really interesting—when you read it, it's dazzling—that the Hopi do not mark time in any way in their language. His idea was that because the grammar does not mark tense in any way, that that means that they have a different way of thinking than Westerners. So they are less concerned with the past, present, and the future and presumably more concerned with a cyclic view of time. You probably have heard that sort of thing described about people of that sort: the cyclic time. Whorf's specific idea was that this is something that is either caused by or in an integral relationship with the actual grammar of the language. He said things along these lines:

> Users of markedly different grammars are pointed by the grammars toward different types of observations and different evaluations of externally similar acts of observation, and hence are not equivalent as observers but must arrive at somewhat different views of the world.

In other words, we see the whole world differently than a Vietnamese person. A Vietnamese person is seeing it through different eyes, and this is because of—or significantly colored by—the fact that Vietnamese grammar has certain differences from English grammar.

Whorf took this pretty far, to some very, very stimulating conclusions: "Newtonian space, time, and matter are no intuitions. They are recepts from culture and language; that's where Newton got them." Newtonian space, time, and matter are not just truth; that's just one of many ways of looking at things, and the reason that Newton came up with that was because he spoke a European language where it is more important to mark tense in terms of past, present, or future than, say, in the Kawésqar language. Then he made statements that have become famous, such as this one; this is the classic Whorf passage:

> We cut nature up, organize it into concepts, and ascribe significances as we do, largely because we are parties to an agreement to organize it in this way—an agreement that holds through our speech community and is codified in the patterns of our language. The agreement is, of course, an implicit and unstated one, but its terms are absolutely obligatory; we cannot talk at all except by subscribing to the organization and classification of data which the agreement decrees.

That's what got everybody really interested when Whorf made his speeches in the '30s—not speeches; talks—and when Whorf did his writings.

If that's true, certainly that is a ball that you want to pick up and run with in turn, just as he had picked up the ball and run with it in response to Sapir's ideas. But there is a problem in terms of biography, and that is that it's often said, for example, that Charles Ives—the American classical composer—actually worked for an insurance company. That's what his job was, and yet he was a classical composer. There is a similar problem with Whorf, because he actually was someone who worked in fire insurance as well, and he was actually just an amateur linguist. Now that doesn't necessarily matter—it might be that he did his homework, and there are talented amateurs all over the place—but the fact is that he didn't really know Hopi very well. It's as simple as that. It's mystifying to me that he allowed it, but he did. If you actually look at Hopi, the idea that there's no indication of time in it just doesn't hold up.

For example, look at this sentence for *Start sharpening your arrows; we're going hunting.* (*Um angwu pay ùuhoy tsuku-toyna-ni; itam maq-to-ni.*) Now I am not going to venture to pronounce this language, but this is Hopi, and what you can see in this sentence, very simply, is that in order to say, "Start sharpening your arrows; we're going hunting," it seems like there's some indication of time. You can talk about not marking the future. Hopi does: We can see that there is this suffix *-ni*, and it translates into *will*. When you say, "Start sharpening your arrows," what you say is literally along the lines of "Have your arrows sharpened before." That means that we see that you do have indications of pastness—you've got a word for *already*; you've got this *beforehand*—whereas Whorf had actually claimed "Hopi has no words, grammatical forms, constructions, or expressions that refer directly to what we call 'time,' or to past, or future, or to enduring or lasting." That's what he said, and it simply isn't true.

Nevertheless, the fact is that the Sapir-Whorf hypothesis, based initially upon this characterization of Hopi, is still presented to undergraduates and still addressed in books written for the public as if it was a going concern. For example, the book that showed that Hopi was different from what Whorf assumed was written the better part of three decades ago, and yet the article in *The New York Times* about the Kawésqar was in 2004. The fact is that if you look at a lot of languages rather than just one—whether or not you've got the data on it right or not—you see that the idea that language channels thought in the way that Whorf was talking about, the magic and determinative way, is difficult to support. For example, in Turkish there are two past tenses, in a way. One of them is what we would call normal, and then there's another one that you use when you're talking about something that you heard about but you didn't actually see. For example, if you say, "I saw," then you say, "*gördüm,*" but if you're talking about "I saw" in the sense of you heard about something that was going on, then you would say, "*görmüşüm.*" It's different. That's called an *evidential marker.*

Some people would say that that has something to do with Turkish culture. I remember once I was far, far, away, and I knew somebody in the Foreign Service who had served in Turkey. He was very taken with the idea that those evidential markers indicated that people in Turkey were uniquely attuned to sussing out what sources of information were. But the fact of the matter is, aren't most people? Who are the incurious people, if you think about it? Any culture that you look at, what is really the reality of remarking that they're attuned to where information came from? That might be rather like saying that people are human.

More to the point, there are evidential markers in all sorts of languages all over the world. One tribal group will have them, and then the next tribal group won't, even though they're living a rather similar life. It's difficult to support if you happen to pull the camera back from just looking at the difference between English speakers and Turkish speakers, if you can say, even, that English speakers are not curious about sources of information. I think a lot of us might have trouble with that.

Or you hear something like Edmund Wilson the literary critic—Bunny Wilson, a very prolific literary critic of the previous century—learned Russian to an extent. Russian is a language where future marking is left to context mostly, just like in Kawésqar. For example, in English we can say, "Tomorrow I take my driving test." That, in Russian, is pretty much the way you use the future. There's a way of indicating it, but typically: "Tomorrow I take my driving test," not "Tomorrow I'm going to take my driving test" or something like that. Wilson thought that was why Russians couldn't keep to a schedule; his idea was that because they don't have any future markers, then they have trouble with that. Then again, the Japanese have that same grammatical feature, and I don't think anybody thinks of the Japanese as laggards. We have a problem with that way of looking at things.

Or try this one: You find this sort of thing said innocently by perfectly logical people, but you have to really examine what a larger picture would reveal. For example, in French there are two words for *to know*. There's *savoir*, which is for knowing something like facts; then there's *connaître*, and that is for knowing a person. That's something that one learns as an English speaker as an interesting difference between English and French. Then you have an enterprising journalist, and he writes a passage like this one (beautifully written, understandable sentiment, but):

> My language allows me, somewhat clumsily, to get the distinction across: on the one hand, factual knowledge; on the other, acquaintanceship and understanding. But to a French speaker, that distinction is central to how the mind interacts with the world.

That means that because French-speaking people have *savoir* and *connaître*, or German people have something like *wissen* and *kennen*, that there is a different way of looking at the world.

Let's examine what the implications of that would be. Let's make it go the other way. In French there is a word *sortir*, and it means a whole lot of things which are covered by different words in English. *Sortir* means *to go out*; that's the sort of dictionary definition that you learn in a French class. But it can also mean *come out*, and so if the drawer came out in an earthquake, "*Le tiroir est sorti de la commode.*" If you are stuck in a hole and you tell someone to "get me out of here," you don't you use their word for *get*; you say, "*Sors-moi d'ici!*" *Sortir*; that's what it means. If you stick out your tongue, "*Sors la langue*"; "Stick out your tongue." All those things are *sortir* in French. We've got all sorts of words; they've just got *sortir*. I don't think—now of course this is a venturesome hypothesis—but I for one do not think that we English speakers are more attuned to the difference between a drawer slipping out of something, being pulled out of a hole, sticking out our tongue, and going out for a night on the town than French speakers. It just doesn't work, despite the fact that they only have one word for those things and we've got several. The simple fact is that to make that claim about *savoir* and *connaître* or *wissen* and *kennen* is exactly the same thing. It requires pulling the lens further back.

Another one that one hears a lot where again we have to look at ourselves and we have to look at the world: There's a journalist whose name is Mark Abley, and he's written a book called *Spoken Here*, which is a wonderful survey of attempts to revitalize dying languages around the world. But he does couch that coverage in an assumption that the grand old Whorfian idea is valid; he's utterly entranced by it. You get to some interesting parts: There is a group of people called the Boro in India, and he lists some words that they have with intriguingly specific meanings. Supposedly, these things reflect their culture. For example, there is *egthu*, and that word means to create a pinching sensation in the armpit. Then there's *khonsay*, which is to pick an object up with care, as it is rare or scarce. That's what that means. There's *onsay*, and that means to pretend to love. I don't know what a Boro accent is, and I shouldn't make one up. *Goblo* means when a child or an infant is fat; they have a word. Then *asusu* is to feel unknown and uneasy in a new place.

As a linguist, I have seen many words like this presented from far-away places. The idea is that if you speak that language, you are uniquely attuned to that particular thing. However, let's look at boring old English; let's look at some of our words. What are some words that we have? Imagine if some Boro people did not know English and they came and interviewed English speakers, and they just took down the first definitions of words that many people would give. We have a word *bonding*, and that's when people who are starting to get to know each other first establish a sense of connection. It's a very specific little moment; we've got a word for it. It's *bonding*. There is a word, *reconciliation*, and that's when a romantic pair has been estranged for a long time and they decide to be together again. That's a definition somebody might give. We have the word *hover*, and so if a male member of a couple stays always a vigilant foot away or so from the woman he's with at a party so that other men will not compete for her—actually, it goes both ways; I've known hovering women.

Those are things that you can say in this wonderful English language, and yet it would be hard to say that those things are evidence of something unique to being an English speaker. Yes, we've got all those meanings, but is that really exotic about us? Are we uniquely sensitive to being covetous of one's mate in a social gathering? Are we uniquely aware of what it's like to get that warm feeling of connecting with someone for the first time? Once again, it's very hard to support, and no experimentation has borne any such thing out. You have to note something else, which is that all of those things are specific meanings that actually are from words that have more general meanings. *Hover*, of course, has a core meaning that is to hang over in a hummingbird kind of way; that's what it means. Someone might give that kind of a party meaning because it came to their mind, especially if they didn't know that they were supposed to be giving the most generalized meanings, and who would unless they were told? Take, for example, the word *consummate*. If somebody asked you what *consummate* meant, I think 99 out of 100 of us would give a particular meaning as to what *consummate* means. Very few of us—I would say 1 out 100—would immediately say, "to bring something to its highest point," which is really what it means. That other meaning is a subset of that. *Bonding*, of course, is sticking something to something else. The issue of having the kind of like "Yay, bond!" that people have over a campfire or at some meeting or something like that is derived.

It seems that that would be highly likely to be the case with the Boro as well. It seems particularly likely, given that we actually have most of those meanings. For example, to kind of rub in the armpits, we have the word *chafe*; we have the word *cinch*. In terms of holding something in a delicate way, we have *wield*. We *wield* something when it's precious or it's rare or it's scarce. We do not have a verb that means to feel unknown and uneasy in a new place, but we express the concept: "I'm not feeling acclimated yet." "Finally, I started to feel acclimated." We have the same sensitivity; it just doesn't happen to be a single verb. To pretend to love, the *onsay*, that's something where I, for one, cannot think of a way of saying that with one word in English. That's pretty good, *feign*, but it's not specifically about love. But you know, things like that happen; there are just chance differences between languages where it's hard to say it's about culture.

So let's imagine that the Boro are just so romantically attuned to the notion of whether or not the lover is true, that sort of thing. OK, now ask a French speaker you know how to say this very simple thing: "Your car is sticking out of the row." Let's say that you have driven your car, and you—*screech*—go into the parking lot, and then you park in the space, but the car's backside is kind of sticking out. If it were a helicopter, you'd see this line and then it's going *weh-weh*, like that; so your car is sticking out. Ask a French person how to say that, and you'll notice that in that language—which is clearly a language just like ours—in that language spoken by people who you know can perceive a badly parked car just like we can, you have to talk around it. There are all sorts of ways that you can say it if you have to, but just to say, "It's sticking out"? No. They can say, "You parked your car wrong," but in terms of there being just a verb that applies to that the way we have it, you'll watch them kind of rolling their eyes and smiling. You can do things like that in a lot of languages with random little lexical gaps, but it doesn't mean that the French don't know how to park cars or that they are less acclimated to it than we English speakers. These things have to be viewed with caution.

It goes on and on. It seems that you could look at English and find English speakers extremely exotic and then come up with very culturally specific aspects of what we do and what we are based on this Whorfian perspective. That's when you suddenly realize that if these things don't feel right applied to us, then what does it mean to apply them to the Kawésqar and the Boro? In English we have ordinal numbers that we mark with *-th*. Four is *fourth*; five is *fifth*—and you can see there's a relationship, even though there's a sound change—or six is *sixth*; or seven is *seventh*. The only exceptions are the first three numbers, and so there's no *oneth*, *twoth*, or *threeth*; you have to say, "first," "second," and "third." That seems so normal to us; we would think, why would a language not have that same sort of thing? In fact, if you look at most languages in the world, the only ordinal number that's different is the one for number one. Looking around the world, you'll see that you'll have one, and then there's something like *first* that's completely different, and then with everything else it matches up nicely. For example, if you look at Hebrew, then you just look at these numbers. This is the numbers from one to seven, and whether you know them or not: *ekhad* is *one*, and then *rishon*, which is clearly just a completely different word, is *first*. But after that, then you've got *shney*, and then *shniya*, that's *second*; and *shalosh*— which always sounds like you're splashing through—which is *three*, and then *shlishit*. You can see there's a relationship. That's the way things are. In French: *un* and then *premier*; and after that *deux, deuxième*; *trois, troisième*. I'm sure you can think of lots of languages where it is that way; German is another one. That's normal.

English has this *first, second, third*; and so why would that be? It may be that English speakers have some kind of heightened awareness of firstness, secondness, and thirdness. If you wanted to take that where a lot of the Whorfian types have often gone—especially in the past—then it would mean that English speakers are obsessed with counting things, and that that's because we are obsessed with acquiring and stomping all over the world and building ships and things like that. But that doesn't really seem to make sense when you look at whole bunch of other languages. For example, the French were jumping all over the world too and, look at them: They just have a word for *first*. Estonian has a word for *first* and *second*, come to think of it: One is *üks*, and then the word for *first* is *esimene*; then two is *kaks*, and then the word for *second* is *teine*. Boy those Estonians sure have been a grabby little country, haven't they, stomping all over the world with their obsession with counting and acquiring things. Obviously, these sorts of things have to be looked at more carefully than they have.

What I've just tried to indicate is that there is a really heartwarming, brain-stimulating notion out there that I think probably hits most people in the same place as ginger snaps, Jell-O, muffins, and back rubs, which is that people speaking the 6,000 languages around the world are all channeled by their grammar into seeing the world in charmingly different ways. You want that to be true; that's the most wonderful idea. If you actually think about the languages of the world, not to mention if you actually look at a great deal of the experimentation on that topic, you see that it just doesn't hold up. That's not only in terms of looking at all these languages, but just in terms of basic intuition. A lot of things about how languages are different are a matter of chance. Chance isn't always fun, but chance has a lot to do with how things change.

This has been Whorfianism part one. In the next lecture, we're going to take this up again, and we're going to look at two things: One is the reason why the Whorfian hypothesis has been so influential and so widely discussed, or one of the reasons. Then we're going to look at the fact that there is research that has especially been done lately that shows that there is a seed of truth in Whorfianism—not the romantic kind of view that Whorf himself put forth upon a different kind of data set than we have. Nevertheless, psychologists are finding that there's something to be said about how grammar might shape thought; it's just that there's not as much to be said as we might hope when we're being fed those muffins.

Lecture Twenty-Nine
Does Language Channel Thought? New Findings

Scope: Continuing the previous lecture's exploration of the Sapir-Whorf hypothesis, this lecture demonstrates that sociological concerns as well as linguistic concerns have determined many of its adherents' approaches. Then we will examine interesting new studies suggesting a less stark version of the Whorfian idea.

Outline

I. The Sapir-Whorf hypothesis is driven by what linguists have rightly done for a long time—shown that there is no such thing as a primitive language—but also by politics. Many of the world's languages are in the process of disappearing, and in response to this crisis some people devoted themselves to showing that indigenous languages are better.

A. Whorf seemed to say that the way the Hopi conceive of time and cyclicity shows "a higher plane of thinking" compared to the conceptions of Westerners.

B. Clyde Kluckhohn and Dorothea Leighton argued that the Navaho had a more insightful view of the forces of nature.

II. Such an exotic view of other languages can distract us from more real issues in the relationship between language and thought.

A. In the Native American languages of the Algonquian family, such as Cree, Ojibwa, and the Powhatan that Pocahontas spoke, person marking is different from English.

1. In one of them, Montagnais, the way you say, "You see me" is:

   Tshi   *ua:pam*   *in*
   you   see   me

2. But the way to say, "I see you" is not to put *I* before the verb and *you* after:

   *In   *ua:pam*   *tshi*   [incorrect]
   I   see   you

3. Instead, you use the *you see me* sentence, but stick a little syllable into it to make it mean *I see you*:

Tshi	ua:pam	**it**	in
you	see		me

4. Journalist Mark Abley proposes that this means that Algonquian language speakers are less self-centered than Europeans and that "to speak properly, in an Algonquian language, is to be aware of the identities and interrelationships of all the people you address."

B. But if *I* is interacting with a *he*, *she*, *it*, or *they*, then *I* has to come first.

1. In Cree, *I frighten them* is:

Ni	se:kih	a	wak
I	frighten		them

2. For *they frighten me*, you can't put *they* first; you make *they* the subject by sticking in a special syllable, known as an *inverse marker*:

Ni	se:kih	**ik**	wak
I	frighten		them

3. Because the *I* has to come first, you might see these speakers as very self-centered. However, given what we see from Montagnais and Cree and this whole group of languages, these speakers are really no more or less attuned to others than the rest of us.

C. The reason that we might want to preserve Algonquian and other languages is because they're interesting—something wonderful and beautiful.

III. If we turn upon our own language the way many of these languages have been presented to us, then you start to realize that something is wrong.

A. The Mohawk word *ka'nikonriio* happens to mean *beautiful* and *good* and also something close to *law*.

B. According to one analysis, the Mohawk way of looking at things fuses legality, beauty, and goodness such that the language itself is a kind of philosophy lesson.

C. The word *stand* is used in many ways in English.

    1. You *stand* on a corner, *stand* rather than sit, and *stand* up for a thesis; something cannot *stand*, and when we are not inclined to let something *stand* we cannot *stand* it. One person *stands* in for another; something noticeable *stands* out; you watch a ball game in the *stands*; and so on.

    2. Yet few would say that these uses of *stand* signify something about the culture of English speakers.

D. There are homonymies like this in any language.

E. English uses *get* in a wide range of meanings that are not found in French *obtenir*, Spanish *conseguir*, German *bekommen*, or Russian *poluchat'*.

    1. To understand something is to *get* it. To overcome something by force is to *get* it—"I'm going to *get* you." To enter into some state is to *get* that way. You *get* someone to do something. You *get* to go to the ball. You even *get* fired and *get* hurt. One might suppose that usage signifies that there is something acquisitive about English speakers.

    2. Yet there are languages spoken by small groups in Southeast Asia that also use *get* in wide ranges of meaning. In Muong, Alak, Brao, and Zhuang, one not only *gets* a present from someone; when one must go home, one *gets* go home; if you can dance, you *get* dance; if you are a slow walker, then one would say that you are someone who *gets* walking slow; if you laugh so much your sides ache, then you laugh *get* your sides aching.

IV. Underlying motivations were revealed in the response to a study designed to show that English speakers are more insightful than Chinese speakers.

    A. Alfred Bloom noted that in Chinese, one must engage in a certain amount of circumlocution to be explicit that something is hypothetical rather than real.

    B. In English we can say, "If you saw my sister, you would know that she was pregnant." But in Chinese, the sentence is rendered as "If you see my sister, you know she is pregnant," and hypothetical readings are determined by context.

C. Bloom did an experiment that showed Chinese speakers less alert to hypotheticality when reading stories in Chinese than English speakers reading the stories in English.

D. However, scholars resisted the notion English speakers are the more insightful ones, arguing that Chinese speakers process hypotheticality via context even if their grammar does not mark it as explicitly as English's.

V. The neo-Whorfians have done work on whether grammar can channel thought in ways less dramatic than the earlier Whorfians were seeking.

    A. The Guugu Yimithirr of Australia do not have terms like *in front of*. Instead, they refer to everything according to points on the compass—*to the north of, to the south of*—regardless of where they are in relation to the object.

        1. If a tree is in front of them but in the global sense to the south of them, they refer to it as south of them.

        2. Some see this as showing that their language just happened not to have terms like *in front of* and *behind* and that their grammar forced them to think of things in terms of compass points.

        3. At least as plausible is that their culture happened to focus on compass points and that determined how their language described position—in short, that it is a cultural issue, not a linguistic issue.

    B. The Pirahã tribe of the Amazon have attracted media attention as a people whose language has no words for colors or numbers.

        1. They are incapable of performing even elementary mathematical tasks; the media has advertised this as evidence that the absence of numbers in the language prevents the speakers from doing math.

        2. However, their lives afford them no reason to manipulate precise numerical concepts.

    C. Research into gender of objects (e.g., by Stanford psychologist Lera Boroditzky) has been more promising.

        1. In German, the word for *key* is masculine (*der Schlüssel*). If you give the key a personal name, Germans tend to have an easier time recalling it if the name is masculine, more readily associate the key with a picture of a man than a woman, and describe it with words like *hard, heavy, jagged, metal, serrated,* and *useful*.

2. In Spanish, the word for *key* is feminine (*la llave*), and Spanish speakers are more comfortable with keys having female names and associating them with pictures of women, and they tend to describe them as *golden, intricate, little, lovely, shiny,* and *tiny.*

D. Research into time as length or volume has also been promising.

1. Stanford psychologist Daniel Casasanto has noted that whereas in English we say, "a long time," in Spanish *tiempo largo* is unusual, and the conventional expression is *mucho tiempo.* In English time is processed as having length, whereas in Spanish it is processed as filling space.

2. Casasanto showed that when shown a gradually lengthening line on a screen, English speakers are better at estimating for how long the line was shown lengthening than how long a jar is shown gradually filling up, whereas Spanish speakers do better when shown the jar.

3. Moreover, speakers of Greek, where time is indicated as length as in English, perform like English speakers, while Indonesian speakers, to whom time is volume, perform like Spanish speakers. This shows that language can color how one views the world.

E. Neo-Whorfian scholarship is indicating interesting phenomena.

1. The findings are not precisely cultural but instead concern subtle thought-pattern differences and rather finely abstract psychological ways in which speakers view the world.

2. The neo-Whorfian work gives a very different picture of how language channels thought than the idea that each language gives speakers a starkly different set of "glasses" through which the world is viewed.

3. The Sapir-Whorf hypothesis as presented by Whorf remains a tantalizing notion, but that does not necessarily mean that it is true.

Essential Reading:

Lucy, *Language Diversity and Thought.*

Supplemental Reading:

Levinson and Gumperz, eds., *Rethinking Linguistic Relativity.*

Questions to Consider:

1. We have seen that, contrary to the claims of earlier Whorfianism, the Hopi language does mark linear time. However, we have now seen that while English speakers think of time as a line, Spanish speakers think of it as a substance. Does this suggest to you that Spanish speakers are, in a general sense, of different mind than English speakers?

2. If you are a native English speaker, do objects have "gender" in your mind? To me, for instance, keys have always struck me as rather feminine objects, while a table is distinctly male. How about you? Can you think of reasons for your assignment of objects to gender classes?

Lecture Twenty-Nine—Transcript
Does Language Channel Thought? New Findings

In the last lecture, we were looking at the Sapir-Whorf hypothesis—the hypothesis that the grammar of your native language channels your thought. We were seeing how that basic idea—although it's been charismatically argued and was especially so by Benjamin Lee Whorf—is difficult to maintain when we apply a wider perspective on the variety among the world's languages and even the arbitrariness that creates that variety. In this lecture I want to continue and look at the argument some more; look at some of the rationale for the popularity of the argument; and see how there's an extent to which it does follow through, but through different kinds of experimentation than have usually been done until relatively recently.

I want to start with the fact that just as in any kind of science, you have to start with some kind of hunch. Rarely do we have some idea just completely out of the blue with no desire to see things happen in one way as opposed to another. When it comes to the language-is-thought hypothesis, a lot of what drives it is a quest to do something that linguists have been doing—and with good reason—for a very long time, and that is showing that there is no such thing as a primitive language. The reason, often, nowadays, that that's seen as something so important to do is because so many of the world's languages are in the process of disappearing. For example, it's been said that of the 6,000 languages that exist now, only one-tenth of them will exist in 100 years, so there really is a crisis along those lines. But as part of the argument that languages are equal, the people who have worked on the language-is-thought hypothesis or who have evaluated it are often devoted to showing that indigenous languages are better—that indigenous languages make their speakers more insightful than we are. The rationale for that is to encourage them to be preserved. However, there are problems with this.

For example, take Benjamin Lee Whorf's work on Hopi. Not only was he showing that the Hopi are different from Westerners in terms of how they conceive of time and the cyclicity, but the idea was also that the Hopi are, we might say, closer to God than we ignorant Westerners. A typical quote would be something like:

> Does the Hopi language show here a higher plane of thinking, a more rational analysis of situations, than our vaunted English? Of

course it does. In this field and in various others, English compared to Hopi is like a bludgeon compared to a rapier.

The intent is laudable in itself, especially in a time when it was much easier, even among some educated people, to dismiss indigenous people as primitive. Nevertheless, what's going on here is that English is being dissed in a way, and I think that at this vantage point in time, we can see that might not be fair. Another quote is:

> Our objectified view of time is, however, favorable to historicity and to everything connected with the keeping of records, while the Hopi view is unfavorable thereto. The latter is too subtle, complex, and ever-developing, supplying no ready-made answer to the question of when "one" event ends and "another" begins.

Once again, we're seeing that the Hopi are being explained as more insightful than we are. This is something that was picked up from Whorf by other researchers. Here are Clyde Kluckhohn and Dorothea Leighton in 1946, and they said (about the Navaho this time):

> We feel that the forces of nature, rather than anything that man does, determine success or failure. ... Many white people have the opposite view; namely, that nature is a malignant force with useful aspects that must be harnessed, and useless, harmful ones that must be shorn of their power. ... Their premise is that nature will destroy them unless they prevent it; the Navahos' is that nature will take care of them if they behave as they should and do as she directs.

That's the frame of reference that a lot of this work has been put forth in. These are galvanizing ideas, and of course we always have to check ourselves for ethnocentrism. However, the result often is in our public discourse a kind of exoticization that I think borders on the condescending. I think it distracts us from real sorts of issues of the relationship between language and thought.

For example, there is a language family called Algonquian, and that is spoken in Canada and in these here United States. It includes various Native American languages such as Cree, Ojibwa, and Powhatan (which Pocahontas spoke; it was an Algonquian language). This is a big family just like Indo-European—actually not as big as that family, but it's another language family. In one of the Algonquian languages, which is called Montagnais, here on the screen you see the way to say, "You see me." It's one word, but I've got the elements separated with dashes here; and so you see that *you see me* is *tshi-ua:pam-in*. While we've got this up on the screen, here's a quick little linguistics lesson: You see those two dots in there? The reason those are there is to indicate that the vowel is long, so that's not punctuation or something like that. Just if you ever see anything like that, now you can have that little linguistics nugget; that means it's long. So *tshi-ua:pam-in*; that's *you see me*. In itself, fine, there you go: *You see me*. That is the way that they say it.

But there's something that's interesting in Algonquian languages and really weird in comparison to ours—I mean, these are languages where I've often wondered, do human beings really use these languages? They actually do; I've watched people speak them. This is something weird coming, so stay with me. The way that you say, "I see you," is not what you'd think. *You see me* is *tshi-ua:pam-in*, but the way to say, "I see you" is not what's on the screen now. It's not **in-ua:pam-tshi*; that is absolutely ridiculous Montagnais. You cannot do that. Here's another little sidebar: You see that asterisk that I put before that sentence? That means that it's wrong. The asterisk doesn't mean that it's at the bottom of the page, nor is it something that I stuck in by accident. That is linguist jargon. That means that you can't say that, so that's why there is that asterisk. Instead the way that you would say "I see you" is very peculiar. Look on the screen: You stick in this little bit of stuff—in this case a little *it*—in between the *see* and the *me*. The sentence stays *you see me*. But if you're going to say, "I see you," the way you do it is to say, "*Tshi-ua:pam-it-in*." The *it* doesn't mean *I*; it just means that you're saying "I see you" rather than "You see me." You put that little marker in. That's just the way that it goes in Montagnais; that's the way that it goes in a good Algonquian language. You can't say, "I see you." You say, "You see *it* I," and then there it is.

Mark Abley is a journalist who has written about language preservation, and his idea is that the presence of this in an Algonquian language means that Algonquian speakers are less self-centered than Europeans because they always put the *you* first. As he puts it, "To speak properly, in an Algonquian language, is to be aware of the identities and interrelationships of all the people who you address." But for one thing, that would seem to describe human beings in general. Who is not aware of those things? In what culture would you notice that they don't seem to quite be able to distinguish between *you* and *I*, or that some people are actually not them, or that there are people who are not the people they are talking to. That would be rather peculiar; even infants do that. There are no people who are that incurious, I would suppose. But more to the point, you've got that same problem that Benjamin Lee Whorf had with Hopi. You have to look at the whole grammar.

For example, in another Algonquian language—Cree—if you say, "I frighten them," then here's the sentence, and it's *Ni-se:kih-a-wak*: *I frighten them*. The *I* comes first, and then there's the *them*. Now if you want to say, "They frighten me," you can't put the *they* first. It's the same thing: The pronouns have to come in a certain order. If you want to say, "They frighten me," you have to stick in one of these markers. "*Ni-se:kih-ik-wak*" is the only way to say "I frighten them"; you can't say, "*Wak-se:kih-ni*." That little marker is called something: It's called an *inverse marker*, and it's something that Algonquian languages have and some other ones have.

It's one thing to say that we want to preserve an Algonquian language because its speakers are more privileged than we are in terms of social sensitivity. But when you look at what happens in Cree, you see that the *I* has to come first. Here's a case where you could see somebody as very self-centered. I think that the answer, given the first data that we see from Montagnais—and then you see how it goes in Cree, and this is the way it is in all of them—is that really they are no more or less attuned to whether someone is you or he or themselves than the rest of us. The reason that we might want to preserve Algonquian languages is because they're interesting. It seems to me that very often the preservation people seem to think that we need to show that the other people are better than us. But to me, the fact that any language has to have its pronouns in a certain order and that if you're trying to say something else you stick in affix, that's pretty neat. I'm all in favor of preserving that just because it's something wonderful and beautiful.

You can see these things going through a lot of analyses of these languages. If we turn it upon on ourselves, and we look at our own languages the way many of these languages have been presented to us—and you see this sort of thing in the press all the time—then you start to realize that something is wrong. For example, let's take another Native American language. One of them is called Mohawk; it has nothing to do with the haircut. These are actual people, and their hair is not like that. The Mohawk speak a language again so complex I can't believe people speak it. I admire any Mohawk person who says, "Good morning." Everything about it is marvelously different and very complex. They have some words, actually quite a few, and one of them is the one that you see on the screen: *ka'nikonriio*. That word happens to mean *beautiful*; it means *good*; and it also means something close to *law*. It has that range of meanings. There has been an analysis of that word that proposes that that word's coverage of those three meanings means that there's something about the Mohawk way of looking at things that fuses legality, beauty, and goodness and that therefore the language in itself is a kind of philosophy lesson.

I can understand how that might move somebody to want to preserve Mohawk, but the problem with this is, think about our own language. Let's take a mundane word like *stand*. You *stand* in a corner; you *stand* up for a thesis; you say that something cannot *stand*. When we're not inclined to let something *stand*, we can't *stand* it. One person *stands* in for another; something noticeable *stands* out; you watch a ball game in the *stands*. You *understand*; you *withstand*; and you have a bodily *stance*. You have a *stance* upon an issue; you can go into a *stand* of trees. You can do the last *stand* of a play in Toledo, Ohio (the tour stopped in Toledo, Ohio; that was its last *stand*). We use *stand* a lot. Imagine if a Mohawk linguist were learning English and English were in danger of dying (which clearly it is not). The idea was to look at the word *stand* and decide that there's some unified conception that we English speakers have that unites bodily position, conviction, toleration, nutrition, theatrical performance, and trees, just because of the way that we use *stand*. Obviously, we don't; it's just that there are these homonymies in any language. I think we would feel somewhat condescended to, or certainly we would feel misanalyzed; I think that that is the case with the Mohawk.

English has a *get* fetish too. We use *get* in all sorts of ways: If you understand something, you *get* it; if you overcome something by force, then you *get* it (you say, "I'm going to *get* you"); to enter into a state is *get* that way (the old expression, "How do you *get* that way"; that's another use of *get*). You *get* someone to do something for you; you *get* to go to the ball; you *get* fired; you *get* hurt. All sorts of *get*; it's interesting how wide the semantic scope of *get* is in English. If you go into a dictionary, look under *get* and it just goes on and on, if it's a large dictionary. It would be almost hard for us to say what *get* meant. If you learn another language, you might want to know how to say *get*. If you're trying to translate your thoughts, which I used to do when I was trying to teach myself languages, you keep running up against *get*. In other languages, it's never really what you need, because in the languages that we learn most often, the word for *get* does not cover that range. If you find out in French that it's *obtenir*, that's really not going to help you when you talk about getting hurt. Or in Spanish *conseguir*, German *bekommen*, and Russian *poluchat'*; none of those are like our *get*.

It would be very easy for a journalist to decide that this means that there is something about our society that's highly acquisitive. Then you go to Southeast Asia, and Southeast Asia has many, many languages in it: Vietnamese, Laotian, Cambodian, and Burmese are only the very, very tip of the iceberg—or I guess I should say tip of the big mountain of soil, because there are no icebergs down there, but tip of something. There are languages spoken in the hills that are known to very few people, and they have names like Muong, Alak, Brao, and Zhuang, and they have a *get* fetish too. They use it kind of differently than us, but you *get* all sorts of things. You don't only *get* a present from someone, but if you go home, you *get* go home. If you can dance, you *get* dance. If you're a slow walker, then you're somebody who *gets* walking slow. If you laugh so much until your sides hurt, then you laugh *get* your sides aching, and so on. Obviously these small hill cultures cannot be considered to have any grand fetish for grabbing things or imperialism or getting or anything like that, so then you're left to explain how come we characterize our language and our souls based on this semantic scope when we would do no such thing for the Zhuang or any of the other people. That kind of inconsistency leads one to think that we are being given a rather arbitrary way of looking at things in favor of something which is important, which is language preservation. But maybe we can preserve the languages just because they're interesting for reasons of the sort that we're seeing in this course.

Where this underlying aspect—this underlying motivation—of the language-is-thought paradigm reveals itself is in what happened when one study was designed to show that it's the English speakers who are more insightful. Alfred Bloom noted that in Chinese—he was working with Mandarin Chinese—you have to kind of talk around things somewhat; you have to engage in a certain amount of circumlocution to get the hypothetical across. For example, in English we can say, "If you saw my sister, you would know that she is pregnant." Now in Chinese, as you're going to see on the screen, the way you render it is something that would translate as *if you see my sister, you know she is pregnant*; that's just there. For us, it's *if you saw my sister, you would know that she is pregnant*. We've got the *would*, and we've got the use of *saw* in the first part; so the idea is that it's hypothetical, and that's something that you have to express. In Chinese, you just have *if you see my sister, you know she is pregnant*. The hypothetically has to be inferred from context. Their sentence for this, it can mean either *if you see my sister, you know she is pregnant*; *if you saw my sister, you would know she was pregnant*; or *if you had seen my sister, you'd have known she was pregnant*. In many ways, Chinese is a very telegraphic language compared to English; more context is needed in many cases compared to the way we use English.

Bloom looked at this as kind of a cold-eyed scientist, and he did an experiment. He claimed that his results showed that Mandarin Chinese speakers were slightly less alert to hypotheticality than English speakers. He was looking at people reading stories. The fact of the matter is that whether or not his data was correct is beside the point in terms of the main lesson that we learn from this, which is that other scholars shot at Alfred Bloom's work like a varmint. There was just no such thing as allowing that this study could possibly be valid. Of course some points were made about his experimentation; there's always room for scholarly debate. But I imagine— I really don't have to imagine—that if he had done a study that showed that Chinese speakers were more alert to something than English speakers, then everybody would have let his work stand, so to speak. It seems that there is an agenda, and I think there are new ways of looking at these things.

Let's look at those. Nowadays there are people who are being called the neo-Whorfians so much that I guess that's an official term—so the neo-Whorfians. There is other work that is being done where people are aware that there have been some distortions in earlier addresses of Whorf's work. Some interesting things are coming up. Some of it is less interesting than others, however; there is one study, for example, that is often brought up that once again shows that there's a really neat language, but it doesn't show that grammar channels thought, in my humble opinion and the less humble opinion of some other people.

For example, in Australia the first Aboriginal language there that was written down—somewhat—when the white man went to Australia was one called Guugu Yimithirr. *Guugu* has nothing to do with babies; that's actually the word for *language*. *Yimi* means *this*; and what it means is "the language with *this*—the word *yimi* for *this*—in it." That's what they call their language, as opposed to other related languages where the word for *this* is something else; so Guugu Yimithirr. It was the first one transcribed. One of the words transcribed in it was a word [gaŋurru], which is *kangaroo*; that came from Guugu Yimithirr. It's interesting not only because it has the word *kangaroo* in it but because of the way direction works. In Guugu Yimithirr, there is no word for *in front of* or *behind*; that doesn't happen. They see everything in terms of the points on the compass, so whether things are north, south, west, or east. If a tree is in front of you, but in the global sense it's to the south of you, you say that the tree is to the south: "The tree is to the south of me." There's no such thing as *in front of me*, even if it is. They see the world in direction, and they feel the direction everywhere they go. They can go for miles and miles and miles; they always know what the direction is, and that's how they relate themselves positionally to everything.

It's been said that their language not having a word for *in front of* or *behind* or *to the side of* is why they do this. Their grammar is channeling the way that they think. Just as plausible is that they culturally have this value of direction and that they see things in that way, and that therefore—big surprise—their language doesn't have *in front of* or *behind*, at least as a dynamic relationship between the two. But the idea that the language just mysteriously got rid of its directional concepts and its spatial-positioning concepts and therefore forced people to think, "Well, then we're just going to have to look to the west and east" is not really a very plausible account. We should preserve Guugu Yimithirr because it's so wonderful that a language is like that—there are many other wonderful things about that language—but not that the language has this bizarre trait that makes its speakers think in a certain way. That's a cultural issue, not a linguistic issue.

Or there are the famous—now famous—Pirahã. These are an Amazonian group who live in the Amazon. The Pirahã have gotten a lot of media attention because they're being studied rather intensely right now. I talked about how there are no people who aren't curious. If there are any people who in a way aren't, it is the Pirahã, according to very extensive study. Nobody knows about any of their ancestors further back than, say, grandparents. If people are dead, they're just dead. There is no foundation myth. They don't have any story about how the Great God Something … for them, that's irrelevant. Missionaries have tried to Christianize them, and when you tell them about the things that Jesus did, they ask—very simply— "So have you ever met this Jesus?" Then, when the missionaries say, "Oh, no. No," then they say, "How do you know what he said?" That's just as far as you can get. For them, it has to be in the present tense. They are not bilingual, for the most part. They speak their language, Pirahã, and speak it well. Most Native Americans in their position also speak—for example, if you're in the Amazon—Portuguese, the national language of Brazil. They don't. There are some of them who speak enough Portuguese to do some bartering and things like that. They are not interested in learning another language; they like their own. Very unusual people.

Their language also has some aspects that are strange from the European point of view. For example, no terms for colors, apparently; something's either dark or it's light. Other than that, you just don't describe it. You might want to say, "It's the color of that bird" if you have to. But for them, the idea of talking about cerise, aquamarine, and cadet blue ... remember the Crayola box? It's a wonderful memory for me, partly because you learned all those colors—I wouldn't know what burnt sienna and raw umber were if it weren't for them—and also because the crayons smelled good. After you watch this, go smell one of your kid's crayons. It's a wonderful smell. Don't bite it, because they do not taste the way they smell, which was always a problem for me. But in any case, they don't have colors; that's just not of interest.

Numbers: They've got *one*; then they've got something that kind of means *two*, although it sort of means *not one*; then they've got *lots*. That's it; they don't have any numbers other than that, and there's one researcher who doesn't think they even have that many numbers. This is a very different place, and what we hear in the media about the Pirahã is that they cannot do math because their language provides them with no numbers. The fact is that if you take these people and try to make them do math, they've never done it before; they show no interest, and they're not very good at it. That's true. But the idea that their language having no numbers is something that caused their lack of ability in math is rather absurd, especially if they've never done it. Rather they do not do math because their lives do not require you to do math. If you're a hunter-gatherer, you might not want to do long division. It might not serve your purposes, and therefore no numbers have arisen in the language as a result of that.

One thing that is interesting about the Pirahã—and this gets back again into what the link between grammar and thought is—is that these people who really are rather unusually incurious as *Homo sapiens* go have the same sorts of evidential markers like we saw in Turkish in the last lecture where people have to specify whether they heard something or whether they actually saw it. Pirahã has evidential markers like that. You have to specify when you speak it where you got the information, despite the fact that they are a rather incurious people. Another fun thing about Pirahã is that they have a pronoun *it*, and they have three pronouns *it*. One *it* means that something is inanimate. Then there are two other *it*'s: One of them refers to things that are aquatic, and then another one refers to things that aren't. That's distinguished in their language. But, anyway, that's the Pirahã.

Here is some neo-Whorfian work that actually is promising. For example, in German the word for *key* is *der Schlüssel*; here it is up on the screen. It's masculine. If you give a key a personal name, Germans have an easier time recalling it if the name is masculine. They more readily associate the key with a picture of a man than a woman. They describe it with words like *hard, heavy, jagged, metal, serrated,* and *useful.* In Spanish, the word for *key—la llave—*is feminine. It's been shown that Spanish speakers are more comfortable with a key wearing a dress, having a female name. They associate a key more readily with pictures of women, and they describe a key as *golden, intricate, little, lovely, shiny,* and so on.

Talk about gaps in conversation: About a year ago, I was sitting with a Dutch woman. We really didn't have anything to talk about, and that made me nervous, and so I said, "Well, you're all Dutch and everything. So how do you feel about a key?" The word for *key* in her language is *der sleutel,* and it's masculine. I wanted to ask her, "Well, what is a key to you?" I remember she had a very cute—I shouldn't say cute, but it was cute—perfect English accent out of an old movie, and she said, "Oh, I think it would be a long, hard key, decorated such as the kind that you would use to open a castle." For her, it's this masculine thing (I assume, the way she described it, that it was a masculine thing). That sort of thing shows that the grammatical gender of objects does seem to have something to do with the way people perceive those objects, that a key's wearing a dress; Germans are much less likely to imagine a key putting on perfume.

Or a new experiment is by the Stanford psychologist Daniel Casasanto, whose food I have eaten: He has done work where he's shown that in English we say, "a long time." In Spanish, you would not say, "*tiempo largo*" usually; usually, you would say, "*mucho tiempo.*" In other words, they say, "a lot of time." For us, it's "a long time"; in Spanish, it's "a lot of time," as if it were piling up in a jar. We think of time as having length, whereas in Spanish time fills space. Casasanto—Daniel—showed that if you show on a screen a line getting longer—if it's kind of *wooo,* like that— if you show it gradually lengthening and you start at a certain place, English speakers are better at estimating how long the line was shown lengthening than how long a jar is shown gradually filling up. In terms of estimating how long this took, an English speaker is better at this than estimating a line rising in a drawn jar like this. Whereas with Spanish speakers, if they are shown this line going like this, they're not as good at estimating the time involved in that happening as they are in being shown something like a jar being gradually filled up. It would seem that that correlates with the fact that we see time as length and they see time as a quantity.

What's interesting is that Greek is like English in terms of saying, "long time," rather than, "a lot of time"; they are better estimating the timing of the line lengthening than the jar filling up. Indonesian has "a lot of time"—for them, time is like water or corn; it's a quantity—and for them, they have an easier time with the jar level rising like that than the long line. This shows—as far as I'm concerned, that convincingly shows—that there's an extent to which the nature of one's vocabulary, or the nature of one's grammar, can condition the way that you think.

But what's important is that that the sorts of things that have been shown—such as imagining a key speaking with a high voice or something like that, or how good you are at timing a line shown lengthening on a computer screen versus water going up in a jar—those things are not precisely cultural. Psychologists will surely have all sorts of interesting things to show about the effects that have been shown in the new neo-Whorfian work. But it would be hard to say that any of those things render the people who have these subtle thought pattern differences from us more anything than us, in terms of anything that would interest us in terms of the diversity of how human beings see the world, in anything but rather finely abstract psychological ways.

I myself am very interested in the neo-Whorfian work, and I think a lot of people will be, but I think it's giving us a very different picture of how language channels thought than the classic version that Benjamin Lee Whorf taught us. Nevertheless, today, if you open up a textbook in anthropology or if you open up a textbook in linguistics, you are almost sure to find the Sapir-Whorf hypothesis as presented by Whorf as a living idea, as something that still has not been disproven. I think that's because it's a very tantalizing notion, but that does not necessarily mean that it's true.

Lecture Thirty
Is Language Going to the Dogs?

Scope: Linguists have had little success in convincing the public that there is no such thing as "bad grammar." This lecture attempts a case for descriptivism over prescriptivism by covering arguments that have not succeeded with the public in the past, questioning why change in English is accepted for the past but not for the present, and revealing some things once thought of as "bad grammar" that now go unnoticed.

Outline

I. Another controversy in the philosophy of language—one that extends to general society, beyond the confines of academia or even journalism—is the issue of *prescriptive* as opposed to *descriptive* approaches to language.

   A. Linguists study language as it is actually spoken. We find that spoken language is thoroughly complex, challenging, and interesting.

   B. This has been the goal of linguistics since its foundation. De Saussure stressed that the study of language should apply to actual spoken language and that writing was a mere approximate reflection of speech.

   C. Yet the general public tends to view casual speech as an imperfect version of written "real" language, riddled with "errors." Linguists' approach to language is descriptive, while laymen's approach tends to be prescriptive.

   D. Linguists present various arguments against prescriptivism, which seem to have limited effectiveness. In this course, I am venturing that we may now be in a position to see the unwitting logical errors in prescriptivism.

   E. Linguists value articulateness and graceful writing composition just as others do. We also espouse that people be taught how to wield language artfully.

F. The question is how we view ordinary language and whether or not it truly makes sense to treat people as making "mistakes." It may be that the descriptive philosophy of language has strengths that are not readily perceivable.

II. Some prescriptive rules are on the ropes and perhaps nearly defunct.

    A. No one taken seriously thinks it's wrong to end a sentence with a preposition anymore, in a case like *That's a store I wouldn't go to.*

    B. Similarly, the grand old rule that one does not split infinitives is on the ropes. In our guts, few of us truly feel that there is anything wrong with where *slowly* is placed in *to slowly realize that my carpets were soaked.* (This is partly because English is a language with the Verb Attraction Parameter set "off," recall, which means that we don't like it when the verb is up before the adverb.)

III. Other prescriptive rules are more tenacious.

    A. Singular *they* is a more serious battle between prescriptivists and descriptivists.

        1. Many insist that it is wrong to say, "If a student comes before I get there, they can slip their test under my office door," because *student* is singular and *they* is "plural."

        2. Linguists traditionally observe that esteemed writers have been using *they* as a gender-neutral singular pronoun for almost a thousand years. For example, the *Sir Amadace* tale from the 1400s had "*Iche mon in thayre degree*" ("Each man in their degree").

        3. If Middle English seems different enough from modern English to be a "different language," we also find the usage in later writers, such as Shakespeare: "There's not a man I meet but doth salute me / As if I were their well-acquainted friend. (*The Comedy of Errors*, 4.3.1–2)

        4. In Thackeray's *Vanity Fair* we find "A person can't help their birth."

5. We can see that this use of *they* is simply a matter of the fact that languages are always in a state of flux. For example, in earlier English second-person pronouns differed according to number and case:

	singular	plural
subject	thou	ye
genitive	thy	your
object	thee	you

6. To a Middle English speaker, our use of *you* forms in the singular would sound barbaric. In fact, here is an English speaker from even later on the issue:

> Is he not a Novice and unmannerly, and an Ideot and a Fool, that speaks *You* to *one*, which is not to be spoken to a *Singular*, but to *many*? O Vulgar Professors and Teachers, that speak Plural, when they should Singular.

> —George Fox, *A Battle-door for Teachers & Professors to Learn Singular and Plural* (1660)

7. Yet it would seem that linguists' arguments have not penetrated on this point.

B. Another argument takes place over using nouns as verbs.
   1. *Impact* comes in for especial condemnation, as in *the new rules are impacting the efficiency of the procedure*.
   2. However, the verbs *view*, *silence*, *worship*, *copy*, *outlaw*, and countless others started as nouns and are now also verbs.
   3. This is because affixes typically differentiate parts of speech, and English has fewer of them than it used to and fewer than its relatives have. In German, *telephone* is *Telefon*, but *to telephone* is *telefonieren*.
   4. In Cantonese Chinese, *lengjái* can mean *good-looking* (adjective), *a good looking person* (noun), or *to become good-looking* (verb).

C. It would appear that people associate these "rules" with propriety and intelligence, with making an effort, and as kind of a privilege.

IV. However, if you went to the trouble to master all those rules, then you also know—especially from this course—that there is history in a language.

    A. The procession from Old, through Middle, to modern English is considered interesting and positive. However, there is a sense that, apparently, about 175 years ago, change was no longer appropriate.

    B. The development of Old into Middle English included the development of auxiliary *do* (*Do we eat apples?*) and the use of -*ing* to mark the present tense, rather than just the explicit progressive.

    C. If these things had not happened, English would be like its relative Frisian, where *Do we eat apples?* is *Ite wy appels?* and *We're eating apples* is *Wy ite appels*.

    D. Yet there was a time when these developments in English were "wrong," dialectal "errors." The question is where we draw the line on when changes like this became "wrong."

V. Words and constructions considered "wrong" as recently as the later 19th century shed light on the arbitrariness of our conception of correctness in language.

    A. Many grammarians considered the following extremely déclassé: *all the time*, *lit*, *washtub*, *standpoint*, *the first two*, *there's a house being built across the street* (instead of *there's a house building across the street*), and *stacked* (instead of *stackèd*).

    B. This meant that this passage would have been considered sloppy and vulgar:

> Let's have a look at the first two chapters I have excerpted, where we learn about the period when the Cross-Bronx Expressway was being built from the standpoint of people who were born in East Tremont and lived there all of their lives.

    C. That sense of vulgarity is a matter of fashion. Trying to stop language from changing is like tilting at windmills or standing in front of a steamroller.

Essential Reading:

Crystal, *The Fight for English*.

Supplemental Reading:

Pinker, "The Language Mavens," in *The Language Instinct.*

Questions to Consider:

1. Dr. Samuel Johnson, esteemed pioneering lexicographer of the English language, used *heerd* as the past tense of *hear* and thought of this as perfectly proper usage. Today, we do not. Johnson would have been shocked to be treated as vulgar for saying, "heerd." Was he?

2. Here are five sentences:

   > You can't simply walk out without paying.

   > You can't up and walk out without paying.

   > You can't merely walk out without paying.

   > You can't always walk out without paying.

   > You just can't walk out without paying.

   Based on the first four sentences, the fifth should be "You can't just walk out without paying," which, for example, is of the same meaning as "You can't simply walk out without paying." Yet people utter the fifth sentence constantly. To my ear, it has always been irritating, although for the reasons elucidated in this and the subsequent lecture I cannot reject it as "wrong." Or is it "wrong"? If so, why, and what about the fact that so many people use it daily who consider themselves to be using "proper English"?

Lecture Thirty—Transcript
Is Language Going to the Dogs?

Another controversy in the philosophy of language—and this is one that extends to general society, beyond the confines of academia or even journalism—is the issue of *prescriptive* as opposed to *descriptive* approaches to language. What I mean by that is that there are those who describe language as it is spoken—casually and in an unmonitored fashion—and those are the descriptivists. That tends to be … as a matter of fact, in terms of what any linguist is trained in, that is a linguist. Then there's the idea that the way people speak is something to be improved; that the way people generally speak is insufficient in some way; and that there is hand-wringing to be done about this. That is the prescriptive tradition. Of course the prescriptive tradition certainly has a major foothold in the way people conceive of how other people speak, and often even how they themselves speak. As we've seen, Ferdinand de Saussure stressed that the study of language be the study of language as it's actually spoken, and that writing was just an approximate reflection of what speech is. But the general public tends to suppose that casual speech is an imperfect version of real language—i.e., the kind of language that we like to see in writing—and that the way that people often speak is full of mistakes—errors.

Linguists have been presenting arguments against prescriptivism for a very long time. Way back in 1950, there was a book called *Leave Your Language Alone*, which was on any well-informed person's coffee table. There was an era when you had Van Cliburn playing the Rachmaninoff piano concerto, and you had *Leave Your Language Alone*, and you smoked; there was a time like that. Everybody read the book, but everybody still came away thinking that they're surrounded by people making errors when they talk. Steven Pinker's book *The Language Instinct* has sold God-knows-how-many copies; everybody says it's so wonderful. He's got one of the most blazingly convincing antiprescriptivist chapters ever written in it. I don't know whether people don't get to it, but that book has not made a dent in people's conception of how these things work. I am venturing that, because of your acquaintance in these lectures with various ideas that are usually only tossed around among linguists, that you might be in a position to see the debate between descriptivist and prescriptivist differently than you may have been before.

Of course linguists value articulateness and graceful writing composition as much as anyone does. We also espouse that people learn how to use language artfully; there's no question there. It's not that there's no room for people being taught how to wield the language in a particular way when they're thinking about it, especially when writing, and even when speaking if one is going to be taught how to do public speaking for example; nothing wrong with that. But the general idea that people in their casual speech are doing something "wrong" is one that is less easy to support when you look at it from, once again—just like the language-is-thought hypothesis—a wider-lens perspective than we are often taught. It may be that the descriptive philosophy of language has strengths that are not readily perceivable to those people who didn't happen to buy this set but maybe will be more so to you all.

There are some rules of this kind that I think we can think of as on the ropes at this point. For example, I'm not sure how many people these days really think that it's wrong to end your sentences in a preposition, because that would mean that it's wrong to say "That's a store I would not go to." Obviously that is a perfectly clean, logical sentence of English. Anybody who really thinks that you're supposed to say "That's a store to which I wouldn't go" is someone who doesn't want friends, and that is not most of us. Therefore I think we can let that one go. Then there is the split-infinitive thing. I think that brings a smile to most of our faces. It's not wrong to say something like, "to slowly realize that your carpets are getting soaked," as happened to me not long ago. It's just the way English is spoken, and some people still have an idea that it's something to be avoided, but very rarely can they tell you why.

It's not necessarily those things that I think are the occasion of serious battles these days between the prescriptivists and the descriptivists; it's other things where it seems that no matter how carefully descriptivists—i.e., linguists—make their argument, the notions just hang on that there's something that linguists aren't knowing, or that linguists are somehow inattendent, or some people even read politics into it when, really, we over here in the linguist world think that we're just arguing from the point view of logic.

Let's take singular *they*: Many insist—my editors, when I'm writing things, insist—that it's wrong to say "If a student comes before I get there, they can slip their test under my office door." I always thought of that as handily gender neutral. If you say, "If a student comes before I get there, *he* can slip their test," that makes it seem like they're all boys, and let's face it, it does not imply both men and women to say, "he"; the first thing you think of is a boy. If you say, "she," then you start wondering about the boys, and frankly it sounds pretentious; "he and she" is clumsy; etc., etc. *They* seems to be rather convenient, but that's supposed to be wrong, and the reason it's supposed to be wrong is that *they* is plural. The reason that you can't say "If a student comes before I get there, they can slip their test under my office door" is because *they* is plural. *They* is plural. Is it?

What a linguist usually does is to show that this usage of *they* in this singular gender-neutral way goes back to Middle English. The thing to do is to put something like this up on the screen. This is the *Sir Amadace* tale, and it's from the 1400s. The kind of thing you can find in *Sir Amadace* is things like this: "Each man in their degree," and the way it came out then was "*Iche mon in thayre degree*." That's what it was. That's *each man in their degree*; they were doing it then. We put that up on the screen; and now I'm saying "Is it wrong to say 'If a student comes before I get there, they can slip their test under my office door'?" My sense is that people still think "Yes, you can't say that because *they* is plural." That's the fact; but it wasn't back in the 1400s.

My sense of these things—I'm trying to put myself into other people's heads; that's what one should do; you have to try to imagine yourself as someone else—I think that people are thinking Middle English was so far away that it was just a different language. I openly admit—maybe this is just me—but because of the spelling differences and things, Middle English always looks drunk to me. It looks like whoever was writing it had had too much to drink or had a stroke or something. The person who said, "*Iche mon in thayre degree*," that's somebody who might as well be speaking Icelandic maybe. It doesn't matter whether *they* was used in that way then.

What about if we take it further? For example, it wasn't only in the 1400s; it was much later. For example, Shakespeare and Thackeray—and these people wrote pretty well; I mean, these are some pretty high writers. In *The Comedy of Errors*, there's "There's not a man I meet but doth salute me / As if I were their well-acquainted friend." That's referring to one person. "There's not a man I meet but doth salute me / As if I were their well-acquainted friend." It's right there; it's not supposed to be vulgar. So Shakespeare does it. Or Thackeray does it in *Vanity Fair*. Don't watch the movie, by the way. Just read the book; it's better. For one thing, in the movie, all the men who are of importance are clean-shaven, whereas actually at the time, an attractive man had ridiculous facial hair. I found that wrong. There are a couple of other things, so read the book. But when you do read the book, you will find things like "A person can't help their birth" (that's the Dutch girl again); so "A person can't help their birth." That's what Thackeray said; that was supposed to be a standard-speaking person, and so Thackeray did it. But on the other hand, we're not supposed to say "Tell the student that they can hand in their paper"; that's somehow wrong. Thackeray did it, but we can't do it.

I might, as a linguist, then say that the fact that we use *they* in the singular is a matter of the fact that languages are always in flux. For example, that includes English. To a Middle English speaker, somebody saying, "Isabelle, you pick up those sticks," would have sounded quite strange, especially in many parts of England. You wouldn't say, "you"; you would say "thou." There was a whole different kind of system. Look at this system; this is the way "you-ness" worked in earlier English. This is people who we could have understood speaking. I'm not talking about way back in Old English; I'm talking about in Middle English varieties. Here you have singular, and you have plural. You have a subject, *thou*; and then you have genitive, *thy*. Or remember the terrible old song, "Drink to Me [Only with] Thine Eyes"? That's an archaic thing. Object was *thee*, and so *I tell thee*, and then, over here in the plural, that was *you*. *You* was actually only the object form. The subject form was *ye*; that's from *hear ye, hear ye*, and then the genitive was *your*. Nowadays, we're using *you* in both the singular and the plural, and we don't have this difference between subject and object either. *You* has just fallen apart and taken over. It's just something that happens in languages.

Now suppose somebody came from the Middle Ages or from the Old English ages, and they're putrid and disoriented, and they're telling us "*You* is only used in the plural" (I have to use to that voice that they all had, "You is only in the plural"). What would that mean to us? It isn't now; now we use *you* in the singular and in the plural. Then it was only used in the plural. We use it our way, and there isn't anything wrong with it.

That returns us to the argument: "If a student comes before I get there, they can slip their test under my office door." Yet I can say all that, and very many people continue to think, "But no, because *they* is plural." That's a little frustrating, because it really doesn't follow in terms of logic; it doesn't penetrate.

Another example: using nouns as verbs. "I don't like it when people say that they're going to *impact* something, because *impact* is a noun." That's just standard. So "I don't like it"; that's what people say, they don't like it. I don't really have any feeling about it here or there, but when you look at a sentence like *the new rules are impacting the efficiency of the procedure*, to say that you don't like what happened to *impact* means that you have a problem with the same thing having happened to *view, silence, worship, copy, outlaw*—all those words began as nouns. There was a time when the idea of *outlawing* something would have sounded very strange. Somebody could have said, "I don't like it when people say, 'I *outlawed* something.'" "Why?" "Because *outlaw* is a noun." We kind of got past that, because, as we've seen in this course, languages change. Languages are always in flux, and in ways that often are something that you might feel like you don't like within the time slice of your life. That's the sociolinguistic variables, for example; so there's *singin'* and there's *singing*. Or there's the vowel change on Martha's Vineyard. What you don't like might just be where the language is going to be tomorrow. Here we are in tomorrow's language, the English of the future—we're all wearing unitards and things buzz—and we have verb: We have *view, silence, worship, copy*, and *outlaw*. If so, then that means that technically to say, "I don't like it when people use *impact* as a verb" is peculiar, because you use every day words that have their source in that exact same thing happening. Basically, English does this because it's a language with relatively few affixes to distinguish parts of speech. It's rather natural for words to slip in this way from one part of speech to another, and it doesn't have to be indicated with an ending.

That is not true, for example, even of English's close relatives, the Germanic languages. In German you can have a *Telefon*, but if you're going to make it into a verb it's *telefonieren*; you can't just *telefon*. That's because German has a lot more of that kind of equipment than we have. But in languages without that kind of equipment, there's all sorts of slipping and sliding around. For example, in Cantonese, there's a word *lengjái*. *Lengjái* means either *good-looking*, and so that's an adjective; or it can mean *a good-looking person*—"a looker," "a hottie," as it's said these days—and that's a noun. Or it can mean *to become good-looking*—"to prettify" or whatever—and that would be a verb. *Lengjái* can be a noun, an adjective, and a verb; very common in the Chinese languages, because they're very low on affixal morphology. No one's writing in to newspapers in China about this kind of thing, but somehow in English we have this idea that it's just wrong when *impact* is used as a verb. "Kathleen, why don't you like it?" "I just don't like it." That won't really do in terms of having a constructive discussion about prescriptivism versus descriptivism, but unfortunately that's often the best that we have.

Again, you have to try to put yourself into people's heads, and I try to in looking at this kind of thing. It would seem that the feeling a person has is that you were in school, and you learned all these rules, and you got graded, etc. You were probably better at it than some people. Now you've got all your ducks in a row—that's what you were told by people who were older than you and had responsibility and authority—and then here somebody comes telling you that all that was wrong, that you're not supposed to pay attention to those things that you learned in school and justifiably felt pretty proud of having mastered. I can imagine that it must be like someone coming along and telling you that it's OK to chew with your mouth open, yet you've learned "lips together, teeth apart," which is not intuitive; there are people from other cultures—especially the men, for example—where clearly chewing with your mouth open is perfectly ordinary. I've been told by some Americans—who unfortunately missed learning the rule—that food tastes better when you chew with your mouth open. I've tried it, and it does. I'm sure that smacking is the natural way you eat. Look at your dog, for example. But we have "lips together, teeth apart." Then someone comes along and says, "Oh, just let it all hang out." It must feel like you're being deprived of something you always thought of as an effort and kind of a privilege. I can understand that completely.

But here's another way that you might look at it, because if you went to the trouble to master all those rules, then you also know that there is history in a language. You especially know that there is history in a language from this course. It's interesting where the problem starts. We know that there was *Beowulf*. *Beowulf* was written in Old English, and Old English was a tongue which looks like German to us on the page; it's clearly completely different from modern English. You've got this noble story, and you imagine illuminated pages and museums you have to go to and stuff like that. That's all considered a noble part of our history. Then we know that there was Middle English, and the first thing we think of is Chaucer. We know that was very different from modern English, and so we might have learned in school to recite the first lines of *The Canterbury Tales*, "Whan that Aprille with his shoures soote," and we always say it with that Swedish lilt, although we have no idea whether people talked that way then. We enjoy that. Read further in *The Canterbury Tales* and it's often more opaque than those first four lines happen to be. We don't see it as a problem that we don't talk like that; that's just fine.

Then there's Shakespeare, and as I've mentioned elsewhere in this course, we understand much less of what he's saying than we like to think we do.

Then there's the King James Bible; nobody talks like that. Then you get up to Jane Austen, and we see Old English to Jane Austen, and it's this noble history of this language that's taking on words and even changing grammatically. It used to be this thing, and now it's this thing; and the soundtrack has like [FANFARE] and is scored in thirds and fourths with French horns and things; it's this wonderful thing. Then, somehow, once we get up to about Jane Austen—once we get up to about 175 years ago—it's supposed to have stopped. Somehow that's it. As soon as you get up to about 175 years ago, it's as if there was some project someone knew all along: We are building what will be modern English as of about Jane Austen's time, and once we get to that exalted spot, we must stop.

The question is, why? What's so good about just that stage of English? Because as de Saussure taught us, languages are always in a state of flux. Language is a lava lamp; of course, he didn't put it that way, but languages are always complex conglomerations of oppositions and signifiers, and they move along. The language is never better or worse; it's just different. It's always a grammar, and grammars are configured in different ways. But somehow, with English: [FANFARE]. I don't see the sense in that, and what I mean is that I don't understand the logic of that. No linguist understands the logic of that. We don't tell Nicholas Sarkozy that he's speaking bad Latin; he's speaking French. That's because we understand—I think we accept—that Latin changed into French. Old English changed into Middle English, changed into our English, and our English will keep going, we assume. If change was OK in 1400, if change was OK in 1700, then what's wrong with change today?

It's something to think about. There are things that we think of as perfectly ordinary English, which really were kind of bizarre when they came in at the time. There's a way that English kind of should be. We have something I've mentioned a few times, this peculiar use of *do*. So *Do you eat apples?* In any self-respecting language, it's *Eat you apples?* That would be a common European thing, or all sorts of ways that languages form questions. But having this *do* is very strange: *I do not eat apples.* What *do*? What's that doing in there? It almost surely has to do with the presence of Celtic languages with that same construction on the island. But the English that was brought to England did not have that use of *do*, and no one was recorded mentioning this sort of thing because there just wasn't as much writing; but certainly when *do* came into the language, it was seen as peculiar.

We can even know what English kind of should be like if things had gone differently. English's closest relative is Frisian. Frisian is a language very much like Dutch, and it's spoken over on the other side of the North Sea in what is today Holland. Good English and good cheese is good English and good Frise; i.e., Frisian. They're very close. Over in Frisian, if you say, "Do we eat apples?" then you just say "*Ite wy appels*?" You can see it right there. That's how it should be in English; it should be *Eat we apples?*

Or something like "What are you doing, Timmy and Jessica?" "We are eating apples." That's very strange in English that we have to specify that we're doing it right then, when in any other language what you would say is, "We eat apples." You might say "I'm in the process of eating apples right now," but that's the marked case. Over in Frisian, if you asked Timmy and Jessica—I imagine they'd be called something like Jop and Tanika or something like that—then you ask, "What are you doing?" It would be "We eat the apples." That's what they would say, not "We are eating the apples"; they don't have that in Frisian. Frisian is the way English kind of should be, but English changed and we don't mind. We are using these kinds of excrescences in our language, and yet we just don't like when *impact* is used as a verb. There's a certain inconsistency in this.

What it comes down to is that you can not like something at this point, and then if you look at a slightly earlier point, you'll see that a lot of what we decide that we don't like now actually was not being looked at. There were other things that were considered not likable that look perfectly OK to us. After Jane Austen—now we're in the late 1800s—there's a squadron of people who are very upset that people are running around saying déclassé things. It's an era very familiar to us, in a way. There are all sorts of things that make you realize that the things that are bothering us now are really just like the fashions that those people were wearing. It will pass. *The House of Mirth*, Edith Wharton's novel—the one that truly shreklic film was made of; I talked about this in an earlier lecture—in the book, Ned [Silverton] is walking down the street and he says, "Fifth Avenue is so imperfectly lighted." Lighted? You think to yourself, "Really, shouldn't it be *lit*?" But he says, no, "Fifth Avenue is so imperfectly lighted." That's because in the late 1800s, *lit* was considered tacky. People were saying they didn't like it; they thought it sounds a little vulgar. Now today we would say, "lit"; "lighted" sounds a little fruity. We can see that really it's just a matter of that Ned wore a certain kind of hat and we wear certain kinds of hats now.

It used to be considered really a little tacky to say "all the time." You're supposed to say, "always." And putting *all the time* in writing? Well, goodness darlings, we do not do that. Of course that's changed, and we kind of figure, what were they getting their knickers in a twist about? There were other things to worry about. It was the Gilded Age, there were poor people, there were no telephones—or telephones were just beginning; there was a Yellow Page at that point—you know there were other things they should have been thinking about. But instead, they're thinking about *all the time.* "Wash tub" was something that you could get smacked on the back of the head for saying in the late 1800s, because it was supposed to be a *washing tub.* Again, trivia—it's just something that shouldn't matter—yet nowadays we have people running around saying, "I don't like it when people say *liaise.*" There are larger problems, and languages always change.

There was one grammarian—kind of sniffy guy with three names and too full of big dinners, probably—who rather extensively argued that *standpoint* (this is a grammarian) is not really a proper word of English because you're not literally standing anywhere. The lack of imagination is interesting that that kind of argument was actually taken seriously. This is one of my favorites: In, like, Abraham Lincoln's time—yes, I said, "like"; language changes—it was said by people who were very precise about language that if you say, "The first two people get a set of dishes," then that is wrong because "the first two" should be "the two first." You're supposed to say, "The two first people will get a set of dishes." According to the grammarians at that time—i.e., the prescriptive grammarians at that time—if you say, "the first two," that's supposed to refer to the first set of two amidst other sets of two. If you say, "first two," then there has to be a second two and a third two. It only would apply to that very unusual situation where you've got sequences of pairs. If you just mean person number 1 and person number 2 in a line of 30, then you're supposed to say "the two first." If you're trying to wrap your mind around that, keep going. If you do, it makes a certain sense, but it clearly didn't have anything to do with anything that spontaneously arose in the communal minds of speakers; i.e., in terms of what Chomsky would call the competence of English speaking. It's really just something somebody made up and kind of imposed on people like a cudgel. People got past that, and now we don't talk about "the two first" at all.

One more example: If you walked by a house in the process of construction in 1850 in America, then the proper thing to say was, "There's a house building across the street." Now we would say "There's a house being built across the street," and we think nothing of it; that's considered proper English. But at the time, "There's a house being built" was considered a little on the edge, a little peculiar, and there were a lot of people who didn't like it. It was something that people joked about; it marked you in terms of class. Or it was something that "silly women" were thought to be characterized by, to say "The house is being built across the street." The language was changing, and ordinary, very intelligent people just didn't like it. Now we look at the yellowing pages of those old journals and books where they talk about those sorts of things and we just think to ourselves, "These are people, post-Industrial Revolution, who have too much time on their hands; they're thinking too hard, and they could be lending themselves to other pursuits such as really thinking about what graceful written expression would be apart from made-up rules like two first versus first two." There are all sorts of things that they could have been doing instead of this resistance of language changing in the present tense, despite thinking of that same language change as marvelous when it's a matter of going from *Beowulf* to Shakespeare to the King James Bible to *Sense and Sensibility*.

To give you a sense of where these people were coming from, here on the screen is a passage that I think is perfectly standard English, but in about 1870 it would have seemed like it was written by somebody who had slightly dirty fingers or maybe hadn't been brought up in a good home. That passage is:

> Let's have a look at the first two chapters I have excerpted, where we learn about the period when the Cross-Bronx Expressway was being built from the standpoint of people who were born in East Tremont and lived there all of their lives.

Another vulgarism in this is *born in*; you were supposed to say, "born at," and people used to have arguments about that. *Born in* is fine now.

> Let's have a look at the first two chapters I have excerpted, where we learn about the period when the Cross-Bronx Expressway was being built from the standpoint of people who were born in East Tremont and lived there all of their lives.

According to the standards reining when Abraham Lincoln was president, I just spoke sloppy language of the streets. Obviously, the sense that that was the case was a matter of fashion; it was a matter of arbitrariness. These are people who, as it were, were standing and tilting in front of a windmill, or were standing in front of a steamroller. You can't stop a language from changing.

The lesson, therefore, is we have to examine why we think something that was so ordinary in the past is only within this particular 175-year window suddenly some kind of scourge. If we fully understand that, then we understand that in the logical sense there's no such thing as "I don't like impact being used as a verb" or really much of anything else that goes on in language. I consider even all of this an incomplete address of the prescriptivist-descriptivist debate, and so we're going to cover a little more of it in the next lecture. However, this is not the next lecture; this is still this one, and so I can't cover it now.

Lecture Thirty-One
Why Languages Are Never Perfect

Scope: This continuation of the previous lecture explores the various imperfections and lapses of logic inherent to English grammar, building to the basic point that there is no human language without such features and that a quest to iron away a select few does not seem useful or promising.

Outline

I. Imperfection is inherent to language.

    A. *Billy and me went to the store* has been judged a mistake, because *me* is an object form rather than a subject form. There is an understandable sense that this usage must not be allowed to pass, as it could be the beginning of a slippery slope.

    B. However, no language is free of wrinkles of this kind. They are common, for example, with pronouns.

    C. In Russian, to refer to yourself and someone else, you refer to yourself as "we" (*мы*; in our Roman alphabet, *my*) and include the word for the other person.

        1. For example, to say, "my wife and I," you would say, "we and my wife": *my s ženoj.*

ja	I	*my*	we
ty	you (singular)	*vy*	you (plural)
on/ona	he/she	*oni*	they

        2. The *we* usage crept in out of a sense that you are referring to two people of which you are one, which is the definition of "we-ness," just as we say, "everybody can have their own piece of cake" because *everybody* brings to mind lots of people. Russians do not consider *my s ženoj* a mistake.

    D. In Hebrew and other Semitic languages, numbers' gender is the opposite of the noun being counted.

        1. A *kibbutz* is masculine. If you put *kibbutz* in the plural, it's *kibbutzim*. But then if you want to talk about three *kibbutzim*, it is *kibbutzim šloša*, with the feminine ending for the number.

2. Bananas are feminine; if you make them plural, you have *bananot*, but then you say, "*bananot šaloš*" with the masculine ending for the number.

II. English is full of imperfections that are rarely noticed as such.

A. Having a conjugational ending in the present only for the third-person singular (e.g., *walk* becomes *walks* only for *he*, *she*, and *it*) is vastly rare and makes no logical sense.

B. Auxiliary *do*, as used with negative sentences (*I **do** not walk*) and interrogative sentences (***Do** I walk?*), makes no logical contribution to meaning.

C. Technically, *aren't I?* "should" be *amn't I?*

D. English is odd—and ambiguous—in not having distinct pronouns for singular and plural *you*.

1. Many other languages use the plural second-person pronoun for either number or politeness, but English is unique in having no difference between singular and plural at all.

2. Yet attempts to fix this imperfection (e.g., *y'all*) are treated as slang.

E. The ending *-ly* makes an adjective into an adverb, as in *strongly*, *helpfully*, *badly*. It also, however, occurs in adjectives such as *portly* and *brotherly*.

III. English has suffixes (which are often not recognized as suffixes) that can no longer be applied to new words.

A. View the following words: fondle, nibble, riddle, dabble, fiddle, diddle, giggle, stipple, tickle, dribble, jiggle, wiggle, trickle, curdle, nipple. All of them have to do with rapid, repetitive movement, a "hummingbird" quality.

B. The *-le* suffix is referred to as a *frequentative* suffix.

C. The occurrence of the suffix is not regular. But with *-le*, as often as not the original word doesn't exist. There are *nip*, *jig*, *dab*, and *curd*. But *nib* and *drib* are marginal, *trick* comes from a different root, and we cannot *fid*, *fond*, *did*, *gig*, *wig*, *rid*, *tick*, or *stip*.

D. Linguists term a suffix like this *nonproductive*: It cannot be applied to new words anymore like *-ed* can.

1. An example is *-dom*. We know that *kingdom* is bimorphemic: There is *king* and *dom*.

2. But there are only so many words with that suffix, e.g., *freedom*, *martyrdom*, and *wisdom*, where the pronunciation of the *wis* root is from before the Great Vowel Shift that rendered *wise* alone as [wajz], showing that *-dom* is from an antique stage of the language.

E. But nonproductiveness creates illogic when the root that an affix is appended to ceases to exist independently.

    1. We know what *ruthless* means, but where's *ruth*?

    2. In the same way, if *wiggle* means to squirm rapidly, then why isn't there a verb to *wig* that refers to slower, undulating motion?

IV. When it comes down to it, we don't think about or even notice these "flaws," because they're really not that important.

    A. If English were anything close to perfect, then this sentence would be correct: ***Amn't** I the one who **have** to **sprink** the second coat of paint on?*

    B. Yet can we really not be vigilant at all? There are two answers to that.

        1. We should be concerned about the artful use of language. Some people are more articulate than others. Some people are clearly better writers than others, and writing definitely needs to be taught. It is a matter of what one is vigilant about.

        2. Despite all the arguments that I just made, there seems to be a fear that if we just let all these changes take place, somehow something bad would happen. However, that has never happened to any recorded language on Earth.

    C. You can see what truly decadent English is really like in Pedro Carolino's *The New Guide of the Conversation in Portuguese and English*, written in the late 1800s by a man under the impression that he could render English by just plugging English words into French sentences.

        1. The entire book is full of the most ridiculously degraded, erroneous English you can possibly imagine.

        2. I think this is what people are afraid of if the language changes.

        3. This never really happens, which we know because we've never seen anything like this despite all the change we have seen.

Essential Reading:

Crystal, *The Fight for English.*

Supplemental Reading:

Bailey, *Nineteenth-Century English.*

Questions to Consider:

1. I fashioned the previous two lectures very carefully as an attempt to make general readers truly understand what linguists see as logical flaws in the idea that speaking "badly" is rife in society. Have I succeeded in your view? If not, why? (And do let me know, for future reference!)

2. For almost any English speaker, there are words or constructions that aesthetically we "do not like." What do you "not like," and does anything you have learned in this course change your feeling about it (or make you not like it more?!)?

Lecture Thirty-One—Transcript
Why Languages Are Never Perfect

My goal in this double lecture is to get across the linguist, descriptivist case in a way that might be effective in ways that other arguments seem not to be. What I stressed in the first half is that language always changes and that what linguists are saying is that it doesn't make sense to resist change today if we don't have any problem with the fact that our very language is the product of change from before. My general experience is that for reasons that I don't completely understand—here's where I can't completely get into people's heads; at least I personally can't—that argument does not always work. Saying language always changes seems to vaguely irritate people somehow; they don't consider that a sufficient argument. If one doesn't, then what I'm inclined to think is that there's another way of looking at it that might seem more compelling to those who are really convinced that prescriptivism is the hallmark of being a civilized person.

That theme—that second observation—is this one: Imperfection is inherent to language. Or to put it another way, all languages have their dings; there's never been a language that didn't have any. It's the very nature of it. It's like a chaotic but beautiful English garden, full of thises and thats, and yet we think of it as a beautiful thing. That's what languages are like, and it's not a matter of whether they should be or shouldn't be; it's what they've always been, no matter what anybody thought. Taking the parts of a language—which may not make strict logical sense—and submitting them to witch-hunting is incoherent in its way because there's never been a language that was anywhere near perfect, so maybe we might revise our conception of what a language is supposed to be.

For example—and here's one of the big bugbears of prescriptivism—there's the idea that if you say, "Billy and me went to the store," then it's a mistake because *me* is an object form instead of being a subject form. There's a sense that we can't let that usage slip; there's a sense that if we let that go, then it might be a slippery slope and we're going to have some sort of chaos. Now that's understandable—I see what people might be worried about—but the fact is that there's no language that's free of wrinkles of that kind, and they're particularly common in pronouns; pronouns churn around. You have to see other examples to understand how worrying about the *Billy and me* case might not be the most fruitful use of one's time.

For example, let's look at Russian, good old Russian. Here are the vanilla pronouns in Russian. You've got *ja* for *I*; you've got *ty* for *you*; you've got *on* and *ona* for *he* and *she*; you've got *my* for *we*; *vy* for *y'all*; and *oni* for *they*. (We'll talk about *y'all*, by the way; that comes into this discussion too, but right now we're doing Russian.) Notice that in Russian the word for *we* is *my*—*my* does not mean *me*; that's a little confusing. *My*, that's right there; we're going to light it up on the screen: *my*. That means *we*. In English one would say, "My wife and I," or one might say, "Me and my wife." The way that you say that in standard Russian is, "We and my wife," and that means *my wife and I*, not *my wife and two other men*. It's *we and the wife*, and so it's *my s ženoj*. That is *my wife and I*: "We and the wife went—the two of us—out strolling in the park." The way that you would say, "he and his wife" is to say in Russian, "they and his wife." It would be *oni s ženoj*. And it's not three people; that's two people: "They and his wife went strolling in the park."

You can imagine how that happened. There's a sense that if you are with your spouse, there is a kind of a "we-ness," and that we-ness crept into what you actually say. This is what's important: That business of *we and the wife*—meaning a man and his wife sitting together on the sofa; *we and the wife did this*—that is not slangy Russian. That's not Boris Yeltsin when he was drunk or something like that. That's not the way they speak Russian way out in Siberia or something. That's standard Russian. That's in *Anna Karenina*. It is an imperfection; it does not really make sense. No one in Russia worries about that, though, because it's just one of the dings of the language.

My cat is really cuter than your cat. My cat is the cutest cat in the world, and she's quite beautiful. She's got big eyes; she's kind of like a feline Ava Gardner, if Ava Gardner were black and stupid. Laura is a gorgeous little dummy, but she does have a tooth that kind of sticks out; she's got a little fang. You only see it if she's on her belly and wants you to pet her, and you can kind of see she's got this funny little tooth. It's a little imperfection. That makes her her. Other than that, she's perfect. She's got that little thing, and now she's getting gingivitis too. It's a shame because it's going to cost money to fix, and you can see it on that little tooth that's coming out. That's like Russian and the *we and the wife*. That's like English and all sorts of little things.

Or some other languages: In Hebrew and other Semitic languages—Arabic has this too—there's something really not right about the numbers. It has to do with masculine and feminine. You've got two genders in Hebrew:

masculine and feminine. If you're talking about somebody's good luck, we often hear it as "*Mazal tov*," but actually if you want to say it in Israeli Hebrew: "*Mazal tov*." The way that comes out is with *tov* in its masculine form, and *mazal* is a masculine noun. Then if you're talking about "good year" colloquially: "*Šana tová*"; but if you want to say it in Israeli Hebrew, it's, "*Šana tová*," and so you have this feminine ending. That's transparent to any of you who happen to know Spanish or something like that. It's *tov, tova*; it works like that.

But for some reason in Hebrew, when you're dealing with the numbers, the numbers have reverse gender. A *kibbutz* is masculine. If you put *kibbutz* in the plural, it's *kibbutzim*. But then if you want to talk about three kibbutzes, it's *kibbutzim šloša*, with the feminine ending. *Bananas* are feminine; if you make them plural, you have *bananot*, but then you say, "*bananot šaloš*" with the masculine number. When you tackle one of these languages, one of the things that is a little confusing is that suddenly the numbers don't work right. There's terminology that tries to keep you from looking at it, like they'll tell you that the numbers with the feminine endings are the masculine ones or something, but you can kind of tell that it's just that the languages, they messed up there, and it just stays that way. No one has a problem with that, and that's because all languages have their little fangs like Laura has.

That means that we have the same sorts of things in English. We don't think of them as imperfections because we're used to them, but really they're kind of strange. For example, *I walk, you walk, she walks, we walk, you all/y'all*—we'll get to it—*walk*, and *they walk*. What's that *-s*? Why? How come it's *he walks*? What's that little thing hanging there for? What other language have you learned where you only have to learn an ending for the third-person singular? Wouldn't it be more logical if it were *I walk, you walk, he walk, we walk, you all walk*, and *they walk*? See how much nicer that is, how much more euphonious it is? But instead, *I walk, you walk, he walks*. ... What? In fact, there is no other known language to me—or to many other linguists—where in the present tense the only marker is on the third-person singular. If you think about it, why would there be? You wouldn't make that up if you were making up a language. If you've learned any other language, the first thing you have to unlearn is that there's going to be this little piece of crap hanging off of the third-person singular. It's an imperfection in the language that is like a fang hanging out of little Laura's mouth, and yet we use it all the time. We just haven't been told about it. I wonder if there are going to be any crusades against that in the newspaper? We just deal with it.

For example, *I am a man. Aren't I a man?* Wait a minute; shouldn't it be *Amn't I a man?* If we're going to talk about logic, I wouldn't say, "I are a man." I don't know of any dialect of English spoken under any rock where anybody would say, "I are a man." Why isn't it *Amn't I a man?* If I say, "Amn't I a man?" I sound like I have a disease. It's *Aren't I a man?* And that's just the way standard English is. That's really imperfect; that's as if Laura had 60 teeth. It doesn't make any sense. There are some dialects in England where they do say, "amn't"; it's considered quaint and evidence that there might be something in the water up there that kind of screws up people's grammar, when actually they seem to be making sense. We don't mind that imperfection.

Never mind that language always changes; another point is that languages are always full of dings, including ones that nobody cares about, and so we might want to be consistent. Let's think about *you*. Why is it that we don't have a distinction between singular *you* and plural *you*? Nobody quite understands why. Shouldn't we still have *thou*? Or if not *thou*, something else? Again, it's a matter of other languages: If you've learned another language, where was the one where you had a difference between *I* and *we*, and then *he* and *she* and *it* in the singular and *they* in the plural, but then suddenly in the second person, no, it's *you*: It's *you* in the singular, *you* in the plural. That is really odd about English. It's not that way in its relatives; it's really not that way, and you know in a way it shouldn't be, but it just is.

Notice what happens when somebody tries to fix it: We've got this *you* in the singular, and *you* in the plural; naturally, speakers all over the world—including here in America—are inclined when there's more than one person to come up with some way to indicate it, and hence you get *you all*, contracted to *y'all*. That's considered something cute that people in the South do or something that black people do, and in general it's considered something kind of quaint and maybe even wrong. Other versions of it such as *yuns* and *yous*, all of those are just seen as kitchen-sink barbarisms, when really it makes it better. Wouldn't it be nice if you had *I*, *you*, *he*, *she*, *it*, *we*, (something), and *they*? What's something going to be? We could just make something up—kloop—but that doesn't really work. Let's make something else up—klep—that doesn't work either. Let's make something up that sounds like English—you all—no, can't have that; nonstandard slang. What's happening to the language? We don't mind that English has this imperfection where there's not enough differentiation between singular and plural in the second person; and so here we are.

Other things: Adverbial ending -ly, and so you have *strongly*, and you have *helpfully*, and you have *badly*, but you also have a -*ly* that's used for adjectives, like *portly* and *brotherly*. That doesn't really make sense. It's supposed to stay where it belongs. If we're supposed to have this perfect language, then the pea juice—I mean juice of peas, the vegetable—is not supposed to kind of sweeten the steak; it's supposed to stay apart. What's *portly*? It's actually kind of confusing sometimes. I remember one time I was working, I had this bizarre summer job, and I had this boss: Among other things, he was a person who had a certain avoirdupois—he was a large individual. I forget why I had reason to refer to it, but I said something along the lines of, "Well especially given that he's rather portly, we blah blah blah blah." The person who I was speaking to was listening to it, and she wasn't sure how that worked. I think that in her brain she wasn't hearing -*ly* as an adjective, and the best she could make of it was that I was saying, "porkly." We had this whole exchange where she seemed to think that I had said something mean about the boss, and gradually I figured it out: She thought I had compared him to a pig and said, "Well given that he's rather 'porkly,' we'd better not." That's just the cause of the confusion in this case.

I want you to look at this bunch of words—they're up on the screen; see them?—*fondle, nibble, riddle, dabble, fiddle, diddle, giggle, stipple, tickle, dribble, jiggle, wiggle, trickle, curdle,* and *nipple.* See all those words there? Those words clearly share something in common, and it's not only aspects of their sound. All of these things, if you think about it—and it's probably the first time anybody has presented you with those words together—but if you think about it, there's a kind of a *lelelelelelelelelelele* ... kind of hummingbird quality to all of those words. In other words, there's a suffix on these words. We're not usually taught it as a suffix, but that -*le* is there, and it does convey a rapid, repeated kind of movement, and it has a name: It's called a *frequentative suffix.* Many languages have them, and in much clearer form than here. What's interesting about this frequentative suffix is that as often as not, the original word doesn't exist. For example, you have *nipple*, and then there's the word *nip*; the relationship between them is clear. Or there is *dab*—which is like what you do when you're fishing—and then there's *dabble*, which you can see as a kind of a hummingbird version of it, and certainly *dapple* would be the same thing; and so it works with those. But then with *nibble*, the word *nib* is not something that we know of as meaning *to clomp down on*. For example, if *nibble* is to kind of go *nomnomnomnomnom*, than *nib* should be to just go *nom*; but it isn't. There's an expression, "Oh, here comes His Nibs." I don't know what it means, and really it's not a part of modern English. *Dribble* is one thing; *drib* is only used in "dribs and drabs." It's not really a word. You can't say, "Oh, look, there's a drib!" What's a *drib*? It's not there; we just have *dribble*. There's *trickle*, but *trick* is not the version of that word that it comes from. There's *trickle*, which means *pitterpitterpit*, like that, and then *trick* is completely different. *Trick* is to deceive; *trickle* does not mean "to go *gotchagotchagotchagotcha*"; that's not it. Really there is no *trick*. You can't *fid*, you can't *fond*, you can't *dib*, you can't *gig*, you can't *wig*, and you can't *stip*; and so the original words don't exist.

What that's called is a suffix that's *nonproductive*—there's some terminology I did not throw at you when we talked about morphology, but now we see it in action—it's nonproductive; therefore it can't be applied to new words anymore. For example, the *-ed* past-tense suffix—spelled *ed*— that is very much productive. Even when new verbs come into the language, such as the hideous and malformed excrescence which is *impact* as a verb, then you can say "This impacted the development of a new sign language" or something like that. That's a *productive* suffix. But there are many suffixes that we know are there—we can see that it's a suffix; we perceive them—but they are what we call not productive; you can't apply them to new words. For example, *kingdom* (the word *kingdom*): We know in morphological terms that it is bimorphemic; it has two morphemes, not one. It's one word, but there is *king* and then there's *dom*, and *-dom* conveys this meaning of *realm*, and it has a more abstract kind of meaning. We know, if we know the language, that there are other words with this *-dom* suffix (*d*, *o*, *m*). You can be *free*, in which case you have your *freedom*; you can play the *martyr* and therefore be indulging in *martyrdom*. Then there's *wisdom*, but in the case of *wisdom* you get a clue that this *-dom* is something that was productive a very long time ago, because it's not *wisedom*, it's *wisdom*. That means that the shift in English vowel sounds—the Great Vowel Shift—had not taken place when the word *wisdom*, which now would be *wisedom*, was created. We see the original vowel sound, or something like it, preserved. That's an indication that *-dom* is old, old news.

We can't apply *-dom* anymore, or if we do it's a joke. I remember one time I stayed in the apartment for a while with this guy. There was something wrong with him—I don't remember what was wrong with him; it was a very long time ago—but there was something about him that especially my girlfriend at the time found vaguely ridiculous, and I was about to buy something ugly for my apartment, once it was ready. I said, "Well, would you think that this would look nice on the wall?" She said, "You know, actually, I think that that would have a certain air of 'Len-dom' about it." The guy's name was Len, and so we laugh because there's no such thing as *Len-dom*; it is a nonproductive suffix. She wouldn't have used those terms, but that is the essence of it.

But the fact is that nonproductiveness creates illogic in a language. Preview: Nonproductive affixation is inherent to a language; if a language has affixes, then some portion of them are going to be nonproductive. It creates illogic in cases like what we're seeing with the frequentative suffix. What we're seeing with the frequentative cases is that you can have the affix appended to a root, and then you have a word; but then suppose the root itself ceases to exist? Then you end up having a ding; you end up having a Laura fang in the language.

For example, we know what *ruthless* means, but where's *ruth*? Clearly, *ruthless* does not mean "being in the state of missing a woman named Ruth." *The poor man was Ruthless after his wife left on her vacation.* Where's *ruth*? If we're going to have a perfectly logical language, if we've got the word *ruthless*, then we should be saying, "Please show me some ruth, because I'm very sick today, and don't make me come in." But, no, we don't really mind. If *wiggle* means to squirm rapidly in that kind of wormy way, then why isn't there a verb *to wig* that means roughly "to do a hula dance"? If *wiggling* is like this, then *wigging* should be like that, but it isn't. We don't walk around thinking about things like this because the language is, one, illogical and, two, it's OK.

For example, if English were anything close to perfect, based on the things that we've seen, then this thing up on the screen would be a normal sentence of English. Instead of saying, "Aren't I the one who has to sprinkle the second coat of paint on?" we would say, "Amn't I the one who have to"—because we wouldn't have this strange third-person singular *s*, let's make it perfect—so "Amn't I the one who have to" and then "sprink the second coat of paint on?" We have *sprinkle*, but where is *sprink*? There should be *sprink*. If is *sprinkling* is to kind of go *dinkydinkydinkydinky*, then *sprink* should be just to paint slowly; and there should be that word: "Amn't I the one who have to sprink the second coat of paint on?" That clearly sounds like a being from the planet Neptune; that's just not our language. Yet that is perfect, logical English.

To the extent that we don't mind not saying, "Amn't I the one who have to sprink the second coat of paint on?" there are all sorts of things that we might not mind, too. When it comes down to it, being upset about the kinds of things that prescriptivists very genuinely see it necessary to be on guard for is very much analogous to watching your five-year-old girl coloring in a book and noticing that she doesn't color within the lines and being, one, angry with her about it and, two, genuinely supposing that she could. It's the exact same thing. You're mad at her, and you're thinking that a five-year-old—who still sometimes walks a little bit unsteadily; there might be some toilet issues still going on; they don't have enormous vocabularies yet; they're five—you're imagining that the five-year-old actually could color the way you do. You're continuing to think that way over a long period, instead of marveling at what a brilliant little creature she is, what an inquisitive little creature she is, at the interesting colors that she does use when she is coloring, either within or outside of the lines. It's really—in my mind; talk about getting into other people's minds—to a descriptivist, to a linguist, or at least to this one, when someone says that it is vulgar and wrong to say, "Billy and me went to the store" because *me* is not a subject, it is exactly equivalent to smacking that little girl on the back of the head and actually thinking that a five-year-old could color within the lines. It just doesn't work that way.

What it comes down to is also, however, a question that people often ask. There's a sense that even if all of this stuff makes a certain sense, can we really not be vigilant at all? There are two answers to that: One of them is that—as I've said before and I really meant—we should be concerned about the artful use of language. Some people are more articulate than others. There's such a thing as learning public speaking; Toastmasters does it. Some people are clearly better writers than others; writing definitely needs to be taught, and in this country it needs to be taught a lot better. All those things are very much true. It's a matter of what one is vigilant about. Second, there seems to be a fear that if we just let all these changes take place, despite all the arguments that I just made, somehow if we really did follow their implications and just let it go, somehow the language would possibly grind down into a handful of dust. In other words, something bad would happen if we allowed it.

The answer to that question is really very simple (you have to open yourself up to the simplicity of this): That's never happened to any recorded language on Earth. We're in a plane, we're flying around the globe—if you're of a certain age, remember the old Universal movie logo—and you're looking at all of the languages of the world (there are 6,000 of them, remember), and you're just thinking about all of them. A linguist, or a certain kind of linguist, can kind of look down at all the languages of the world. You can fly all around—you can go to the Pirahã; you can go into the mountains of Turkey—there is no language that we have ever found where because people weren't vigilant enough, there was only one vowel, and nouns and verbs had all collapsed together, and people had a hard time communicating without supplementing it with sign language or having very articulate facial expressions.

If English were in danger of undergoing that, then I assume that would have happened at least once. Really I would think that if there were a danger of a language grinding down into dust, or anything similar, it would happen a lot, but what's particularly interesting is that it hasn't happened even once. For example, Old English to Middle English to early modern English: It didn't happen then, and people weren't running around during the reign of Old English complaining about the mistakes that people were making being about to kill the language. It just kind of kept going. The reason that we know the language won't grind down into dust is simply because that never happened. Now we might say "Suppose it does happen?" In which case the answer would be "Why would that happen only to this one of the 6,000 languages that are on earth now?" (Remember that there were a whole bunch of them depending on what you call stages of a language during the past 150,000 years that human beings have lived.) Why would it only happen to this one? People are worried about it happening to this one, of course, but that doesn't mean that it's more likely to happen to this one. It might really be that the worry could be better placed.

Here is another answer to the issue, which is that you can see what decadent English is really like in one of the most wonderful books ever written. There was a man in the late 1800s; his name was Pedro Carolino, and he was Portuguese. He wrote a book called *The New Guide of the Conversation in Portuguese and English*. Even the title is wrong. Pedro Carolino decided to write this guidebook to English with these long word lists and dialogues and proverbs. It becomes clear as you read the book that not only did he not speak English, he didn't even read English. He knew nothing about the language; he just had the strange notion that he could actually look at French, plug English words into French sentences, and that somehow that actually was English. This wasn't something some medieval did, or somebody back in the days of the ancients; he did this like 10 minutes ago. This was in what he thought of as the modern world. You have this entire book full of the most ridiculously degraded, erroneous English you can possibly imagine. This is what I think people are afraid of if the language changes, but it never really happens, and we know it because we never see anything like this.

For example—just a quick example of what Pedro Carolino thought was English—there's a whole series of dialogues, and this one is called "Of the Fishing." These two men are fishing: "That pond it seems me many multiplied of fishes. Let us amuse rather to the fishing." Then the other person says, "I do like-it too much." Then the other person says, "Here, there is a wand and some hooks. Silence! There is a superb perch. Give me quick the rod. Ah! There is, it is a lamprey." I don't know why they find a lamprey, but they do. Next, "You mistake you, it is a frog! Dip again it in the water. Perhaps I will do best to fish with the leap." I don't know what a "leap" is, but that's what he put in. Then, finally, the ride out of this articulate dialogue: "Try it! I desire that you may be more happy and more skillful who a certain fisher, what have fished all day without to can take nothing." It's a whole book full of that. Obviously that is never going to happen to the English language, and in terms of the things that we're worried about, we can think of there being a watch cry. The watch cry is, "Where's *ruth*?" It's that whole *ruthless* issue. If you don't mind that, then why mind all these other things? Where's *ruth*? In the '50s we were told *Leave Your Language Alone*, and nobody listened. Pedro Carolino should have left our language alone, and I think that we can too.

What we should really—watch this transition I'm about to do—what we should really do is we should attend in particular to gracefulness in writing. In fact, because the development of writing is a topic that's always of interest, I have decided that in the next lecture we are going to address the development of writing.

Lecture Thirty-Two
The Evolution of Writing

Scope: This lecture explains how writing emerged in the Middle East around 3500 B.C.E. A picture-based system gradually became one in which concepts were represented by abstract cuneiforms. Shortly afterward, Egyptian hieroglyphics emerged, then developed into a less graphically complex hieratic system, which in turn developed into an alphabetic system, eventually the source of the Roman alphabet.

Outline

I. If human language had only existed for 24 hours, then writing would have been invented around 11:10 pm. Even today, only about 200 languages have a literature and speakers who are used to seeing their language on the page.

II. The first known writing system developed around 3500 B.C.E. in what is today Iraq and Iran.

   A. It is called *cuneiform* writing, and the characters were pressed into clay.

   B. Clay tokens from Susa correspond to early cuneiform and therefore are thought to have been the precursor of the writing system.

   C. The first written language was Sumerian, a language with no known relatives. Later other leading languages of the Fertile Crescent were written in cuneiform, including Akkadian.

   D. In the earliest cuneiform writing, the symbols are literal pictures. They gradually evolved into abstract symbols composed of strokes.

   E. Literal (*pictographic*) symbols often developed into abstract (*ideographic*) ones. Thus as the symbol for *head* evolved into an abstract symbol, it also came to mean *front* as well as *head*.

   F. Pictograms also developed into syllables.

   1. The symbol for *arrow* was pronounced [ši].

   2. The Sumerian word for *life* also happened to be [ši], and thus this symbol also came to mean *life*, and then to mean the syllable [ši] as it occurred in other words.

III. In Egyptian hieroglyphics, similarly abstract relationships appear between writing and language.

    A. Egyptian hieroglyphics were long assumed to have developed about five centuries after cuneiforms, but a 1998 finding suggests that the two systems may have arisen around the same time.

    B. The hieroglyphics were the writing system not for Arabic but for the Coptic language, a now-extinct member of the family that the Semitic languages belong to.

    C. Just as in cuneiform, pictograms were also used as ideograms, such as the pictogram for *hand* coming to also mean *power*.

    D. Pictograms were also used to indicate syllables and consonants. The symbol for *mouth* also stood for the *r* sound.

    E. Hieroglyphics had a symbol consisting of a branch plus the symbols for *h* and *t*. The word *hti'* meant *carve* or *retreat* in Coptic: with the knife, that symbol means *carve*; with a pair of legs, *retreat*.

    F. There was a simpler *hieratic* script, written with ink on papyrus, for everyday use.

IV. The decipherment of Egyptian hieroglyphics was quite a challenge.

    A. It was first thought that hieroglyphics were pictures of events already familiar to the Egyptians.

    B. The key to deciphering them was the discovery in 1799 of the Rosetta Stone, which had the same text in Greek, hieroglyphics, and hieratic.

    C. Physicist and physician Thomas Young (1773–1829) noticed that the cartouches in the hieroglyphic text corresponded to royal names.

        1. Young pieced together one that contained symbols for the Greek name *Ptolemy*.

        2. However, he assumed that this phonetic rendition of speech was done only for foreign names.

    D. Prodigy Jean-François Champollion (1790–1832) noted that there were also cartouches in hieroglyphic writing from before Greco-Roman contact, ruling out Young's explanation.

E. In one such cartouche, it was already known that the final two symbols stood for the *s* sound. Champollion, who was familiar with Coptic, supposed that the leftmost symbol stood for a sun and would be pronounced *ra*. This led him to see that the cartouche spelled out *Rameses*.

F. This showed that the hieroglyphics were written partly according to a rebus principle—a combination of pictorial representations, syllabic representations, and single consonant sounds.

V. The emergence of alphabet is a continuation of this story.

A. The Phoenicians, a trading people, invented an alphabet in about 900 B.C.E., deriving it partly from the Egyptians' hieratic script.

    1. They translated the meaning of a symbol in Egyptian into Phoenician and then made that symbol stand for the first letter in that word.

    2. The idea of having symbols stand for the first letter of what they represented in this fashion likely began as a shorthand used by scribes for Egypt's growing multinational mercenary army.

B. The Phoenicians did not indicate vowels.

    1. For example, *aleph* stood for a glottal stop rather than *a*.

    2. The modern Hebrew alphabet is still based on the same principle, with only partial indication of vowels; for *bakol mikhtav*, only *bkl mkhtv* is written (right to left): ‏בכל מכתב‎.

C. The Phoenicians passed this system to the Greeks, who adopted some signs to indicate vowels.

    1. Thus the Phoenician *daleth* became Greek's delta.

    2. Note the fate of *daleth* in various offshoot alphabets: Greek, Δ; Hebrew, ד; Arabic, ﺩ; and Russian, Д.

D. The Phoenician alphabet traveled much further than Greece and was the foundation for the writing systems of Arabic, Hebrew, and languages of India, Southeast Asia, and Mongolia.

    1. The correspondence to sounds made it easy to learn.

    2. The Phoenicians traveled throughout the Mediterranean and as far northwest as Ireland, which strengthened their influence.

E. This first alphabet opened writing to a wider class range of people and helped make democratization possible in many areas.

F. The alphabet also contributed to the battle between descriptivists and prescriptivists that we discussed in previous lectures.

Essential Reading:

Robinson, *The Story of Writing.*

Supplemental Reading:

Sacks, *Letter Perfect.*

Questions to Consider:

1. From the perspective conditioned by the Roman alphabet, it can look almost counterintuitive that earlier writing systems were so unconcerned with transcribing speech precisely and consistently and that this remains true of some systems today. Yet the English alphabet is by no means a precise transcription system: We have not consummated the pathway one can see from Egyptian hieroglyphics. Də ju θɪŋk ɪʔ wʊd bi bɛst ɪf ɪŋlɪʃ wər rɪʔən fənɛdɪkli?

2. Have you ever noticed that Hebrew letters look like they would be good to eat? They would make a fine ingredient in a hearty winter stew.

Lecture Thirty-Two—Transcript
The Evolution of Writing

Imagine if language—human language—had only existed for 24 hours. If human language had only existed for 24 hours, then writing would have been invented around 11:10 pm; so that's how late writing comes in terms of human language. Language is, in essence, spoken. Even today, the vast majority of the world's languages are not written in any real way. There are only about 200 languages where there's really what you would call a literature and speakers are used to seeing them on the page. Otherwise somebody may have done a Bible translation, maybe there are some stories, maybe there are some signs, or something like that; but for the most part it's an oral language—it's spoken—and people are bemused to see it on the page. This means that writing is derived; you can call it marked, even. Writing is the secondary kind of expression of language; the real one is speaking. An analogy would be dance notation. You know there are ways of notating dances. You can do a Balanchine dance, even though he's not here to tell us how to do it—sometimes from one of his old grand ballerinas— but these things have been or are being written down, so that you can take what's on the page and dance from it. But none of us are under the impression that dance notation is dance; we know that that's just something on paper, not quite alive, a little bit artificial. The real thing is dancing.

In the same way, writing is not language; it's a representation on the page of language. As such it's actually not surprising that it took a while for it to emerge. For most of the existence of human language, all one did was what I'm doing: You just spoke; there was no such thing as scratching representations of it onto flat surfaces and passing them around; there was no need, and that didn't happen. As a result, the first known writing system for us comes along around 3500 B.C.E. in what is today Iraq and Iran. The kind of writing that it is, is called cuneiform, and it's pressed into clay. You can see an example of that here. Quite pretty, isn't it? That is cuneiform. As far as how that started, what we know is that there have been found little clay tokens that seem to signify various things. There's a correspondence between a lot of the little clay tokens that you could hold in your hand and early cuneiform writing. It seems that the original idea was here we have these clay tokens, which stand for things—which can count things or symbolize what should be inside of a container or something like that. Then someone had the idea of etching a representation of those little clay tokens into clay, rather than actually having to handle them themselves. Those clay tokens were found, for example, in Susa, in Iran. That's one of the former capitals, of a sort, of old Persia. Language change: Susa is now called Shush, and so we have a shift from the alveolar to alveopalatal. That is how it seems to have begun.

In the early cuneiform writing, what we see is literal pictures of things, as you can imagine if you were trying to come up with a way of writing, if you can put yourself into the head of somebody who's trying to come up with a way of writing for they very, very, very first time in human history that we know of. Very gradually, these representations evolved into abstract symbols for things that you wouldn't know what they were if you weren't told. For example, the symbol for bird: You see its development from early to later cuneiform. The first sign, it's quite clear that that's a bird. But then there are various distortions, where after awhile what you've got is a kind of glyph for a bird; that happened over time. Or in the same way, there was an original sign for woman, and it developed in this same abstract way. What you got was, on paper, a development of abstract signifiers for signifieds. It's not completely arbitrary for a drawing of a graceful flying thing to correspond to a bird, but it is quite abstract when it becomes something that you wouldn't know what it was unless you were told. And so that happened.

What also happened that mirrored the kind of thing that happens in spoken language change is that the literal symbols, which are called *pictographic*, often developed into abstract ones, and those are called *idiographic*; i.e., about ideas. For example, the symbol for *head* evolved into an abstract symbol, and the abstract symbol meant *front* as well as *head*. You had that same development from the concrete to the abstract that we've seen in grammaticalization in the development of cuneiform. You can see how the head is here. The head changes its orientation, and so pretty soon not only do you have a different kind of symbol, but it has a grammaticalized meaning in terms of *front* or *in front of*, in particular.

What I have left out so far in terms of cuneiform is, what language was this? I think we can guess that it wasn't English, because we were not in England. However, we do know what this language was: It was a language called Sumerian. Sumerian is a language with no known relatives, but we have a pretty good idea of what it was like because of these cuneiform representations. Cuneiform was later used to write many other languages in the area such as Akkadian, which was the leading Semitic language of its time—Semitic having Arabic and Hebrew in it—and later even Hittite, which was an early Indo-European language. But at first it is the writing system for the now-extinct language called Sumerian.

In Sumerian, the word for *arrow* was [ši]. There was a symbol for that, and you can see the relationship with arrow. Something started happening: The word for *life* also happened to be [ši], so there are situations like that in all languages. The symbol that had originally been used just for *arrow* started being used for *life* as well. Then the next mental step was to think that, whenever the syllable [ši] occurs within a word, that you might use this symbol here, originally only meaning *arrow* but then coming to mean *life*, then coming to mean the sequence of sounds [ši]. You had a situation where at first people were just drawing pictures of things, as you might imagine a child doing or somebody doing when they first develop a writing system. Then we have a new development where people start to see more abstract relationships between what they're putting on paper and the language that is actually spoken. In cuneiform this is about as far as it went, but more happened in the world of Egyptian hieroglyphics.

Hieroglyphics, in terms of the factoid, were long assumed to have developed about five centuries after cuneiforms, but there was a discovery in 1998 that suggests that hieroglyphics and cuneiforms may have developed around the same time. There is certainly no reason that they would not have. It used to be that cuneiforms were always discussed first because they were first; they may not have been. But in any case I'm adhering to tradition by starting with them.

Hieroglyphics were a different system, and hieroglyphics—despite the fact that they were used in Egypt—were not used to write Arabic, because Arabic had not spread to Egypt yet with the spreading of Islam; that was something that happened after A.D. 600. At this point the language spoken in Egypt was called Coptic. I'm calling Semitic a family, but actually Semitic is a subfamily within an actual family called Afro-Asiatic; Coptic is one of the other branches. That was the language that hieroglyphics were being used to write. We had the same kind of situation where you had pictograms being used as ideograms. Here we can see the pictogram for *hand*, and it's quite obvious why that's a hand because it's a picture of a hand. Then that also came to mean *power*, and so that's a more abstract meaning and an abstract representation as well. This is the sort of thing that happened both in cuneiform and in hieroglyphics; it seems to be natural to process writing systems that way over time.

Then pictograms were also used in hieroglyphics to indicate syllables—just like we saw with the [ši] in Sumerian—and then also consonants, just consonants alone. Here you see the symbol for *mouth*, which is *ro*. After a while, it also came to stand for just the *r* sound, as we might think, but not everybody thought that as immediately as we would; as we might think, they did that. What's interesting is that really you would think at this point that the people using this system would realize that if *ro* can mean just *r*, then why don't we make all of this simpler and start having a symbol correspond to a sound? They didn't do that. It's interesting how that kind of thing can happen throughout history, that we can look back and see people just on the verge of what would seem to be an obvious solution or an obvious development, and somehow it doesn't happen. It doesn't occur to them as quickly as we might think.

One of the weirdest things about early talkies—talking about like from 1927 to early '33—is that despite the fact that they are talkies, they are strangely silent movies in some ways, because you're not allowed to play music in the background. There is a sense that even though in silent films—silent films were never silent; you had at least somebody banging on the piano, and maybe an orchestra swelling underneath—and the idea was that there was this abstract music playing while people were walking down the street, but once you were in the world of the talkies, there was a sense that it would be unnatural to have background music. People are kind of walking around, and you can kind of hear their shoes clopping and their dresses kind of swishing, but there's no music to cover any of this up. If they want some music, then somebody will say, "Well, let's turn on the radio," and they'll go *click* and then this music comes on. But it has to be actual music; there's no such thing as just walking down the street with music. You're thinking, "If you guys were having music in your silent movies 10 minutes ago, why don't you have those same orchestras playing music now, like in our movies, and it enhances our movies so much?" They could have, but it just didn't occur to them.

In the same way in hieroglyphics, they could transcribe consonants, but we think, "So therefore it's alphabet time, folks," but not to them. They liked things the way they were. For example—it was kind of ingenious in its way—here is a branch (so there's this branch thing here), and then underneath it are the symbols for *h* and *t*. The word *hti'*—if that's how it sounded; we can only guess—that meant *wood*. It also happened to mean— *hti'*—*retreat* in Coptic. The way that they handled it was that you could have this branch, plus this *h* and this *t*, and if you put a knife next to it, then it meant *carve*; if you put a pair of these "boots are made for walking" legs next to it, then you could indicate *retreat*. All of that is very clever—a little clumsy, frankly. This was an elite activity. This was not the sort of thing that was taught to what was considered the masses; there was a class of scribes who were taught very carefully how to do this. This was not a very democratic writing system, but they had it.

As time went by, as you can imagine human beings would do—we've all seen hieroglyphics and they're pretty elaborate—if the occasion arises that you want to write something faster than what would be involved in scribing something on the side of some obelisk or something like that, maybe there's going to be some sort of shorthand, and there was; there was something called the *hieratic* script, and this was when you were writing hieroglyphics in ink on papyrus. This was for everyday use, and you can see that these are simplified hieroglyphics. That is the hieratic script.

It's interesting: What does all this stuff say? We certainly can't tell. It looks like a bunch of very pretty pictures with people holding their arms in peculiar ways, and there are cats and things. How do we figure out what this means? It was quite a challenge. It used to be—people were long aware that there was this writing in the remains of ancient Egypt—but it was thought that it must just be a bunch of pictures. That was not such an unreasonable thing to think; it was thought that people were kind of drawing pictures of stuff that happened, and it all made sense to them because they already knew what happened, and then we were kind of left with the challenge of figuring out what all these pictures were saying. Then there was also the sense, which still reigns with us today to an extent, that people in the past were somehow more simple-minded. It was assumed that there wasn't any kind of actual transcription of language going on.

It was only when the Rosetta Stone was discovered in 1799 that there started to be an idea that there might be something more going on and that one could try to do a decipherment—if one thought there was any deciphering to be done—and have some sort of intelligent and useful evidence to work with. The Rosetta Stone had the same text in Greek—and there was no problem figuring out what that meant—and then in hieroglyphic and hieratic. It's clear, when you see the Rosetta Stone—as you're seeing it now—you get the feeling that it's the same text in those three kinds of writing, so this gives you an opportunity to figure out what the hieroglyphics and the corresponding hieratics might be saying.

But imagine what the challenge of that would be. You've got these things there, but you don't know the writing system. Imagine, for example, if nobody knew Russian and nobody knew the Cyrillic alphabet. Here you've got, "I like five newspapers," and then underneath it is what you see here; that's the Russian for it. As it happens—here's another screen—here I can show you that what that says is, "Five newspapers to me please themselves." More specifically, it's "five of-newspapers." Remember that crazy thing from the de Saussure lecture where the genitive plural has no marker? This is that in use, to make it seem less abstract. "Five of-newspapers," and then the way that you say, "I like," is "to-me please-themselves"; and so, пять газет мне нравуются (*pyat' gazet mne nravuyutsya*). That's the way it works. To go back to the first screen of this, how are you going to figure out what's going on linguistically when you can't decode this alphabet and you don't know any Russian?

The way this ended up working was rather interesting, and it helped that there was a knowledge of Coptic. They did have a certain leg up. But figuring out what the correspondence was between that and this writing system was hardly easy. What happened was begun by Thomas Young. Thomas Young was a physicist and a physician. As one of these polymaths—in this time, when it was easier to know everything—this man didn't just know one kind of Aramaic; he knew two kinds of Aramaic. He knew a whole bunch of other languages; he apparently discovered the fact that our ocular perception is a matter of the combination of three basic colors; he identified various diseases; and he took it upon himself to figure out what was going on with the Rosetta Stone. He noticed that there were these, what's called cartouches. The cartouches are that there are certain words in hieroglyphics that are encased in these pretty little things that look kind of like St. Joseph's aspirin on a pedestal; so that was there. Looking at Greek—where, say for example, Ptolemy's name appeared—and then looking at the hieroglyphics in the cartouches, he made the guess that what's in the cartouches must correspond, for example, to the names of these Greek figures. He looked at, for example, this one, and he figured out that this was actually indicating Ptolemy. He figured it out phonetically; he could see which sounds corresponded, and that seemed to work for Greek names.

But Thomas Young—and he was a brilliant man—he stopped there. He assumed that the cartouches were the one place where there was any kind of transcription of language. He thought all the rest was still just kind of random pictures, and he figured that this was the way that they managed the challenge of writing a foreign name. It was kind of like the way talkies were, in '32 and '33: Some of them were moving along. You have this movie where there's, for our standard, mysteriously little music. You have people turning on the radio, and for some reason nobody does any announcing on the radio. It's just this music, but you have to at least pretend. Then at one point in, for example, *Dinner at Eight*—that's my favorite old movie; that's 1933—Millicent Jordan is having a party, and she has a string orchestra. She says, "Well, play boys"—that's Billie Burke— and so they start playing. Kind of mysteriously, for the next 15 minutes of the movie the string orchestra's songs always precisely parallel the emotional tone of whatever scene is going on. Somehow they know the conversations people are having in every room. They're almost to the point where they realize that a movie is supposed to have music, but still it has to be literal. Thomas Young was like the *Dinner at Eight*, and he just let it go.

Then we come to the prodigy, and that's the person who actually figured this out. That is Jean-François Champollion. He noticed something crucial: He noticed that there were cartouches in hieroglyphic writing that came from before Greco-Roman contact. So before the Egyptians had contact with the people across the pond, there were still cartouches. That meant that it couldn't be just that the cartouches were translations of names like Ptolemy.

One of those cartouches was this one; you can see this here. Champollion was one of these people: He also had taken it upon himself to master two varieties of Aramaic; he also had the Latin and the Greek; he had some Chinese, Persian, Sanskrit, you name it; and that included Coptic. He took a look at this thing. Thomas Young had already figured out that the two final syllables stood for [s]; he got that. Champollion knew Coptic, and he figured the leftmost symbol, because it looks like a sun—and you can see that here—in Coptic, sun is *ra*, and so this must be *ra*. He knew, OK, this must be *ra ... s*. Then he thought: "Who would that be? What Egyptian figure would it be where you'd have *ra ... s*?" He thought, "Oh, wait a minute, Rameses!" So *Ra-me-ses*. By deducing, he could figure out what the rest of the cartouche was saying, and so this meant something very important. It meant that there wasn't just some cute little code that they were using in cartouches to transcribe names of famous people from across the pond; it was actually a system that was in use for the entire writing system.

This meant that he had cracked the key. All of hieroglyphics were written in this rebus-like kind of patterning, where you have this combination of pictorial representations, and then syllabic representations, and then single consonant sounds. He cracked it. He fainted, incidentally. He fainted a lot. He was made a professor at 17; when he got the news, he fell down on the floor. When he first began to discover that there was something going on other than just big names from across the pond, he fainted and was in bed for days. When he cracked it, he fainted again. A very delicate man; brilliant people tend to be. In any case, this was the beginning of truly understanding hieroglyphics. Poor Jean-François died at 41, but people continued after him. Now we know what those hieroglyphics said.

But in terms of a writing system, if we're going to be a little ethnocentric—and let's harmlessly be a little ethnocentric for a bit—what about alphabet? When did what we think of as real writing come along? Of course that's not fair, because there were thriving writing systems that are not alphabetic in this world, such as the Chinese and Japanese one; but when did ours come along? We have a right to have some sort of self-interest. That is a continuation of this story. The Egyptians had their hieratic script. Another group in this story is the Phoenicians, and the Phoenicians were Semitic-language speakers, so we're in that family that is Arabic, Hebrew, and also Akkadian, the dead one. The Phoenicians are down southerly and southeasterly across the pond from Greece and Rome. They invented their alphabet around 900 B.C.E., maybe a couple centuries earlier. They derived it partly from Egyptian's hieratic script.

What they did was they translated the meaning of a symbol in Egyptian into Phoenician, and then they made that symbol stand for the first letter in that word. This was a massive revolution, because that's the beginning of getting toward what we call writing. You can see that happening here on the screen. This was a big idea. As far as we know, the idea of having symbols stand for the first letter of what they represented started as some kind of shorthand when there was a need for more writing in Egypt's growing army—Egypt had a growing army—but they did not take the ball and run with it. For Egypt, it was just kind of an eccentricity, something that you do on the fly. For the Phoenicians, they figured out, why don't we just have it be this way all the time?

The Phoenicians did not indicate, in their system, vowels. For them, they just used consonants, and there's a certain sense in that; it's perfectly legible that way. For them, *aleph*—which we take to mean *a*—actually indicated a glottal stop: [ʔ]. For them, [ʔ] was a real sound, so that's what it originally indicated. That kind of alphabet still works; Hebrew is partly that way. If we look on the screen now at some modern Israeli Hebrew, then we have לנו

בכל מכתב אתה מביא (*bakol mikhtav atah miveeya la chun*); that's "Each letter that you bring to us." Just look at the first two words; and so בכל מכתב (*bakol mikhtav*). The *kol* that I'm saying is not indicated here. What the first word says is *bkl*, and you just have to know what the vowels are. The second word is *mkhtv*, and one just has to know that it's *mikhtav*; those aren't indicated. You can indicate the vowels in various ways in this script; however, all of it is very much abbreviated compared to what we are used to. That is something that originally began when the Phoenicians created the first writing system where you had any kind of correspondence in a regular and universal way between symbols and sounds.

The Phoenicians passed this system along to the Greeks, and the Greeks adopted some of the signs to indicate vowels. You can see how in Greek, Phoenicians' *daleth*—which was a *door*—became Greek's delta. Here is where a true alphabet begins. This is the *King Kong* (I mean the movie). *King Kong* was one of the first movies where they gave up the idea that the music is coming from a string orchestra or a radio, and they just played some darn music and saw that it really enhanced things. If they're in the jungle, and there's this big rubber model of an ape chasing after you, where's the music going to be coming from? There's nowhere to plug in a radio, and they certainly didn't bring a string orchestra. They had to just give in, and that helped them to get the idea, and the next thing you know, by the mid-'30s they're actually playing some music in the movies. The Greeks were the equivalent.

Daleth has had a fate in various alphabets, and that's because the Phoenician alphabet traveled much further than Greece. It was the foundation of the writing systems now used for not only Hebrew but Arabic and languages as far afield from its origins as India and Southeast Asia and even Mongolia. It all starts with the Phoenicians. The reason that Phoenicians' writing system spread so fast is connected partly to the fact that it was relatively easy to learn. Learning how to scribe cuneiforms and hieroglyphics must have been a glorious nightmare, just as learning the Chinese writing system is today. No disrespect intended, but that's one knuckle-cracking way of writing. Whereas if you're just dealing with correspondence to sound, there is no language that has hundreds of thousands of sounds, and so you have a much easier system.

The Phoenicians were incredible travelers. They traveled throughout the Mediterranean, and there's evidence of them as far up northwest as Ireland. If you get a kick out of "who'd of thunk it" theories, there was recently discovered in some silt, way up as far as Denmark, shards of Phoenician pottery. We don't know yet whether the Phoenicians actually traveled all the way up that way, but it would not be utterly impossible in terms of folkloristic sources and in terms of their technology. It's been shown that with the technology available at the time, there were people who did sail equivalent distances and dealt with worse meteorological conditions. Maybe the Phoenicians got up there, but they definitely traveled far and wide. That strengthened their influence; if anybody's writing system was going to take fire, it was likely to be theirs.

In any case, having an alphabet at last was part of democratization in many areas. It helped to open up writing to a larger class of people, instead of it being a matter of a small scribal class transcribing for the purposes of business and for royal affairs. It's possible that if the only kind of writing system we still had was like hieroglyphics—such as the Chinese writing system—then developments in the world may have been different in terms of the development of a middle class, in terms of the spread of literacy; and so it was very important what the Phoenicians and the Greeks did.

In addition, it's only when there's a writing system and widespread literacy that a stage of the language is preserved on paper forever, and then as time goes on, people start comparing what's written with the way people talk and start having feelings about how language change is inappropriate, because there's a "real form" of the language. The sense that there's a real form of the language that's always just out of reach comes mostly from there being language down on the page. Small indigenous groups have little spats about what form is the right one to use, but not nearly as much as people in societies where there is widespread literacy in a language, and centuries' worth of representations of that language. Not only did the development of an alphabet have major social repercussions in the development of many countries in the world, but it had a lot to do with the development of the battle between descriptivists and prescriptivists that we discussed in the previous lectures.

Lecture Thirty-Three
Writing Systems

Scope: Writing is interesting not only in how it evolved but also in its worldwide variety. This lecture presents the Chinese, Japanese, Korean, and Arabic writing systems and describes the decoding of the extinct Greek writing system Linear B.

Outline

I. As we have seen, the alphabetic approach to writing was not immediately intuitive to humans, and even today nonalphabetic writing systems thrive around the world. In this lecture we will take a look at some writing systems that operate on principles quite different from our own.

II. Chinese is a system reminiscent of hieroglyphics and cuneiform. It is based on a combination of *logographic* and linguistic elements.

    A. The earliest known Chinese writing directly related to the modern system is divinations inscribed into ox scapulae and tortoise shells from about 1200 B.C.E., called the oracle bone script.

    B. This makes Chinese writing the oldest still in use (as opposed to the earliest known, which is Sumerian cuneiform).

    C. It is often thought that Chinese writing consists simply of *pictograms*, or of pictograms and *ideograms*.

    1. There are indeed such elements, such as these for *sun*, 日; *moon*, 月; and *mountain*, 山.

    2. However, these are only a sliver of the writing system. More often, the symbols are used in combinations, such as *sun* plus *moon* (日 plus 月) to mean *bright* (明) or *woman* plus *woman* (女 plus 女) to mean *quarrel*.

    D. Most often, however, the system is based on sound as well, like cuneiform and hieroglyphics.

    1. There are about 300 semantic *radicals* (200 in use today) used for common words like *person*, *water*, and *wood*.

    2. These are combined with *phonetic determinatives*, which represent how the word sounds.

3. For example, the word for *hand* is a semantic radical, and *shake* might be written by combining the semantic radical for *hand*, 扌, with a phonetic determinative, 敖 (*áo*), that represents how the word for *shake* sounds.

4. Such a written symbol would connote "the word having to do with hand that sounds like *áo*."

E. However, sound changes over time have made the correspondences inexact. Although in some instances all of the pictophonetic compounds for a given phonetic determinative continue to have the same sounds and differ only in tone, the relationships are often less regular and tidy.

F. Also, the relationship between the meaning of the semantic radical and the word created by combining it with a phonetic determinative is not always clear anymore, as in the word for *cat*, 猫, where the semantic radical 犭 once meant *worm* but now refers to all animals.

G. Basic literacy in Chinese means familiarity with about 2,000 characters; technically there are about 50,000.

H. One advantage is that the system can be used with all of the Chinese varieties. For example, recall the various words for *I* in Chinese. In all of these varieties, it is written as 我.

III. Chinese has influenced many other writing systems. One is Japanese, which combines Chinese symbols, *kanji*, with two *syllabaries*.

A. The *hiragana* is used to indicate grammatical material.

あいうえお

かきくけこ...

B. The *katakana* is used to transcribe foreign words.

アイウエオ

カキクケコ...

C. Here is Japanese for *Kellogg's breakfast*, with all three writing systems: ケロッグの朝飯.

D. Japanese also contains many Chinese words in its spoken language, which influences the writing system. For example, the Japanese word for *rain* is *ame*, and is written thus: 雨.

E. However, the word for *downpour* is *taiu*, a word from Chinese. *Taiu* is written as the symbol for *big* and the symbol for *rain*, thus: 大雨.

F. But this means that in this symbol, the *ame* kanji stands for the *-u* in *taiu*. Also, the first symbol is pronounced "*tai*" when used in words originally from Chinese but as "*ōkii*" in native Japanese words.

IV. Korean writing looks completely different from Chinese and Japanese.

    A. The Korean writing system (called *han'gŭl*) is based, like the Japanese hiragana and the katakana, on the syllable. *Bada* ("sea") is written ba-da: 바다.

    B. There are also symbols for consonants alone.
        1. *Balam* ("wind") is written ba-lam, 바람, where the little square, ㅁ, is just the consonant [m].
        2. The English word "hip-hop" might be written 힙합, where the ㅂ at the bottom is the consonant [p].

V. Arabic writing can look quite impenetrable, but it is actually quite systematic.

    A. The Arabic writing system is of a type called an *abjad*, where generally signs refer to consonants rather than vowels. Here is "he wrote," *katab* (going right to left):

كتب

    B. One is expected to know and fill in the vowel sounds.
        1. However, for long vowel sounds, there are letters to indicate them; for example, the *aa* sound is a stroke: ا
        2. Book is *kitaab*, where the stroke in the middle indicates the *aa* (long [a]) sound:

كتاب

    C. There are optional signs for short vowels, and even for omission of vowels (when a little circle is used), but these are mostly used in religious or highly explicit writing.

D. Arabic letters occur in different forms, depending on whether they are used alone, at the beginning of a word, in the middle, or at the end.

    1. For example, note how the letter for [b] (the symbol with a single dot at bottom) is different at the end of the previous two words, as opposed to in the middle of *Al 'Arabiyya* ("the Arabic language"):

ةيبرع لا

    2. The letter for the glottal stop, for instance, takes these forms:

alone	ع
first	ء
middle	ـمـ
end	ج

VI. Linear B, a precursor to the Greek alphabet, was deciphered in the 20th century.

    A. It used to be thought that what is described in the *Iliad* and the *Odyssey* were mythical events, but Heinrich Schliemann (1822–1890) discovered Troy near Turkey in the late 1800s.

    B. Sir Arthur Evans (1851–1941) wanted to know more of this period in Greek history, which would have been about 1500–1100 B.C.E. He found elaborate remains on Crete, including a script called Linear B.

    C. It was assumed that Linear B was a lost Cretan language, in part because the Minoan civilization looked more advanced than the Mycenaean, even when more Linear B was discovered in Greece itself. There were actually fierce academic debates over this.

    D. Brooklyn College classicist Alice Kober (1906–1950) theorized that the writing was syllabic, because alphabets tend to have 20–40 symbols and syllabaries 50–100; Linear B had 90.

    E. She also noted that many words formed triplets.

        1. This suggested that Linear B was an inflected language, and one could infer that the third syllables had the same consonant as in these hypothetical words:

            pasa**da**nu
            pasa**da**ni
            pasa**du**

2. She also noticed that where two words had the same ending but different third members, then this must mean different consonant/same vowel between equivalent syllables in the same word:

> pasa**d**anu
> hiru**w**anu

F. Then architect Michael Ventris (1922–1956) deduced that there must be signs for just vowels—and that you would logically find them only at the beginning of words.

1. He noticed three words that occurred often, including one beginning with a vowel. Amnisos was one important town in the area, and thus he deduced the symbols for *a*, *mi*, *ni*, *so*.

2. Then he noted that another word had the same *so*, and that the other signs had the same vowel (based on being third syllables in "triplet" words). Thus he knew that it was *o*, *o*, *so*, which fit with Knossos.

3. Finally, he could decipher that the words at the bottom of inventories were TOSO and TOSA, which were Greek for *total* (*tossos*, *tossa*). Linear B was a form of Greek.

G. Linear B represents Greek as it was spoken 500 years before classical Greek, and therefore it recorded an earlier stage of the language.

Essential Reading:

Sampson, *Writing Systems*.

Supplemental Reading:

Singh, *The Code Book*.

Questions to Consider:

1. The Chinese and Japanese writing systems are both beautiful and cumbersome. Students in China and Japan take longer to learn to read on a sophisticated level than do students in countries with alphabetic or syllabic writing systems, and the systems are massively difficult to master for adult foreigners. There have always been suggestions that the Chinese switch to a system based on the Roman alphabet, countered by an argument that the writing system is a cultural hallmark. What side of that argument would you fall on?

2. To the layman, written Chinese and Japanese tend to look similar. Based on this lecture, you might find them easier to distinguish. What would the most obvious feature be that would distinguish Japanese writing from Chinese writing?

Lecture Thirty-Three—Transcript
Writing Systems

One thing we saw in the last lecture is that the alphabetic approach to writing is not something that was immediately intuitive to human beings and that even today that is not the basis of great many writing systems in the world. In general, the development of writing systems and writing systems themselves are interesting not only in terms of the fact that they represent a clinal procession towards an alphabetic system but just in the sheer variety of them that are still thriving today, based on all sorts of perspectives, all sorts of linkages of writing with the sounds that come out of our mouths. In this lecture, we will take a look at some other writing systems around the world that operate on principles very different from what we naturally think of as ordinary in a society where our writing system happens to be an alphabet.

I think that, in terms of just appreciating diversity in terms of writing systems, that it certainly helps to have a sense of what's going on with the Chinese writing system. This is because it's very much around us in most places in the United States—it's increasingly around us in many ways—and it's easily misinterpreted what that system is. I think that there's a folk sense that we have an alphabet, and the Chinese system is based on pictures. Of course there is an element of truth in that, but pictures alone would really only take a writing system so far. We saw, for example, that that was not what was going on except in a very approximate sense with Egyptian hieroglyphics. It's the same way with the Chinese writing system. In fact, it's very reminiscent of hieroglyphics and cuneiform in that it's based on a combination of *logographic* symbols—and that is symbols that are based on pictures or that singly represent an idea—but then also linguistic elements. That is the Chinese writing system.

What is it when you see a sign written in Chinese? If you can tell that what the sign says is something like, "fresh fish," and you think, "Well, they've got something for *fresh* and something for *fish*," what about if you have occasion to look over someone's shoulder if you're on a subway—you can see what city I probably live in—and you see that they are reading a book in Chinese? It's not just "fresh fish" or "savings bank," but it's "brrrr," "brrrr," "brrrr." In other words, it's a whole writing system of a whole language. What is that stuff? What is on those pages?

The fact is that, as far as we know, the earliest Chinese writing that is identifiable as directly related to the Chinese writing system is actually written on turtle shells and shoulder bones from oxen; it's called the oracle bone script. It dates from about 1200 B.C.E. What it is, is divinations and things. This is not people writing novels; it's not people writing "savings bank" or anything like that; writing in this society was still something that was very ceremonial, very utilitarian, and very elite. On these shells and bones we see this system, which is clearly the direct precursor of Chinese of today. What that means is that the Chinese writing system is the oldest system still in use. As we've seen, there are writing systems that are documented from before that, such as the Sumerian and the hieroglyphic that we saw, but the oldest one that's still in use is good old Chinese.

When you look at these, or if you were a little boy in the early '70s and you were taken to Chinatown by your parents and they gave you a little book called something like *Chinese for Beginners* and you learned a few of the very basic symbols—that boy was me—it's easy to think that what the Chinese system is, is just a bunch of pictures. Of course to an extent it is. There are elements like that. Here is the one for *sun*, and that looks kind of like a sun: 日. Here is the one for *moon*: 月. They're very beautiful, aren't they? There's a calligraphy—that's not the subject of this lecture, but as you can see it's quite an art to render these, much more than our kind of boring Roman alphabet. Here is the symbol for *mountain*: 山; you can see how that was the mountain. So there's a relationship between these things and the things that they are. As you might predict, in earlier renditions of these symbols they looked more like what they are supposed to represent.

There are these pictograms; however, those pictograms are really only a sliver of the writing system. One estimate is four percent of the entire writing system. You can only get so far with that. For example, if you're going to use these pictures, or even pictures of ideas, what would your picture of *hint* be? *Hint*? It's a very simple thing, and we all know what a *hint* is. Draw one. How are you going to do that? Or how would you draw a *such*? You want to say, "such a good time," "such an ancient script," how do you draw *such*? Have you ever seen a *such* running around? You can't. Clearly there are more systems that we're going to need than that.

Very often there are combinations of symbols, as you might think. If you combine the one for *sun* and *moon*, then you get *bright*: 明. If you combine—and I did not make up this system; I know this is a little infelicitous—but if you combine a symbol for *woman*, 女, and another symbol for *woman*, then it means *quarrel*. Men fight, too, but that is what the symbol is. You have those combinations. But even that is only a sliver of the writing system, because even then, how would you combine two symbols to mean *such*? A *mountain* and a *bicycle*? Clearly we need more than that.

What the heart of the Chinese system is, it's something kind of like what we saw with the hieroglyphics: You combine two different kinds of symbols, or, in the terminology that's used, you combine two different kinds of *radicals*. There are about 300 of what are called semantic radicals; there are only really about 200 that are commonly used today. These semantic radicals, these symbols, are used for common words like *person*, *water*, or *wood*; then these are combined with what are called *phonetic determinatives*. What these represent—these symbols represent—is a sound, so there is representation of sound in this writing system. If you look here at the way *shake* is indicated, for example: How do you draw a *shake*? It's easy to imagine drawing Dagwood with some lines or something, but that's clearly very local to American, pop-drawing stuff. How do you draw *shake*?

As it happens, in Chinese there is a limited collection of syllables. It's all based on syllables that begin with a consonant, and for the most part a vowel is all you've got at the end. You might have an [m] or an [n], but that's about it. There's only so much you can do with that, and so one syllable can mean an awful lot of things. For example, the syllable *áo*, 敖, can mean all sorts of things in Chinese, and the difference is encoded partly by context but especially by tone.

Here we're talking about writing. In terms of tone and writing, there are many ways that you can approach it. The way to write *shake* is that you use the phonetic determinative that means *áo* in the mind of anybody who's reading in this system, and then you combine that with the semantic radical for *hand*: 扌. It means the word pronounced *áo* that has to do with hand, and that will take you to *shake*. That's how this sort of thing works in Chinese. Most of what you would see somebody reading—if you're looking over their shoulder on the subway and they're reading a whole novel—what it is, is those kinds of combinations.

All of that is very elegant, but it is also quite challenging in that Chinese, like any language, has changed over time, and so the correspondences are inexact. There's an inherent arbitrariness; for example, *áo* and then a *hand*, and it doesn't necessarily mean *shaking*. Why does the hand shake? There are reasons hands might shake, but lots of things shake. It would work just as well if maybe it were a *leaf*, but it doesn't happen to be a leaf; you just happen to know.

Then also sound change has made it a little messier. If we look in this chart at column A, and we see what happens to the phonetic symbol for *áo* and how you can show which *áo* is meant by using different semantic radicals, you see that if we put it into this chart—which is already simplifying things a bit—that it all looks very tidy. But then, if we swoop over to column D and we illuminate it like this, we can see that things are really messier, actually, most of the time. Here we have a phonetic determinative, which is *fŭ*. We can see that if you use the *fŭ* that has to do with *wood*—and here's your semantic radical for wood: 木—then you get the word for *trellis*. Notice that it's not *log* or *ski* or something like that, but still, *trellis*; it makes a certain sense. But then, when you've got the phonetic determinative for *fŭ* and you combine it with *hand* (扌), it means *catch*, and that's good, but the word now is actually pronounced "boo." Or if you have the word pronounced "foo" that has to do with *water* (氵), that's how they write *creek*, but the word today is not pronounced "foo," it's pronounced "poo," and so on.

This sort of thing gets worse and worse and worse, and so there's an awful lot of things in the Chinese writing system that you have to know what is on the page is best described as a guide to what is actually being communicated. There are all sorts of things, like for example this is the symbol for *cat*, 猫, and the semantic radical is the one used for *animal*: 犭. But that semantic radical actually means *worm*, and so the sign for *cat* has to do with a *worm*. A cat's not a worm. What's cute about the sign for *cat*, though, is that it's pronounced "mao," and that sounds kind of like "meow." I'll bet there's a reason for that.

In any case, basic literacy in Chinese means that you have to know about 2,000 characters. There are technically about 50,000 of them, but of course that's getting into the very scholarly and/or poetic registers. But one advantage of the Chinese writing system is that because of the way it's structured, it can be used for all of the Chinese varieties. Remember, we had a lecture where we talked about how the word for *I* is very different in all of the different varieties of Chinese, which are really separate languages and languages with often highly divergent dialects. You look at all of these different words for *I* that you will find all over China; all of them can be written everywhere in China with this symbol: 我. This is the symbol for *wo* ([uo]) in Mandarin; this is the symbol for *ngo* ([ŋo]) in Cantonese. This is the symbol for *I*, and that can be used across that great land.

That's how the Chinese system works. It's a marvelous mess, and I mean both of those words. It's a mess; I think most Chinese people would agree. It is also marvelous. It's a thing of great beauty; if you master it, which I have not, you have really accomplished quite a bit. It's wonderful to draw. It's being compelling in that way has meant that it has actually affected the writing systems of many other places. One of them is Japan. The Japanese writing system—talk about a marvelous mess—is a glorious nightmare. It is generally agreed to be one of the most complex—if not the most complex— writing systems in human civilization. It combines Chinese symbols, which in Japanese are called *kanji*, with not one but two other writing systems used alongside of it. You've got the Chinese symbols, and that's why Japanese looks kind of like Chinese to us. But if you look over somebody's shoulder and saw "brrrr," "brrrr," "brrrr" and you see that, the way I do it is that you see that it's not as thick as Chinese. It seems like they're not all pictures, and you see this other stuff in it; that's when you know that the person is reading in Japanese. It's because there are these two other systems. Both of them are *syllabaries*. They are not alphabetic systems; they indicate by syllable. One of them is called the *hiragana*, and it's used to indicate grammatical material. In this course you know what the difference is: There are content words, and then there is grammatical material. For example *walk*, that's content. *Walked*? Well, the *-ed*, that is a grammatical ending. That sort of thing in Japanese is indicated not with pictures, not with logograms; that is indicated with the *hiragana* syllabary.

For example, our stereotypic Japanese sentence that we've used, *Pam bought the book in Tokyo* (*Pam wa Tokyo ni hon o katta*): The *-ta*, for example, is their version of the *-ed* ending. *Bought* is *katta*. The *-ta* is indicated with the hiragana, even though there is a nice Chinese-derived kanji symbol for *buy*. That's the hiragana.

Then there's another syllabary—a whole different syllabary; a whole different set of symbols—called the *katakana*, and that's used to transcribe foreign words. You can see the katakana here, and they would use this to write things like—and now anything I think of ends up dating the course— so I'll just say, "Superman." *Superman* would be written in katakana. Or let's date the course: Gerald Ford, when they were going to write about him, he was written about in katakana, because there's no kanji; there's no Chinese symbol for *Gerald Ford*. You have these three different systems all working together. It's a marvelous thing that Japanese is read by people very casually.

For example, this is Japanese for *Kellogg's breakfast*. *Kellogg's* is of course a foreign word, and so that is written in the katakana. These symbols are ケロッグ, "keh-loo-guh-guh," and so you have a double *g*, and so that's in there, too. That's in the katakana. Then this little thing that looks kind of like—well it doesn't look like anything—but see this thing that's being highlighted, の, that is in hiragana because that's grammatical. It's a *Kellogg's breakfast*; well, you put it that way in Japanese, too, and so the *'s* ending—although for them it's the separate word *no*—Kellogg *no*, that *no* is a piece of grammar—that's written in hiragana. These symbols are not all qualitatively the same; even right here we've got two different writing systems. Then for *breakfast* you've got *asa gohan*, 朝飯, and these, these look busier; these are originally from Chinese. The first one is *asa*, and that's *morning*, and you can see that there's a kind of a sun in it. Then there's *gohan*, and if you think that this little thing here looks kind of like a rice cooker, then that can help your memory because actually this does mean *rice*. "Morning rice" is how you say, "breakfast," because obviously there is a certain rice-ness about the culture. Here you have the katakana and the hiragana and the kanji, all used just in some tacky ad, just to say, "Kellogg's breakfast." You need all of that stuff.

Japanese has got these three different systems. Then in addition there is the Chinese issue and pronunciation. What I mean by that is that in the Japanese language, about 60 percent of the vocabulary is originally from Chinese due to previous relationship. That is why there are all these kanji in the Japanese system. It ends up creating problems like this: Here is the Japanese symbol for *rain*: 雨. Here it is; it's my favorite one. See how it actually is rain being seen through the windows? Isn't that pretty? It's like you're inside. That is pronounced "ame"; that's the Japanese version. If you want to write *downpour*, then you end up having this symbol: 大雨. You see that the *rain* is still there, and then that first symbol means *big*. However, the problem is that this time—when we're looking at it in this particular way—it has to be pronounced in the Chinese way; that's just the way it is. The Chinese way to pronounce this *rain* symbol happens to be "-u." This thing in the front means *big*. There's a Japanese word for *big*— *ōkii*—but in Chinese it's pronounced "tai"; in Japanese, therefore, you pronounce this "taiu"; there's no "ame" at all. The symbols are recognizable, but this rainy-day window has a whole different pronunciation when it's in one of the Chinese pronunciation words. These are things that you just have to know, and nevertheless there are people in Japan reading all the time under no impression that there is anything really impressive about what they're doing. But there very much is; it is really something to me that there's enough diversity in human nature that this can be a writing system that doesn't hurt people. That's Japanese.

If I mention the Japanese writing system, I know what you're wondering. I know what the natural sequence of these things is, and we know our geography, so let us go across the sea, and now we're in Korea. They do a whole different thing with their writing system. It's called *han'gŭl*, and it is syllabically based as well. If you see Korean, and if you want to know the difference between Chinese, Japanese, and Korean—and I think a modern American citizen might want to—Chinese looks real busy; Japanese has these kind of simpler syllabary symbols in it; Korean is completely different. Korean has the look that you see here. What you see here is *bada*, 바다, and that means *sea*. You have a symbol for the syllable *ba*, 바, and a symbol for the syllable *da*, 다. Of course you can have symbols for consonants independently by themselves. With *wind* you've got *balam*, 바람, and you see that you have *la* up top, 라, and then we've got this little square in here, ㅁ, and that means [m]; and so you've got these two syllables.

Based on this principle, you could write "hip-hop." I don't think they do— well, maybe they do. If you were going to do it, you would do it this way, where you have *hee* (히), *p* (ㅂ), *hah* (하), *p* (ㅂ) in these two kind of squares here: 힙합. Of course in the way the alphabet is written, you don't have these squares, but what you have is these signs for different syllables. That's how the Korean writing system works. Chinese is Chinese; Japanese is the one with three systems all working together; and then Korean is a whole different kind of symbol. Those are not kanji; those are not hiragana or katakana.

Another writing system is the Arabic one. This is also one that we see around us all of the time. It can look quite impenetrable, and it's not. Not only is it beautiful, but it's actually quite systematic. It's relatively easy to understand, once you wrap your mind around certain differences that we don't necessarily expect. The Arabic writing system is one that has been for about the past 12 years called an *abjad*, and that means that the signs generally refer to consonants rather than vowels. Abjad comes from the fact that while we talk about our ABCs and the alphabet, the *a, b, j, d* is the way that you do the Arabic alphabet in some situations; and so abjad. And so,

"He wrote" in Arabic is *katab*. You see this [k] (ك), [t] (ت), [b] (ب) (going right to left, كتب), and you just have to know that there is this [a], [a].

There are ways of indicating long vowels; in Arabic there are long and short vowels, and this is an important distinction. For example, the word for *book* is *kitaab*, with a long [a]. Here is how that's indicated (ا), and you can see that there is, in addition to the [k], [t], and the [b], in between the [t] and the [b] you've got this indication which is for [a]: كتاب. That's only for long [a], though. As far as the short vowels, there are symbols. That is mainly used in religious or highly explicit writing. In general, you are just supposed to know when it comes to the short vowels. That works; that seems perfectly natural to Arabic speakers. And it is; it's just a different way of indicating things than the alphabetic system.

What challenges some people about learning the Arabic writing system is that the letters occur in different forms depending on whether they are in isolation, whether they're at the beginning of the word, whether they're at the end of it, or whether they're in the middle. You can look at how there is this letter for [b] at the end of the previous two words, and so you see this sort of … I guess you'd call it a bathtub with a dot under it. But then here's how you write *the Arabic language*, and so *Al 'Arabiyya*, العربية, and you see that where the [b] is supposed to be, it's a different kind of shape: ب. So when many people talk about Arabic being hard, it's because the layman often thinks of the writing as the language, and what does throw people at the beginning is these different forms of the letters. It can get rather noisome to the foreigner. For example, here, for the glottal stop—which is indicated in Arabic in a way that it isn't in English, like notice what I just said, "which is indicated"; I didn't say, "whichisiiindicated"; I said, "which is indicated"; I actually did the glottal stop—well, in Arabic you actually have to indicate that in the writing. If it's alone, it looks like this: ع. If it's first, then it looks like this: ع. Completely different. If it's in the middle then—oh Lord—you've got that: ـه. And if it's at the end then, well, it's completely different: ع. You do have to master that. It's not as hard as it looks, though. Once you have mastered that, Arabic writing system has a very pleasing grace to it. Especially if you're coming to it as something exotic from our alphabetic system, as I'm sure you all know, it also can be quite beautiful. It's worth learning how to read it. It's all around us these days, and to actually look at it written and have those words say something instead of it looking like *awooawooawah*, which is what it does look like to us, is a very gratifying experience.

In any case, we have seen that it can be very difficult to untangle what a nonalphabetic writing system is, and we've seen what went into figuring out how hieroglyphics were represented to the language. However, even a syllabary can be difficult to figure out. For example, the decipherment of what's called Linear B, which was found on Crete, was an interesting story. It used to be thought—and this is by perfectly sophisticated people—that if you were reading the *Iliad* or the *Odyssey*, that these were just mythical events, that none of this stuff ever happened. Just like hieroglyphics were thought to be just kind of impressionistic pictures of thoughts and that's it, it was thought that people had made up these stories, but it had nothing to do with actual life. But Heinrich Schliemann found in the 1800s that there were remains on Troy, near Turkey, which actually indicated these kinds of events, and also in the Mycenaean region in Greece. Sir Arthur Evans, who was a British archeologist, picked up this ball and ran with it. He wanted to know more about these things happening in Greece. This would have been between about 1500 and 1100 B.C.E. He concentrated on Crete, and what he found was that there were remains of a Greek civilization, the Mycenaean civilization, but if you dug—literally dug—then you found that there were obvious remains of a different, and in many ways more advanced, civilization that is known as the Minoan civilization.

One of the traits of these Minoan remains was these tablets, and here was this script, and there it was. Linear B, it came to be called. The first thought was that Linear B was some lost Cretan language. They even found remains of it over in Greece later, too, but it was still thought that this was some sort of Cretan language, and it was thought that it must have reflected that language because the Minoan civilization looked in many ways more advanced than the Mycenaean. There were big debates over this.

Then people started looking at Linear B, and they started realizing that it might be possible to interpret what it actually said. There was some interesting, ingenious work done. For example, Alice Kober was a Brooklyn College classicist, and that name sounds like what it was. If your name was Alice Kober, *k-o-b-e-r*, you were a Brooklyn College classicist in the 1930s and '40s, which is what she was. She thought about the fact that an alphabet tends to have, say, 20–40 symbols; for example, in English that's the way it is. If you are a syllabary—and of course many syllabaries were known even then just like they are now—then chances are that you have 50–100 symbols. Linear B had 90. Alice Kober thought, "Well, maybe this a syllabary, and how are we going to figure out what these words mean?"

She noticed that you could see triplets of words that were clearly related, like up here on the screen (see outline, VI.E). If you're seeing Linear B, and you don't know what it indicates, you do see that there's some sort of relationship here. One of those symbols does look like a daiquiri, and we now know that it was actually the indication of *ki*—the syllable *ki*—but yes, it looks like a daiquiri. Anyway, there are these triplets.

One thing that Alice Kober came up with—and this was really something, given that she went from nothing—she figured that it must be that this is a language with endings. Her idea was suppose, for example, that it was something like this, and so you have *pasadanu*, *pasadani*, *pasadu*. All endings don't have to be the same length, but she thought if that's true then we know that the third member in these triplets must begin with the same consonant. That's something, certainly, from nothing. Then she noticed that there are these other cases where you have what looks like it would be the same ending, but then the third members are different. For example, you would see triplets like this. She thought, "Maybe that means that it's the same endings, but that then this third syllable begins with a different consonant than in the set of first triplets." You might have *pasadanu*, and then *hiruwanu*; like that. She came up with this insight that that must be the sort of thing that's going on. She didn't know what the syllables were, and unfortunately before she could figure it out—and I'm pretty sure that she would have figured it out—she was carried away from us by a disease. It stopped there for a bit.

But then there was Michael Ventris; he was a young architect. If you were a young architect in the middle of the 20th century, then your name definitely was going to be Michael Ventris. You can see pictures of him; he looked kind of glamorous. He looks like he was going to play James Bond, if he had lived so long. (That was just some foreshadowing.) In any case, he thought, "If this is a syllabary, then there must be signs for just vowels." There's no language where everything is a consonant and a vowel; in any language, you're going to have syllables like [a], [e], [i], [o], [u] all alone as well. He figured—and this was good too; he was not just an empty pretty face—he figured you would find those at the beginning of a word. It's probably going to be something like *okahan*—I'm just making up that word.

He looked around and he saw one word that seemed to come up again and again, and he thought, "What is an important place in the area that might come up again and again and again?" There are only so many. He thought, "What about Amnisos? That's one place, and that begins with a vowel." He thought, "If this spelled Amnisos, then this symbol would be *a, mi, ni, so*—something like that." Then he noticed that there was another word that had this same symbol that he was thinking might mean *so*, and then, using the Alice Kober-style deduction, he figured out that there were some other signs that would have the same vowel in them—based on this same deduction about what might endings be—and so he thought, "Then this word is going to be *o, o, so*." What does that fit? There was the city Knossos, and so he decided this must be *ko, no, so*. He thought, "If that's what those mean, then what's this little word that you always see at the bottom of the tablets?" There was *toso, tosa*; those mean *total* in Greek. Michael Ventris had figured out that this Linear B script was not decoration and not some strangely missing Cretan tongue but that it actually was the Greek language. Specifically, it was Greek 500 years before the previously earliest known stage of Greek, our familiar classical Greek that Homer wrote in. Michael Ventris figured this out and died in a car accident.

That brings us to the end of this lecture. In the next lecture, we will take a look at a language which is effectively unwritten, and we will see what it's like to actually be a linguist.

Lecture Thirty-Four
Doing Linguistics—With a Head Start

Scope: This lecture brings the viewer into what it is to actually be a linguist. Namely, I will share a few of the things I have discovered about the grammar of a hybrid between English, Portuguese, and African languages, showing that what linguistics is about is something more than exploring what I just wrote.

Outline

I. Saramaccan is a creole language spoken in the inland region of the South American country of Suriname.

   A. Saramaccan developed among slaves who escaped from plantations and settled in the rainforest interior.

   B. The creole developed among slaves who were exposed to both English and Portuguese. Therefore, its core words are from English, and it has many words from Portuguese because there were Portuguese plantation owners as well.

   C. The Dutch took over Suriname in 1667, and so Saramaccan also has Dutch words.

   D. Its grammar is based partly on English and partly on the African language the most slaves spoke natively, Fongbe, spoken in Togo and Benin.

   E. Saramaccan is neither Fongbe with European words nor a "baby English"; it is a hybrid language with a complex grammar of its own.

   F. I have written a grammatical description of Saramaccan. In this lecture I will show you a few things about the language that demonstrate what linguistics actual do.

II. A language will challenge you to figure out the order underneath what looks like chaos.

   A. The Saramaccan word for *eat* is *njã*.

> *Mi njã di fuuta.*
> I eat the fruit.

B. However, there is an odd quirk: Whenever the word for *it* comes after *njā̆*, there is suddenly an odd little *m*:

> *Mi njā̆mɛ̃.*
> I ate it.

C. To a linguist, this *m* is not just "there." Rather, we can imagine that the "real" situation is *Mi njā̆ ɛ̃* and that the inserted *m* is something "derived." In the conception we have learned in this course, there is an underlying form and a surface form: /njā̆ ɛ̃/ became [njā̆mɛ̃], *eat it.*

D. However, the linguist wants to know the reason for this. It turns out that the reason in this case gives us a clue to the past. The *m* has something in common with the vowel in *njā̆*: *m* is a nasal sound and *ā̆* is a nasalized vowel.

E. Often when something doesn't make sense in a language, it's because something is being dragged along from the past. One way we can look at this *m* is that *njā̆mɛ̃* reflects something old in Saramaccan. For example, we could suppose that the word was once *njam.*

F. In this case, we would assume that what began as *njam* became *njā̆* over time as the *a* assimilated to the nasal quality of the *m* and the *m* disappeared. This is common in languages: Latin has *bonum*, French has *bon* ([bɔ̃]).

G. This *njā̆mɛ̃* teaches us, then, that even though the word is pronounced [njā̆] phonetically, that underlyingly, phonemically, it is /njam/, even though you would never know this from the way it usually pronounced—except when that *it* word follows it.

H. There is one more word in Saramaccan that has the same property, the word for *beat*, *fɔ̃*. Followed by the *it* word, that *m* appears: /fɔ̃ ɛ̃/ becomes [fɔ̃mɛ̃], *beat it.* Thus underlying the word is [fom].

I. If this is true, then we would expect that in earlier documents of Saramaccan, we would find these forms.
  1. And we do. Here in a Saramaccan-German dictionary compiled by missionaries in 1779, we find this entry: *fumm* schlagen, stampfen
  2. Moreover, the word for *eat* is *njam* in Jamaican patois and many other related English creoles of the Caribbean.

3. In Saramaccan, the [m] has dropped off and left behind a *tincture* of itself.

J. This is part of what it means to document the phonology of Saramaccan. What we hear or see is not always what is going on underneath, and the difference is often a clue to history.

III. Creole languages like Saramaccan begin when slaves need a way to express themselves very quickly, and they become real languages rather quickly.

A. In the early 1600s there was no such thing as Saramaccan or any precursor.

B. Yet by about 1670, that language existed in its full form.

IV. To the extent that Saramaccan has been documented (sparsely but indicatively), we can actually see grammar developing.

A. Recall how in a previous lecture we saw a new information marker in Saramaccan, *nɔ́ɔ*. How do we know it's a new information marker?

B. In an exchange I had with one of the Saramaccan speakers I work with, he said that he would be waiting for my call, using *nɔ́ɔ*:

> *A   búnu.* **Nɔ́ɔ**   *mi   ó   tá   háika   i.*
> it   good   I   will be   listen   you
>
> *Good. So I'll be listening for you* (i.e., *waiting for your answer*).

    1. But later in the conversation, basically repeating that, he did not use *nɔ́ɔ*:

> *A búnu, mi ó   tá háika dí kái fii   tidé   néti.*
> it good I   will be listen the call yours today night
>
> *Good, I'll be listening* (*waiting*) *for your call tonight.*

    2. This was because the first time he said it, his waiting for my call was new information. The second time, it wasn't.

C. *Nɔ́ɔ* is not, as it is reasonable to suppose, just the word for *now*. For one, the actual word for *now* in Saramaccan is *nɔ́unɔ́u*.

D. In addition, the *now* translation doesn't work in the way *nɔ́ɔ* is typically used. In lecture we listen to a segment of a folktale in Saramaccan, where *nɔ́ɔ* is used whenever information is new.

E. The question is where this word came from, if Saramaccan's words are based mostly on English.

    1. One way to find out is to see what the equivalent word looks like in a closely related language.

    2. Sranan is another Suriname creole, the modern descendant of the English creole that was part of the mix that made Saramaccan.

    3. In Sranan, where Saramaccan uses *nɔ́ɔ*, Sranan uses *nomo*.

F. *Nomo* looks like it started as *no more*, and this is confirmed in C. L. Schumann's 18th-century documentation of Sranan:

No	**morro**	*hulanga*	*tem*	*ju sa*	*libi*	*dea*?
no	more	how-long	time	you	live	there?

So how long are you going to live hereabouts?

G. Why would *no more* become a pragmatic marker of new information? In fact, there is something similar in modern English, in the way *no* is used in casual conversation to start a new topic. I once had an exchange that went like this:

    J: So you spent six years in New York, nine in L.A., and then … Toledo.

    T: (laughter) No, it was really hard at first, but after a while the low cost of living starts to become really attractive.

H. The fate of *no more* in Saramaccan is a prime demonstration of how grammaticalization creates language, and even how grammaticalization must have taken human language from simple words for things and concepts to having words to indicate new information, interrogation, and more.

V. A final aspect of Saramaccan grammar that can give us a sense of letting the language speak for itself is the way that Saramaccan uses its word for *throw*, which is *túwɛ*:

Mi	*túwɛ*	*di*	*súndju*.
I	throw	DEF	dirt

I threw the dirty thing.

A. It can be used in a serial construction:

A	*ba*	*pɔtɔpɔtɔ*	*túwɛ*	*a*	*wáta*.
he	carry	mud	throw	LOC	water

He carried mud to the water (and threw it in).

B. However, its usage often seems to strain logic. For example, do you precisely throw someone when you push them down?

> *Kobí tɔ́tɔ   dí   wómi túwɛ.*
> Kobi push DEF man throw
>
> *Kobi pushed the man down.*

C. Then *throw* seems even less intuitive in sentences involving cutting down trees or shooting an animal:

> *A   kóti dí   páu   túwɛ.*
> he cut   DEF tree throw
>
> *He cut the tree down.*

> *Mi súti dí   píngo túwɛ.*
> I   shoot DEF pig   throw
>
> *I shot the pig (and hit him).*

D. Even stranger are cases in which throw is used serially with a verb that itself has a meaning close to that of throw:

> *Vínde ɛ̃ túwɛ   gó naandɛ́.*
> throw it throw go there
>
> *Throw it over (onto) there.*

E. The verb's actual function is to mark the end of a trajectory that an object has traveled. The verb *throw* has grammaticalized so far from its original meaning that it is barely recognizable.

1. I asked one of my informants whether this following sentence meant that he actually threw the dog; it didn't:

> *Mi tɔ́tɔ dí   dágu túwɛ a   dí wáta.*
> I   push the dog throw in the water.
>
> *I pushed the dog into the water.*

2. This means that two of the sentences we already saw "translate" differently than they look:

> *A   ba   pɔtɔpɔtɔ túwɛ   a   wáta.*
> he carry mud   throw LOC water
>
> *He carried mud to the water (and threw it in).*

> *Kobí tɔ́tɔ dí   wómi   túwɛ.*
> Kobi push DEF man   throw
>
> *Kobi pushed the man down.*

F. The closest English equivalent is the difference between *I pushed the dog in the water* (which could mean that you did the pushing while you and the dog were both in the water) and *I pushed the dog into the water*. However, in English marking that difference is highly optional.

G. In a very short time, Saramaccan has developed grammatical distinctions that we would not think of.

Supplemental Reading:

McWhorter and Good, *Saramaccan Grammar*.

Questions to Consider:

1. Saramaccan speakers now say, "*nɔ́ɔ*" to introduce new information. They once said, "*nɔ́ɔmɔ*." The standard pronunciation of *Manhattan* is [mænhaʔən]. Yet many pronounce it as [mæ̃hã̃ʔæ̃]. If it's just no big thing that standard Saramaccan for new information is *nɔ́ɔ*, then why it is it worthy of notice that so many people say [mæ̃hã̃ʔæ̃]?

Lecture Thirty-Four—Transcript
Doing Linguistics—With a Head Start

In this lecture and the next one, I'd like to give you a taste of what it is that many linguists actually do. What is it to create a grammatical description of a language? How was it that all of these sentence structures and grammatical features that I've been throwing at you were discovered? What is the process? I think a useful language to give you your first taste of that in is a language I've referred to a fair amount in the course, which is called Saramaccan. Saramaccan is spoken in the South American country of Suriname, and you can see it here on the map. It's spoken in the interior. That is away from the coast; that is for our purposes southward. It was developed by slaves—African slaves—who had been brought to Suriname to plantations that were out on the coast, and they escaped into the interior, and their descendants are still living there today.

The language of the plantations that the first slaves brought to Suriname were exposed to was English. There was a protolanguage that developed among the slaves there. The core of Saramaccan's vocabulary is derived from English. There were also Portuguese plantations in Suriname, and the people who created the Saramaccan language were actually from those plantations, although they used the protolanguage as a basis; and so there also are a lot of Portuguese-derived words in the language. Then the language's grammar is very much based upon a language called Fongbe, which is spoken today in Togo and Benin in West Africa. Grammatically, the language is quite different from English or Portuguese, but its vocabulary is mostly—of course, there are many African words in it—but most of the vocabulary is derived from English and Portuguese.

As a result of that history, Saramaccan is a language where at least the words will often look rather familiar to us, and so we can just look at what's going on with the grammar. It's a way of getting your feet wet. A language that develops like Saramaccan did is called a creole language; it's a hybrid language. As we'll see, it's also a language that had to start from something very basic and become the very unbasic thing that an actual spoken language that people live in is. Saramaccan is not "baby English" or baby anything else; it's got a grammar of its own. I have written a grammatical description of Saramaccan. A colleague of mine did the phonology, and I did the rest, and so I'll show you what linguists do, and along the way you'll see a little bit of what I have done.

We're just going to look at a few of the features of Saramaccan, this being a language which I presume very few of you are native to. This is what it means to do a grammatical description. This is how a language will challenge you, and give you the task of trying to figure out what the order is underneath what looks like chaos. For example, in Saramaccan, the word for *to eat* is *njă*—that's with a nasal vowel. That word happens to be derived from African languages. If you want to say, "I ate the fruit" or "I eat the fruit," then you have this sentence here: *Mi njă di fuuta*. See what I mean about how these words are relatively recognizable? *Mi* means *I*—I don't think that's such a stretch—then *di* is *the*; *fuuta* is *fruit*. The phonology is different—many adaptations have happened—but these are words that an English speaker can wrap their head around. And so, *eat*: *Mi njă di fuuta*.

That *njă* seems OK—that's what the word is—but there's this strange quirk, which is that if you say, "eat it," and you use the word *it*, which is *ɛ̃*, suddenly there's this little [m]. If you say, "I eat it," then you say, "*Mi njằmɛ̃*"; you don't say, "*Mi njă ɛ̃*"—which would seem to be what you say—you say, "*Mi njằmɛ̃*."

You don't just look at that [m] and say, "Well, there it is." In this language when you put *it* after the word *eat*, there's an [m]. Why? One always asks, "Why?" One of my advisors had *why* in big letters up on the blackboard in his office all the time. The question is, is there a reason for this? Is it really just an accident? I mean, there are accidents, but why would that be? Might that not tell us something that might be interesting?

If you are putting on your linguist hat, then you look at that *njằmɛ̃* and you start thinking about this basic difference between the underlying and the surface. We can sense that on some level it should be *mi njă ɛ̃*. What in the world is that [m] doing in there? It looks like phonemically it's /njă ɛ̃/ > [njằmɛ̃], so see that there, and remember our formalism: You use slashes for phonemic representations; then in the brackets is what comes out on the surface, the phonetic representation, and suddenly it's [njằmɛ̃].

What's going on there? You take a look at it. It used to be you would write it down in a pad; nowadays I guess people are doing it on their laptops. But you look at it and you think, "This [m] has something in common with the vowel that comes before it, because the vowel is nasalized: [ằ]." We know that [m] is not just the letter that comes after *l* and before *n*; we know that [m] is a nasal consonant, a bilabial nasal consonant. There's something going on here. Then we might recall that when something doesn't make sense in a language, often it's because something is being dragged along from the past. For example, remember our question, "Where's Ruth?" in terms of the fact that there's *ruthless*, but there's no *ruth*? There did used to be a word *ruth*; and so the fact that now we have this *ruthless* and no word *ruth* is an accident. In the same way, if we look at [m] being a nasal consonant and [ã] being a nasal vowel, there might be a reason. Something might be going on; something might be being dragged along from the past.

That's when we think about the assimilation that we saw as a normal process of historical change of the diachronic of a language. For example, let's imagine that there was an original situation where it was just an ordinary vanilla vowel like [a] and it was followed by this consonant [m]. Let's say that something happens that happens all the time, which is that final sounds often drop out. For example, think of how we spell *name*, and then think of how we say it. Did you hear me pronounce an *e*? The *e* is long gone. That's because these things go away.

Suppose we say that the [m] fell away, as final sounds tend to do, but let's imagine that it left behind a calling card or a footprint. Let's say that [m] smelled bad, and it left behind its odor. If it did that, then what it would leave behind is nasality. What started out as *njam*, becomes *njã*. The [m] is gone, but it's still got that nasal-ness. We can even cheat; we know that happens in language change all the time. The word for *good* in Latin was *bonum*; now the word for *good* in French is *bon*. If you've taken French, you know there's this *n* written, but did you say [bɔn]? No, you use the [n], actually, when you're pronouncing the feminine form: *bonne*. There's an [n], but with the masculine form—[bɔ̃]—it's really just a nasalized, open (i.e., lax) *o* sound.

That sort of thing happens. It's not that there's something weird about French; it looks like that probably happened in Saramaccan as well. What this means is that even though we are pronouncing this word [njã] on the surface, it seems like actually underlyingly, even when it's by itself, there's this /m/. Phonemically it's /njam/ and then phonetically it's [njã], and we know this because when that *it* comes after it, it kind of messes things up, and the /m/ ends up popping up. You're looking at the underlying reality coming up on the surface now and then; and so therefore *njãmɛ̃*." You would never know that unless there was this *it* situation where suddenly the [m] reappeared, and so history makes itself known in the present.

What's interesting is that there is one more word in Saramaccan that has the same property. It's another verb, and it also happens to be another one that is African-derived, and that is the word *fõ*, which means *to beat*. If you take *fõ* and you follow it with the *it* word, then you have that same thing. And so: *Mi fõmɛ̃*; all of a sudden there's this [m]. It's interesting: Not only might we suppose that this word phonemically is /fum/ or /fom/ rather than /fõ/, but history ought to be able to tell us something about this. As it happens, we do have some historical documentation in these languages. That is not often common in languages that are mostly just spoken like Saramaccan, but there were missionaries, German-speaking missionaries, who went to Suriname as early as the late 1700s. There's a dictionary—really what we could a word list, but a big fat word list; they called it a dictionary—of Saramaccan taken down by these missionaries. You can go way back into this book, and you can look up the entry for *to beat*, and you actually see this right here: It's "*fumm*—schlagen, stampfen"; so that's *to beat*; *to stamp on*. It's right there. What those Germans heard way back 200-plus years ago, was [fum]; they were hearing the consonant. It has since dropped off, and so now if you ask a Saramaccan what it is, they say, "*fõ*." In other words, the language has changed. You don't even need this ancient dictionary to know that there used to be that [m] on the end because it pops up when you say, "Beat it"; "*fõmɛ̃*." You only know it now because of what happens when that *it* comes.

There are other clues that this is the right analysis, as we would say. There are many creoles with an English basis with a sprinkling of African words spoken in the New World and beyond that. In a great many of them, the word for eat is not *njã*; it's *njam*. Those of you who have any familiarity with Jamaican patois might remember that you talk about *njaming* on something. The Saramaccan situation is just derived, as we say. *Njam* in Jamaican is less advanced than in Saramaccan where the [m] has dropped off, as sounds often do, and left behind a *tincture* of itself—*t-i-n-c-t-u-r-e*; good word—on the vowel. Just based on that queer little thing that happens when you use *it* with those two words, you know that these are words that phonemically are ones that have a final nasal consonant, even though they come out on the surface without it. That is part of the grammar of these languages; that is part of the phonology of these languages. It's not just a sequence of sounds. Stuff goes on; and that's one of the things that has.

There's something else that a creole language like this is useful for, and that is that these are languages which begin when slaves need a way to express themselves very quickly, and then they become real languages. When people need real languages, they develop a real language rather quickly. We can know that in the early 1600s there was no such thing as Saramaccan or any precursor to it. We can know, through various kinds of deduction, that by about 1670 there very much was that language in its full form. We see it actually written out for the first time in—the earliest documentation as of like 10 minutes ago—1709, so then we know that the language exists. Then you get actual longer documentation of it throughout the 1700s and into the 1800s. It's a language which has had to become a real language very quickly. To the extent that that's been documented—which is often sparse but indicative—we can actually see grammar developing, and we can extrapolate from that how grammar has developed in other, older languages.

Remember that in a previous lecture—it seems so long ago now, doesn't it? Unless you've actually sat and done these in a marathon, in which case, I don't know whether I'm flattered or alarmed—but in a very previous lecture there was what we called a new information marker, *nóo*. The way that we knew that it was a new information marker was, for example, when I was talking to one of my Saramaccan informants, we call them; that has nothing to do with a detective movie or *Get Smart*; we call the people we consult to get information from informants. I've been trying not to say that. I'm going to start saying it: my informant. I was working with one of my informants, and he said that he would be waiting for my call. He said, "*A búnu. Nóo mi ó tá háika i.*" That's good—*A búnu, búnu, good, bueno*—remember? That's kind of familiar; that's from Portuguese. Then he said, "*Nóo mi ó tá háika i.*" *I will be listening for you, I'll be waiting* was just *mi ó tá háika i*, but then there's this *nóo*. It's the sort of thing where if you're thinking of it as just some kind of English—which it isn't remotely—but if you're thinking of language as the way English works, you hear this *nóo* and you think, "That's nothing. He's just kind of saying *um*." But then it's this *nóo*, but rarely is it just *um*; you have to let the language speak for itself. A little later in the conversation—because as we've seen, so much of conversation is about repetition, so much of conversation is phatic (*p-h-a-t-i-c*), that was going on here—and he said, again, later, "*A búnu*," very good; "*mi ó tá háika dí kái fíi,*" I'll be waiting for your call; "*tidé néti,*" tonight. This time he said more or less the same thing, but there was no *nóo*. I just thought that was kind of interesting.

If you look at the way *nóo* is used in general, you see that what it is, is it's a marker of information that is new rather than is given. This is something that is very systematic in the language. You listen to it and you think, especially if so many of the words are derived from English, doesn't it mean *now*? Isn't it that he's saying, "Now I'll be waiting for your call"? But the thing is, there already is a word for *now* in Saramaccan, you can see it here; and so somebody's saying, "You know, if it wasn't raining then we would be playing now." The word is *nóunóu*. *Nɔɔ* is one thing, it's got a long, open "o"; that does not spell *nu*. Remember, this is completely neutral IPA kind of transcription, and so *nɔɔ*. Then *now* is *nóunóu*, and so it's completely different. In general, the *now* translation doesn't work if you look at the way it's actually used in the language.

Instead of listening to me speaking my competent but obviously nonnative Saramaccan—Saramaccan speakers tell me, "Oh, you can really talk, John," which is exactly what people mean when they say, "You speak badly but well enough to converse with us, and isn't that cute"—let's listen to somebody who actually speaks the language. This is a gentleman, and he is doing two things: I don't know why he was watching *Beverly Hills, 90210* in an apartment in Amsterdam in 1992, but he seemed to really like the show, and he's telling a story. It's a folk tale about a jaguar who is enduring a famine and decides that the way he's going to get food is to play dead so that all of the neighbor animals will come in and weep and wail and mourn for his death. Then he'll get up with a club and beat them all senseless and eat them; that's what the story is about. You have to hear it told; it's actually very charming. But here is him—here is he to be prescriptive— here is him describing this story.

> *Já sî hángi dé ku u? Wá sondî u njã. Mi ó pɛέ wã kóni, mi ó pɛέ, mi ó ganjã dédɛ. Nɔɔ mi ó kándi a mîndi wósu. Nɔɔ i butá wã kódjo, wã kódjo a bándja, wã kódjo a bándja. Nɔɔ I kái woló, kɛέ.*

You see the hunger we are suffering from? We don't have anything to eat. I'm going to play a trick, I'm going to play. I'm going to pretend I'm dead. I'll lay down in the middle of the house. You put a stick, a stick to the side, a stick to the side. Then you call "Alas!" you cry.

That is that bloody little tale. The question is: What's *nɔɔ*? It's this new information marker. It's something quite unlike English; it's part of a whole little module of the grammar, as we say, of marking new information in ways that English doesn't. Where did that come from? What's *nɔɔ*? One way that you can find out is you can look at related languages where maybe there'll be more of a clue.

I talked about how there was this protolanguage on the coast in Suriname; this is a protocreole. That one lives today. It's still living on the coast; it's the lingua franca of Suriname, and it's called Sranan. That's still around.

There is something like *nóo* in Sranan, except it's a different word; it's *nomo*. Here is a piece of modern Sranan, and there's a story being told. There's something interesting about the story. The person says, "I let the boss fire me; he didn't want to pay me anymore, so I didn't work for him anymore." (*M tek ontslag a bas, a no wan pai moro, da m n e-wroko dj ên moro.*) That's one sentence. Then the next sentence means, *The people told me*—and you can see the words underneath—*The people told me, "It's not slavery time anymore; you're right."* (**Nomo** *den sma tai mi tak: W a no sraften, j a leti.*) Except I'll bet their voices didn't go up like that. "The people told me, 'It's not slavery time anymore; you're right.'" My voice does that more as I get older; it wasn't during my adolescence.

In any case, you see the translation. Notice that I don't have the *nomo* here translated at all. That's because even in the original source that this is from, where this whole text is very usefully given a translation, it is highly unclear what this *nomo* means. That's because it's highly unclear, when you're trying to translate into English, what a new information marker would mean. We don't have a word that serves that function. There are all sorts of ways you can get into it—*however, besides, well*—but none of them really convey what this thing is, which is a piece of a grammar, a pragmatic marker, that English largely leaves to context or has whole expressions for, such as *now we're going to talk about this* or *on another topic*, or something like that.

If you see it here, and if you look in other texts, you see that *nomo* is the same thing as *nóo*. Now that gives us more of a hint as to where this *nóo* in Saramaccan must have come from, because apparently *nóo* is a derived version of *nomo*. Apparently the consonant between the vowels dropped out—that happens all the time—and so originally it's *nomo*. What's *nomo*? You kind of think, "Maybe it's *no more*," because actually in these Suriname creoles, final consonants—consonants that are final in their syllable—are not generally something that one wants, or they only happen in rapid speech. You can see some of if in Sranan. And so, *no more* would come out as *nomo*. Of course, think of Southern English or Black English—always think beyond print when you're doing things like this.

The question is, why would *nomo* be this marker of new information? The fact of the matter is that even when you look in 18th-century documents of Sranan, you can see *no more* being used in this way, and they're even writing it that way; and so it's *no morro* in these documents, so you can see that here: **No morro** *hulanga tem ju sa libi dea?*. Here, I'm using the translation, *So how long are you going to live hereabouts?* Actually that *so* is my attempt to kind of convey new-information-ness, because actually in the translation into German in the original source it's left untranslated. Once again a Westerner can't render it, but actually it has a function.

In any case, the fact of the matter is that it's not that hard to imagine how *no more* would have come to be used in that way, because if you think about it, this is something that we do in modern spoken English all the time. This is a conversation I had about a year ago. Someone was telling me that they had originally lived in various places, and now they were settled down in Toledo.

I said, "So, you spent six years in New York, nine in Los Angeles, and then … Toledo?"

She kind of laughed, [laughs], "No, it was really hard at first, but after a while the low cost of living starts to become really attractive."

We listened to everything she said except, "No." Think about how often that's done nowadays. "So, you spent six years in New York, nine in L.A., and then Toledo?" [Laughs] "No, it was really hard at first but …" Why *no*? That's something that people do; my sense of it is, 45 and under, very common to change the subject with *no*. She wasn't denying anything; she wasn't saying, "I deny what you say." That *no* is something that people in full agreement use in modern English all the time as a way of going to a new topic in an unobtrusive way. It would appear that that exact thing happened in early Suriname creoles. If we see just this *nɔ́ɔ*, that's something that can kind of give us a clue, but we wouldn't know from that alone that it came from *no more*, and it would be easy to go off on the wrong path. Something that's happening actually in modern English is something that the Suriname creoles actually seem to have figured out over 200 years ago. That's something else that has been discovered in Saramaccan—new information marking, and originally from a use of *no more*, which itself specifically is not something that was in English or Portuguese or any of the African languages in question. This language developed grammar.

A final aspect of Saramaccan grammar that can give us a sense of what it's like to actually let the language speak for itself—and don't think of it as just a kind of European language—is the way that Saramaccan uses its word for *to throw*. This is really peculiar. It really threw me for a while, so to speak; interesting. The word is *túwɛ*, which is originally from *throw away*, but it is used for throwing. If you want to say, "I threw the dirty thing," then you say, "*Mi túwɛ di súndju*"; *súndju* is "dirty thing." You throw it; OK, good.

There's a word. You can also use it in what's called a serial verb construction in Saramaccan; so you can run verbs together. We've seen this before in the course. If you want to say, "He carried mud to the water"—the idea being that he carried it in a bucket, and we went over to the water, kind of threw it into the water—then you say, "*A ba pɔtɔpɔtɔ túwɛ a wáta.*" *Ba* is *carry*, you just have to know; *pɔtɔpɔtɔ* is *mud*, that's an African word. *A ba pɔtɔpɔtɔ túwɛ a wáta*; *he carry mud throw to water*.

There you might think, "OK, that describes somebody carrying the mud, standing on the shore, and then throwing it into the water." But sometimes the use of *throw* gets a little peculiar, and it's easy to just kind of wave it away as static, kind of like that stray autumn leaf that's still in your yard in March or something like that. But things start to kind of pile up on one another.

For example, to say, "Kobi pushed the man down," the way that you say it is, "*Kobi tɔ́tɔ dí wómi túwɛ.*" *Tɔ́tɔ* is *push*, and so *Kobi tɔ́tɔ dí wómi túwɛ. Kobi pushed the man throw.* You think to yourself, "You know, I suppose if you push somebody down, it could be interpreted as also including the throwing, but it's a little forced." You push a person down, and down they go: *splat*. It's not, I push you, and then grab you and hurl you as well, unless you're really some sort of completist, but most people are not. Or if you talk to Saramaccans about cutting down trees—I've never cut down a single tree, and I'm pretty sure I never will. I'm never going to cut down a tree. I'm never going to ski because it's crazy, and I don't think I will ever have any reason to cut down a tree. In Saramaccan culture, they do cut down trees, and they talk about it, and you can learn a lot about grammar from it. The way that you cut a tree down is "*A kóti dí páu túwɛ*": *He cut the tree throw*. That's really … maybe you can think of the hacking the tree down as a kind of throwing via the ax or something like that, but again, it's a little weird. It got to the point where I was thinking, "I don't think I'm letting this language speak for itself. Nobody's throwing trees. Why are they using the word in that way?"

Then, if you are living in the rainforest, you have got to shoot things—including pigs—and the word for shooting a pig dead is, "I shot the pig throw." You don't throw the pig; you shoot it, and you don't want to go near a wild animal. There's no throwing involved. I started wondering, "What's this *túwɛ*? Why is it?"

One day with my favorite informant—the one who can always explain things because he actually speaks completely fluent English, Dutch, Sranan, and Saramaccan—I balled up a piece of paper and I threw it into the next office, and there was nobody in the next office.

I looked at Kachung. "What did I just do?"

We talked about various things, and here it was, the sentence: "*Vínde ̃ɛ túwɛ gó naandé*": *Throw it over into there*. What was weird about this one is that the way that translates is *throw it*, *throw there*. I said, "Why are you saying *throw* twice? You already said *vínde*, so why is it 'Throw it, throw there'?"

He said, "John, I don't know."

I asked some other informants, "What's *túwɛ* in this sentence? You *shot the pig throw*. Don't you mean you *shot the pig fall* or something like that? The pig falls." They don't know.

Then I started looking at all of the sentences that have this *túwɛ* thing in it, and I thought, "Is this what it is?" I was working with my informants again, and I said, "Now imagine something." This was in the wake of the *Titanic* movie; interesting story. There actually are black and white shots of the Titanic, of what's going on on the upper deck before everybody left. In one of them somebody's walking a little dog, and so I thought about that. I said, "Suppose you were on the Titanic, and there's this little Scottie dog, and you take that dog and you push that dog off of the ship into the water, so it's like 'Yip! Splash,' down. How would you describe what that was?"

I got the answer. It's *Mi tótɔ dí dágu túwɛ a dí wáta*; (*Tótɔ* does not mean Toto; that's just a complete coincidence.) *Mi tótɔ*. "I push the dog," *Mi tótɔ dí dágu túwɛ a dí wáta*, "throw in the water." Obviously if you push the dog and it's on its way down into the brine, you're not going to then reach over and catch it and throw it to make sure that it gets down to the water. You've done your job by pushing the dog. First I asked again, "What's the *túwɛ*?" It was like asking us what *even* means in *he didn't even show up to the meeting*. We don't know what it means; we know what the sentence means.

What it is, is that there is a usage of *throw* in Saramaccan that is used to indicate the end of a trajectory of movement; this has to be indicated. Throwing is one way to initiate a trajectory of movement, and so you can see how *throw* would grammaticalize in this way. This is an indication of grammaticalization in Saramaccan to indicate a shade of meaning that would not occur to us. When you *push the dog throw into the water*, what that means is that you pushed the dog into the water and it landed. That means we can go back to some of the other sentences where we thought we knew what *túwε* meant, even though it's kind of clumsy: *He carried mud throw into the water*. That means he carried the mud up to the water. If you push the man down, and you push the man throw, that indicates just as when you're cutting a tree down, that the tree then came to rest on the ground.

English can indicate that: *I pushed the dog in the water*; *I pushed the dog into the water*. Think about the two. If you say, "I pushed the dog in the water," I think our first sense of what that means is that we pushed the dog from the Titanic—and we immediately think of the Titanic—and that it landed in the water. But saying, "I pushed the dog in the water" could theoretically mean that I was down in the water, and the dog is swimming beside me, and in addition to the dog and me suffering, I then pushed the dog for some reason. That's what it could mean. If I say, "I pushed the dog into the water," then there's no way that you can think that you were in the water with the dog. That *-to* in that case indicates not only that you may have been inside the water, but that there was an end of the trajectory into— "Yipe, yipe, yipe, yipe!" *Kapow*!—the water.

We, in English, would never think of it; imagine somebody asking us—if we were informants—"What does *-to* mean in *I pushed the dog into the water*? We don't do it all the time in English; in Saramaccan you absolutely have to do that. Nevertheless, this is an indication of grammar; this is in an indication that this is a language which in a very short time has had to develop grammatical distinctions that we would not think of.

Now that we've done that in Saramaccan, where the words themselves are usually pretty easy for us to wrap our heads around, let's see what this is like when we're really examining a language that to us, at first, looks like Martian.

Lecture Thirty-Five
Doing Linguistics—From the Ground Up

Scope: This lecture allows you to make a brief foray into an obscure, difficult, and peculiar language as if you were a linguist encountering it for the first time. The language is Kabardian, spoken in the Caucasus Mountains of Russia, and its sound system and syntax show various concepts we have seen in this course "in action."

Outline

I. Now that you have been exposed to the kinds of analysis that linguists do, let's take a look at a language where the words are completely unrelated to their equivalents in English to get closer to what someone documenting a grammar actually does.

    A. The language we will refer to is Kabardian, spoken in Russia in the Caucasus Mountains by about 300,000 people. There are three small families of languages spoken in the Caucasus, and Kabardian belongs to the Northwest Caucasian family.

    B. Many speakers of Kabardian and its close relative Adyge (also referred to as dialects of a single language, Circassian) live in Turkey. Their ancestors fled the Caucasus in 1864 to escape Russian Christian rule.

II. Kabardian has many sounds that are quite different from the ones that we are used to.

    A. First look at these six phrases of Kabardian (as found in Colarusso's Kabardian grammar).

        1. [ƛapśra žəĝgʷáaśamra]
            Tlepsh and the Lady Tree

        2. [náhrthar zəx̂ʷáy psaw yahx̂ʷəyś'rǝy ƛapś]
            Tlepsh couldn't make the Nahrts the things that they needed in life.

        3. [yəś'án yəməɣʷatə́žəw]
            He couldn't find the necessary knowledge.

        4. [q'aànarǝ́y zaš x̌ʷahś]
            He remained in this quandary until he grew desperate.

5. [x̂ʷaməšakʸə́z śə́x̂ʷəm]
   When he could no longer endure this situation, …
6. [satanaygʷaaśam dayž k'warəy yaƛaʔʷáhś]
   … he went to Lady Satanaya and beseeched her.

B. The first thing you will notice is that Kabardian has quite a few
sounds that English does not—48 consonants, compared to 25 in
English. We are in a position to understand that this means that
Kabardian fills in the phonetic "grid" from Lecture Three in
different ways than English. (I have not included all of
Kabardian's consonants; this grid is composed of consonants
Kabardian shares with English plus Kabardian ones we will
encounter in this lecture.)

		Place of Articulation									
		Front————————————————————————————————Back									
Manner of Articulation		bilabial	labiodental	alveolar	lateral	palatoalveolar	alveopalatal	velar	uvular	pharyngeal	laryngeal
	voiceless stops	p		t				k			ʔ
	voiced stops	b		d				g			
	ejective stops			c'					q'		
	voiceless fricative		f	s		ʃ	ś	xʷ		ḥ	h
	voiced fricative		v	z	λ	ʒ			ɣ, ɣʷ		
	ejective fricative				ƛ'		ś'			ḥ	
	nasals	m		n							
	rhotic liquid			r							
	glides	w		j							

253

C. In English there are velar sounds and then what can be classified as glottal ones.

D. However, in Kabardian there are three places of articulation behind the velar.

    1. The backmost is the *laryngeal*, where our familiar h and glottal stop are pronounced.

    2. In Kabardian there is also a *pharyngeal* fricative, [ḥ], a throaty sound.

    3. Then there are sounds made with the uvula, including a fricative, [ɣ].

E. In addition, there is a manner of articulation foreign to English in Kabardian: *ejectives*, pronounced with an extra push and indicated with an apostrophe. There is, for example, a uvular ejective stop [q']; Similarly, the [c'] symbol stands for a *ts* sound, but ejective.

F. Kabardian does not have a lateral liquid [l]. Its laterals are fricatives: voiced ([λ]) and ejective ([λ']).

G. Kabardian distinguishes between *palatoalveolar* and alveopalatal sounds. Note the [ś] sound, pronounced with the tongue on the lower teeth, distinct from our [s] and from [ʃ]. Then there is also an ejective variant, [ś'].

H. Some consonants have variations pronounced with the lips rounded; this is indicated with the superscripted *w*; for example, [xʷ]. [x], incidentally, is the velar fricative in *Bach*.

I. In the recorded sample of Kabardian played in this lecture, we can hear these sounds actually being produced. (The text is above at II.A.)

III. Often something that looks insignificant is actually important to a language.

    A. We can see this using the following sentences.

        1. [λ'əm pśaaśar yəλaaɣʷəaɣs]
        The man saw a woman.

        2. [pśaaśar yəś'an]
        He knows the woman.

        3. [pśaaśa yəʔa sət q'awɣʷatəw]
        The woman says, "What must you find?"

        4. [λ'ə yəʔa śəm ɣʷənar q'asɣʷatəw]
        The man says, "I must find the edge of the earth …

5. [nahrtham ś'anəγa shən]

"… to bring knowledge to the Nahrts. …"

6. [wagʷəm vaagʷahar wasγacəx̂ ʷəns]

"I will show you the stars in the sky."

B. We can deduce that the word that the first two sentences have in common means *woman*. We can then deduce that the second word in the third sentence means *says*. This then allows us to deduce that the first word of the fourth sentence means *man*.

C. This means that the first sentence is "man woman saw," and thus we know that Kabardian is an SOV language, placing its verbs last.

D. The words for *man* and *woman* have endings in some cases and not in others. The difference between how *woman* is used in the first two sentences and how it is used in the third one is that in the third it is a subject, while it is an object in the first two. Thus we know that the object marker in Kabardian is [r].

E. However, *man* is used as a subject in both the first and the fourth sentences. The difference in usage is that the man does something to something in the first one but not in the fourth. This is the ergativity we saw in Lecture Nine: In Kabardian, subjects are marked differently when they are agents as opposed to playing other semantic roles.

F. If Kabardian is SOV, then according to the universal tendencies we saw in Lecture Fifteen, it ought to be head-final in other aspects of its word order. For example, recall the Ethiopian languages in that lecture, such as Harari, which is SOV and has the following traits: adjective-noun, genitive-noun, postpositions.

G. This can help us find out what the adpositions are in Kabardian. The sixth sentence is useful. Knowing that objects come before the verb, we can figure out what the words mean. We know that the object will end in [r] because of [pśaaśar]. This means that the word for *stars* must be [vaagʷahar].

H. We expect that there will be postpositions rather than prepositions, such that we could guess that in [wagʷəm] either [əm] or [m] has some kind of locative meaning: *sky in* rather than *in the sky*, like *Tokyo ni*, "in Tokyo," in Japanese.

I. This can then help us figure out what the genitive is.

1. We expect it to come before the noun as in Harari, as in *the boy's house* rather than *the house of the boy*.

2. In the fourth sentence, we see *the edge of the earth* is [śəm ɣʷənar]. The first word, [śəm], has a final [m], suggesting something affixal like the one in [wagʷəm] in the sixth sentence.

3. It is not a stretch to imagine that the word for *in* and the word for *of* are the same in Kabardian, just as in French *à Paris* can mean both "to Paris" and "in Paris." Thus [śəm ɣʷənar] means *earth of edge* or *the earth's edge*.

IV. Looking at how to make a word in Kabardian is useful in showing the difference between underlying sound structure and surface sound structure.

A. *You gave it to me* is one word: [q'əsawtəayś]

1. The components (morphemes) of this word are the following:

[q'ə]	it involves you
[s]	me
[a]	to
[w]	you
[tə]	give
[aɣ]	PAST
[ś]	affirmative

2. Note that there is a prefix that indicates that what happened applies to "you," which lends this sentence the actual meaning of *you **lent** it to me*—if you give it with the idea that you'll get it back, then it is relevant to you. Languages mark a vast range of semantic, or in this case pragmatic, distinctions.

3. Note also a suffix indicating that a sentence is affirmative; there is a different one for the negative, an opposition in the Saussurean sense. There is also an *infix* (which comes in the middle of a word).

4. However, the word as I have shown it would sound absurd if actually uttered. It is only a phonemic representation. How it actually comes out on the surface is:

phonemic	/q'ə-s-a-w-tə-aɣ-ś/
phonetic	[q'ɪzzæpʰtʰɑś]

B. Note that in the phonemic representation, and in all of the six sentences, there are only two vowels, /ə/ and /a/. The sentences are in phonemic representation, and in fact, Kabardian only has those two vowels underlyingly.

C. Other vowel sounds emerge because of phonological rules that turn /ə/ and /a/ into different sounds depending on what consonants they occur next to.

D. Another rule regularly makes consonants have the same voicing as the next one. This makes the /s/ into a [z] because a vowel is ahead, and in Kabardian, what happens to /w/ under such conditions is that it becomes a [pʰ].

E. Other consonants disappear regularly, in the process altering a vowel that is left behind and again resulting in a difference between the phonemic and the phonetic.

V. The marvel of something like Kabardian is that no one knew the real system of this language until the analysis of scholars such as John Colarusso. This is the sort of thing that linguists do, documenting how the languages of the world have changed and how they exist in the present context.

Supplemental Reading:

Colarusso, *A Grammar of the Kabardian Language.*

Questions to Consider:

1. What are the words for *I* and *you* in Kabardian, based on the sentences we have seen?

2. There is one derivational morpheme in this data (review the difference between derivational and inflectional in Lecture Fifteen). Can you find it?

Lecture Thirty-Five—Transcript
Doing Linguistics—From the Ground Up

Now that we have looked at how people do linguistic analysis of a language where many of the words are relatively familiar to us, let's get a sense of what it's like to work with a language that is truly completely foreign to us, where the words and their shapes are completely unrelated to their equivalents in English. This is what it's like if you go into a community where there is a hitherto undocumented language—or a language which has only been documented slightly or been documented by linguists working from a very different tradition from yours—and you want to get down in black and white how this language's grammar works. Of course the purest situation is when no one has documented a language before; of course in real life there are various gray zones. But let's imagine what it would be like if we were going to do, from the ground up, a linguistic analysis of, for example, Kabardian. Our language will be Kabardian.

Kabardian is spoken in Russia in the Caucasus Mountains by, depending on how you count it, about 300,000 people. Sometimes you'll see indicated in a book that there is a family of languages called the Caucasian languages. More properly in the Caucasus Mountains, which is really not a very large region at all—I mean, it's really about the size of the office park I'm in right now—but the Caucasus Mountains actually is home to three language families, which are not related in any significant way. It's not really that there's a Caucasian language family; there are three of those families, and Kabardian belongs to the Northwest Caucasian family. This is a very mountainous region. I would say that the only one of these languages that has any kind of shop-window status is Georgian, because of Georgia's geopolitical position and the way it tends to make the news because of the various unfortunate events. But other than Georgian, there are a great many languages in the Caucasus Mountains. Kabardian is one of them. There are other speakers of Kabardian in Turkey, and also of its close relative Adyge. Actually many Kabardian speakers fled Christian rule in 1864 when Russia took over the Caucasus area. Together Kabardian and Adyge are often referred to as Circassian—as the language Circassian—but we're going to refer to what we're working with today as Kabardian.

Kabardian is basically very, very, very, very different from anything that we learn as a language if we've got a European perspective. These are people who are expressing themselves every day with richness and nuance, but all of the underlying assumptions we make about how you get yourself across in a language are different. Let's first look—let's just look—at sentences in Kabardian. You can see these here; it's the beginning of one of their tales, "Tlepsh and the Lady Tree":

> Tlepsh couldn't make the Nahrts the things that they needed in life. He couldn't find the necessary knowledge. He remained in this quandary until he grew desperate. When he could no longer endure this situation, he went to Lady Satanaya and beseeched her.

In these sentences, the first thing that we should note is that there are many sounds in this language that are quite different from the ones that we are used to. The fact is that actually, I don't speak Kabardian. My parents spoke it at home when they didn't want us to understand, but I never learned the language itself. However, there are people who can render the tone, and so instead of me approximating it—you're going to hear enough of that as we go on—let's hear the language actually spoken properly in this sample. This is somebody actually reading "Tlepsh and the Lady Tree."

> "ƛapśra žəĝgʷáaśamra." náhrthar zəx̂ʷáy psaw yahx̂ʷəyś'rɂy ƛapś. yəś'án yəməɣʷatɔ́žəw. q'aànarɔ́y zaš x̌ʷahś. x̂ʷaməšakʸɔ́z śɔ́x̌ʷəm, satanaygʷaaśam dayž k'warəy yaƛaɂʷáhś.

Notice how quickly that went by. Writing is very artificial, and you see these not five but six sentences on the page, and you think it's going to be *boom, boom boom, ba-doom, da da da da ...* but it isn't. Actually it goes by. I'm going to give you a chance to follow again. Here is this, actually uttered, and here's "Tlepsh and the Lady Tree."

> "ƛapśra žəĝgʷáaśamra." náhrthar zəx̂ʷáy psaw yahx̂ʷəyś'rɂy ƛapś. yəś'án yəməɣʷatɔ́žəw. q'aànarɔ́y zaš x̌ʷahś. x̂ʷaməšakʸɔ́z śɔ́x̌ʷəm, satanaygʷaaśam dayž k'warəy yaƛaɂʷáhś.

You will notice that there are many sounds that English doesn't have. We're in a position to understand that this means that Kabardian fills in the phonetic grid that we saw from English back in the early lectures in a different way than in English. Here we see some Kabardian consonants; this is by no means all of Kabardian's consonants. What I have in this grid is the consonants that Kabardian happens to share with English, plus some Kabardian ones that we'll encounter in this lecture. To show you the whole fearsome thing, in terms of the unfamiliarity of it, it would be as chaotic as looking at the contents of a silverware drawer spilled down a staircase;

there's no point in that. But you will see that Kabardian does have 48 consonants, whereas English has 25. There's just a richness here.

Kabardian, for example, has more going on over on the right in terms of places of articulation. In English, we saw that there are velar sounds—for example, our [k] and our [g] are velar stops—then, behind that—they're rightward on our grid—there are ones that can be called glottal ones. However, in Kabardian, once you go behind velar you've got three places of articulation. The backmost is the *laryngeal*, and that's where the [h] and the glottal stop ([ʔ]) that are familiar to us are pronounced; so "huh," "uh"; that's the laryngeal. But in Kabardian, there's more that goes on. There is a *pharyngeal* region where they have a pharyngeal fricative ([ḥ]), which is kind of like *chhhoh*. Arabic has that too; it's the "throaty sound." That has a true status, a phonemic status, in Kabardian, too. It's not just a funny sound you make; it is actually part of expression. Then, in addition to this distinction between laryngeal and pharyngeal, there is *uvular*. The uvula, recall, is the little sort of punching bag that hangs back behind the soft palate that we have no reason to think about much that often gets kind of played around with in cartoons whenever one character goes into another one's mouth. But actually that can be used as an articulator in producing sounds. Not in English but in Kabardian there is a fricative, and that is made with the uvula ([ɣ]). And so we have our uvular region.

We have different places of articulation, and then there are manners of articulation. That's down the left vertical axis of our grid that we've seen so often. There are manners of articulation that are quite foreign to English. For example, there are *ejectives*. Ejectives are pronounced with a kind of an extra push; ejective consonants. They are often conventionally indicated with an apostrophe. There is a uvular ejective stop—of all things—that's indicated with *q* plus the apostrophe; roughly *clop*, like that. Or there is the *c* symbol. Now remember, [k] in any kind of IPA is how you indicate what is often indicated with a *c* sign in English; so *cat* in IPA begins with a [k]. There is a [c] in an IPA; it is *tzt*, and so roughly what we think of as *ts*, but tighter than that. Then there is an ejective [c], [c']—and so *tzt!*, like that—and that is an actual sound.

What Kabardian does not have that we have is there is no such thing as a lateral liquid [l]. There is no just *lily*; that's just not there. They have a lateral sound ([λ]), but it's not liquid, it's a fricative; there's friction. Roughly, you press air past the sides of your tongue. It goes kind of like this; it's roughly this—*hlllll*—kind of like that. That's the *l*. Then there's an ejective one as well ([λ']), so kind of like *hl!*, like that. These are all normal sounds. When a Kabardian speaker speaks, they don't make funny faces and lean forward and get ready and drink coffee. All of this is just what is done.

Even back up in place, in Kabardian there's a difference between palatoalveolar sounds—which we have seen, and so that would include things like [ʃ]—and then alveopalatal sounds, which basically just means that in between alveolar and alveopalatal, there is something that is neither one nor the other; and so they subdivide that region in terms of places of articulation in the mouth more finely. For example, we've got our nice [ś] sound. You pronounce it by sticking your tongue on the lower teeth, kind of like *sssth*; like that. So there's [ś], there's [ʃ], and there's [ʒ]. So, [ś], [ʒ], [ʃ]: All of those are phonemically different, and so it's not that [ś] is just a strange way of going [s]; it makes for a difference in meaning. This is how languages differ from one another.

It should be said, it is a little unpopular among linguists to say that one language is more complex than another, or it has been until maybe about eight or nine years ago. Now there's a crack in the dam, because frankly some languages are more complex than other ones. Kabardian is really, really complex. I mean in terms of just the sound system alone, I think any sane person would agree that there's something different between English and this. That doesn't mean that Kabardian speakers do not speak their language with ease—babies can master just about anything, as matter of fact anything when it comes to language—but in terms of coming to this from a second-language speaker's perspective, I get the feeling that a Kabardian speaker would have an easier time with what I'm doing than I would have with this. Nevertheless, there are these sounds. Of course then you have for this alveopalatal an ejective variant, and so you have [ś] or your have [ś'], and that makes a difference.

Then you have some consonants where there's a variation where you round the lips when you produce the consonant. I talked about how from the perspective of English it's kind of exotic to have a velar fricative. We have velar stops like [k] and [g], but then if you don't close all the way, you get [x]. For example, that is the velar fricative in *Bach* if you want to pronounce it the right way. In Kabardian, not only do you have that sound—for them that's vanilla—but then there's another version where you actually have to round your lips while you do it, and so it's [xʷ]. That is something that is done; it's indicated with a superscripted *w*, and that is actually a phonemic distinction in this language. And so instead of listening to me do all these things, here, one more time, is the recorded sample.

"ƛapśra žəĝgʷáaśamra." náhrthar zəx̂ʷáy psaw yahx̂ʷəyś'rɔ́y ƛapś. yəś'án yəməɣʷatɔ́žəw. q'aànarɔ́y zaš x̌ʷahś. x̂ʷaməšak'yɔ́z śɔ́x̌ʷəm, satanaygʷaaśam dayž k'warəy yaƛaʔʷáhś.

Now let's look at some sentences in Kabardian. How does this language work? What we want to do is we want to look at these six other sentences and we're going to see what kind of grammar we can pull out of these sentences without knowing very much except what the sentences mean. This is often a situation that there is in a language; a language will be only very fitfully documented. Maybe somebody will have recorded somebody telling a folk tale and then have that person tell them what it meant in the language that the person doing the research meant, but then nobody's ever actually worked out what the grammar of the language was. That's a position that one is often in as a linguist for getting a foothold. Let's say that in Kabardian that is where you were, and so you saw these simple sentences.

> The man saw a woman. He knows the woman. The woman says, "What must you find?" The man says, "I must find the edge of the earth, to bring knowledge to the Nahrts." [The Nahrts are people in the folk tale.] "I will show you the stars in the sky."

> ƛ'əm pśaaśar ɣ ƛaaɣʷəays. pśaaśar ɣs''an. pśaaśa ɣ ʔa: st q'awɣʷatəw? ƛ'ə yəʔa: śəm ɣʷənar q'asɣʷatəw, nahrtham ś'anəɣa sḥən. wagʷəm vaagʷahar wasɣacəx̂ ʷəns.

You've got these six, and you've got the Kabardian for it. What's going on here? What kind of grammar is there in this language? If we look at the first two sentences, one thing that we can tell is that if one of them means *the man saw a woman* and one of them means *he knows the woman*, and we look at what those two sentences have in common, then with very little knowledge we can deduce that this [pśaaśar] means *woman*. We've got that word; that's one word that we have. Along those same lines, if we have this sentence—the third one, where it's *The woman says, "What must you find?"*—we can see that it's [pśaaśa yəʔa], now we can reasonably suppose that [yəʔa] means *says*; so we've got that there. Once we know those two things, then we can deduce that in this fourth sentence, where we've got *says* again, this [yəʔa]—and we can assume that it means *says* here, too—then we can assume that the word for *man* is what's indicated here with this lateral fricative ejective and where the vowel is a schwa, approximately, [λ'ə], and that's for a basic word like *man*. We can assume that that is the word for *man*.

If we can do that, then it means that in the first sentence what we're seeing, because we see [λ'əm]—don't worry about the [m] at the end of it; we'll get to that—we can see that it means *man woman saw*; that's how that translates. If the first sentence, where we have these three words, if it turns out that it's the third word and the last word that means *saw*, then we know that this is what we've seen: one of those [languages] that's verb final. Its word order is SOV. We know that right there. As we've seen, you can tell a lot about a language—you know places to go—just knowing that it's verb final. But we've got that based on just figuring out what the words for *man* and *woman* and *says* are in these early sentences.

Then there's the whole issue of what qualifies as the stray autumn leaf in the yard in March. What we have to think about is that often something that looks insignificant or just makes it look like somehow there's more variation in this language than in ours is actually something important. For example, we can look at the word for *woman* in the first three sentences. In the first two it's [pśaaśar], but then in the third one actually it's [pśaaśa] and there's no [r]. We can see that the first sentence means *the man saw a woman*. Then in the second one, we see that we have something that looks like some kind of verb. Then we have in the third one, *the woman says*. What can you deduce from that? It seems like in the third sentence *woman* is a subject, but in the first sentence, certainly, *woman* would have to be an object. Therefore, we know from the first and second sentences, as opposed to the third sentence, that there is an object marker in this language. We've got some case marking, and it would appear at least for the word *woman* to be [r], which indicates our accusative, our object. And so, [r] is our object marker in Kabardian. That's one thing that we can figure out in terms of things that vary.

Then, look at the first sentence, and we have this word for *man*, which is [λ'əm], with this [m]. Then in the fourth sentence it doesn't have that [m] on the end: *the man says*. But in this case we're not talking about subject and object, because in both of those sentences the man is the subject. If you are the layperson, then you just look at that and you think, "Well, you know, it just is. In the first one there's this [m] because maybe they like saying [m] or something, and then over here there's a shorter version. Maybe it's kind of the slang version to leave off the [m], or something like that." That is a last-ditch analysis because you all, y'all—you're not allowed to say that—you are not laypersons anymore. Lay people? Lay folks. You are people who have gotten through 34 and a half lectures of this course. Therefore, you know—or you may recall—that there are subjects and there are subjects. For example, in, *the man saw a woman*, the man did something to the woman; something happened to the woman as a result of the man being there and doing stuff. Whereas in *the man says*, he just kind of said something. That is, there is a difference between a subject that affects an object and a subject that's just kind of there experiencing things or not affecting an object.

We have seen that before; that's the ergativity marking. There are many, many, many languages in the world where how you express a subject is different depending on whether or not there is a patient in the sentence. Is it an agent? Did the boy kick the ball? Then that's one way that you mark a subject. Is the boy just sleeping? Is the boy just saying? Then the boy is marked in a different way. We know from this—just from the way man is marked here and then not marked where there's no object—that Kabardian is an ergative language; so we can see that just from there.

Let's go back to the SOV part. We're looking at how this is a language that puts its verbs on the end. Back in Lecture Fifteen, we learned that if a language puts its verbs on the end—if a language is SOV in particular—then there are certain things that we can predict will be the case. For one thing, where we have prepositions, it's going to have postpositions. This is a language where the genitive is going to come before the noun. You're not going to say, "the book of the boy"; you're going to say, "the boy's book." We saw this in an Ethiopian language called Harari, and we're going to repeat that. Here's a little chart of how Harari—a good, well-behaved SOV language—pans out (see Lecture Fifteen). That's not just Harari; remember, we were seeing pattern.

This gives us clues as to where to look for things in Kabardian, and here the sixth sentence is useful for us. For example, look at *I will show you the stars in the sky*. We know that objects come before the verb, and we also know that the object marker from the [pśaaśar]—*woman*—is [r]. If *the stars* is the object marker in sentence six, then we know that [vaagʷahar] is our object; it must mean *stars*. This is an SOV language—the verb is at the end—and so the last word must be the verb. All that's left for [wagʷəm], this first word, to connote would be *the stars in the sky*. We expect that there are going to be postpositions in this language. If the middle word means *stars*, then [wagʷəm] is going to mean *in the sky*; let's assume that it's going to be *sky in*. Just like we have *Tokyo ni*—"Tokyo in"—in Japanese because it's an SOV language and therefore it has postpositions because it's head final, let's assume that that's the case in Kabardian. We don't know this yet, but let's just imagine that either [əm] or just maybe the [m] alone is going to be our adposition in this language.

Then what about the genitive? We're going to assume that it's going to come before the noun, and so it's going to be something like *boy's house*. Looking up in four, we can see that *the edge of the earth* is going to be [śəm ɣʷənar]; roughly, like that. *I must find* is going to be the verb at the end. If that's true, then we would expect that *edge of the earth* would come out as *earth's edge*, and there would be some sort of genitive marker. Here, look at how there's this [m] on the end of *earth*. That's not really that surprising, because we're thinking, "Are *of* and *in*—as in *in the sky*—going to be indicated with the same marker?" The thing is, yeah, that makes perfect sense, because there are languages like French where *à Paris* could mean both "to Paris" and "in Paris," and so in this language we have this little [m], and that is our indication of the genitive as well. Using all of these deductions to follow one from the other, you can figure out a lot about Kabardian also using generalizations that have been found from other languages.

The final thing to look at in Kabardian is how you make a word in this language. The reason that we want to look at that is because documenting a language is also a matter of looking at its phonology, and what that means is looking at the difference between how words are generated underlyingly versus the way that they come out on the surface. Let's look at a word like *you gave it to me*. I do mean word and not sentence: In Kabardian all of that is one word; this is one of those languages. *You gave it to me*. That comes out on the underlying level as /q'ə-s-a-w-tə-aɣ-ś/; like that. Here's what those morphemes mean: We're going to start with the /s/; /s/ is *me*. The /a/ is *to*, familiar from Romance, but actually an accidental correspondence. The /w/ is *you*; /tə/ and just /tə/ alone is *give*; /aɣ / is past; and /ś / is the affirmative marker. That part there is kind of like *me you gave, yes*. That's what it means.

The /q'ə/ in the beginning is really interesting. What that little morpheme indicates is that this business of you giving it to me is something that is particularly relevant to you, and is something that you keep thinking about after it happens. I swear that's what it means. In adding that morpheme, this sentence actually means *you lent it to me*. That's how that is conveyed, because if you give it with the idea being that you're expecting to get it back and that the whole thing is kind of loaded, then it's relevant to you. The way to indicate that meaning in Kabardian is to put /q'ə/ at the head of a sentence having to do with giving. As I have noted in this course, what semantic or pragmatic concepts a language chooses to express overtly is something very idiosyncratic to each language, and what European languages tend to express is but one complex of many choices.

Then notice that there's this suffix at the end; that indicates the affirmative. Kabardian also has a negative suffix like that, and also an infix, and so you have a kind of a paradigmatic alternation that's in opposition in the Saussurian sense that is indicated between whether something is in the affirmative or the negative. We European language speakers figure that if it's in the affirmative that you can leave that there, but that's kind of the default. In most languages it is, but a language might mark both affirmative and the negative, and Kabardian does.

But more to the point is that to actually say, /q'ə-s-a-w-tə-ay-ś/ would sound absurd, even if rendered in the proper accent by a native speaker. No one would say that; that's the underlying representation. The actual sentence, which is all one word in this language, is something quite different. You see it on the screen; approximately, [q'ɪzzæpʰtʰaś]. This is something quite different from /q'ə-s-a-w-tə-ay-ś/, and we can even hear it. All sorts of things have happened because there are various processes that occur between the underlying form that's abstractly in people's heads and the way someone would actually say it.

For example, notice that in the phonemic representation—and actually this is true of all the Kabardian that we have seen—there are only two vowels: /ə/ and /a/; /ə/ is a schwa, and then there's /a/. That is something that is true in more than one language of the Caucasus, that underlyingly—according to most analyses—there are actually only two vowels. You see that in the phonetic form you've got your lax *i* up ahead, the [ɪ]. And then you've got your [æ], the kind of ugly English vowel; well, Kabardian has it too. Other things happen. All of that just happens as the result of the proximity of other consonants and the consonants coloring the vowels. Phonemically, there are only two vowels in Kabardian, even though phonetically there end up being many more. So the /q'ə/ morpheme—which is the one that indicates future relevance to you when you give it to me—actually comes out on the surface as [q'ɪ]. That's a regular process. You don't say [q'ə]; you have to say [q'ɪ].

We have the /a/—which means *to*—that ends up coming out as [æ] because of the processes that go from the phonological to the phonetic.

There's another rule that regularly makes consonants have the same voicing as the next one. For example, we see that the morpheme for *me* was /s/; an /s/, so to speak, on the phonemic level. Phonetically, it comes out as a [z] because that is the voiced rendition of /s/. Then you get things that are less intuitive to us but very normal in terms of how languages work. Because of that same kind of a process, what is a /w/—a bilabial glide, a /w/ sound on the phonemic level, which means *you*—that comes out as a [pʰ]. So, in [q'ɪzzæpʰtʰaś], what you're seeing in the [pʰ] is a remnant of what used to be a /w/. In terms of thinking of just alphabet, that makes no sense at all of course; but [pʰ] and [w] are both bilabial sounds, and so there is going to be a complementary relationship between them in some languages. You see this distance between the phonemic and the phonetic.

Then there are sounds which between the phonemic and the phonetic disappear regularly. We saw how in Saramaccan with those two verbs, *njã* and *fɔ̃*, that there is a final nasal consonant that almost always disappears when the word is rendered on the surface. Here in good old Kabardian, you see in the phonemic representation that the second-to-last consonant is one that disappears on the phonetic level, so you do not have that /ɣ/ here. However, notice—and this is the sort of thing that one has to attend to with things like this—there are two different *a* symbols involved. Here on the phonemic level, you see this third from the end, you have what we think of as kind of the print *a*. That's your ordinary vanilla [a], vanilla to a European speaker. The other *a*—you see it's different in the phonetic ([ɑ])—that's an [a] that's pronounced further back: "ah," like that. If you're a native French speaker in particular, it's the "ah" that you use when talking about a *soul*—*l'âme*—that's back there. What actually has happened is that that consonant—that consonant that we have as second to the right in the phonemic, that's a backy consonant; that one is one of those that's pronounced in the back of the mouth—it disappears, but it left its scent upon that vowel /a/ that preceded it by making that vowel further back. The next thing you know, you've got this difference between phonemic and phonetic.

The marvel of something like Kabardian is that no one knew this before a certain point. For example, I've been using the analysis of John Colarusso, who has done the most study of Kabardian. There was a time when no one knew this, and people went around saying, "They're going to say, 'You gave it to me,' then they say [qʼɪzzæpʰtʰaś]; that's what they say." The fact that underlyingly it's something as different as /qʼə-s-a-w-tə-ay-ś/ is not something anybody is going to sit and tell you. You have to get people to talk slowly, but more often you have to look at all sorts of other things going on in the language to reconstruct what is underlying versus what is said. What is the real system of this language? Nor will any layman be able to tell you, "Oh yes, we're an ergative language." Or, "Oh yes, we mark subjects differently depending on whether or not there is a patient or an object in the sentence." They'll just say, "We just say it." That's how we all feel about our languages unless we've happened to analyze them.

This is the sort of thing that linguists actually do in documenting the languages of the world, and how they've changed, and how they exist in the present context. In the next lecture, we're going to pull the camera back even further and examine theories as to how this thing called human language evolved in the first place.

Lecture Thirty-Six
The Evolution of Language

Scope: Current work exploring the question as to how language emerged in humans includes many different theories. Ray Jackendoff, for example, has developed a theory of language in which the steps of evolution would have proceeded from units of meaning to their encapsulation in "rules," a rule being anything from a word to an idiom to a grammatical process. We will also encounter work suggesting that syntax was modeled on the structure of syllables and other work suggesting that words emerged as bits of song. Explaining the origins of language means explaining not just words and writing but also the hierarchy of subsystems and their constraints that we have seen throughout this course.

Outline

I. In the past there were so many speculative proposals as to how language emerged in human beings that in 1866 the Linguistics Society of Paris banned all papers on the topic.

   A. More recently, Noam Chomsky, the father of modern syntactic theory, has generally had little sustained interest in how language emerged, which has discouraged study of the subject.

   B. However, over the past two decades there has been a reemergence in the study of the evolution of language.

II. Some speculations focus on how the first words began.

   A. Reading University linguist Steven Mithen and Cardiff University linguist Alison Wray hypothesize that our initial propensity for singing may have led to the extrapolation of words.

   B. There would have been, for instance, a warble *tebima* for when one wanted to give something to a woman, and there was another warble for when you wanted to tell someone to share something with a woman: *kumapi*.

   1. *Tebima* and *kumapi* would not be "words" or "sentences" but just calls.

   2. But suppose a smart human noticed that both calls had -*ma*- in them and abstracted that *ma* could be taken to mean just *her*?

C. This idea is supported by how mothers speak to their children in a singsong tone.

D. We can demonstrate that "musical" intuition could have generated animal-name calls; there's evidence that people can "feel" an animal name's meaning in a foreign language just by its ring.

    1. The South American Huambisa tribe call one bird a *chunchuíkit* and one fish a *máuts*.

    2. Among a group of American students tested, 98 percent could tell that a *chunchuíkit* was a bird and a *máuts* a fish.

E. Current research into whether language and music are generated in the same part of the brain points mainly to the intonational aspects of language.

F. In terms of the mastery of grammar, language and music do not overlap in the brain to the extent that we might expect.

III. The work of Brandeis linguist Ray Jackendoff offers one of the most useful proposals for how language emerged.

    A. Chomskyan syntactic theory specifies that syntax is the primary process in the generation of a sentence and that interpretation of the meaning of the words once they are placed in order is a secondary process.

    B. Jackendoff, like many linguists, has proposed that semantics are, in fact, the beginning of the process.

    C. The components of meaning are then translated into *rules*, a word Jackendoff intends in a particular way: words, expressions, or even grammatical processes that are memorized, set, or regular. Thus a single word is a rule, as is an idiom like *kick the bucket*, which does not mean what its words do and is in effect a single word; as is a set construction like *What is Chastity Bono doing in a place like this?*; and as is a regular process like adding *-ed* to a verb to mark the past.

    D. To Jackendoff, syntax is a grand process called *UNIFY* that combines all of the rule-based elements.

    E. After this, phonology is applied to the string of words that results.

        1. Phonology can work against the syntax.

        2. When we utter, "The man's coming," the *'s* is attached to *man* rather than *coming*, even though the [s] is the remnant of the verb *is*, such that we would expect it to stick to the other verbal form.

IV. Jackendoff's syntax seems to correspond to what the evolution of a language would be like.

    A. Jackendoff notes that there are real-world phenomena that seem to indicate steps along the way to humans' modern language capacity.

    B. Evidence of meaning being first seems to come from manifestations of language in damaged human beings or animals.

        1. Aphasics can lose the ability to use grammar but still retain a full vocabulary. This suggests that concepts alone are a fundamental stage in how language is produced.

        2. Vervet monkeys in Africa have three separate alarm calls for leopards, snakes, and eagles, which can be taken as their having "words" for those concepts.

        3. Dogs can master the meaning of as many as hundreds of words—but not syntax.

    C. There is evidence of less advanced levels of syntax (i.e., without UNIFY).

        1. Apes can be taught sign language or to signal with words marked visually on typing keys. They can learn hundreds of words and can string them together in simple ways.

        2. However, they do not distinguish between nouns and noun phrases or verbs and verb phrases, nor do they mark tense.

        3. People who learn second languages without explicit teaching often settle at a level lacking the more complex aspects of the language's syntax, eschewing inflectional suffixes and embedded sentences of all kinds, leaving out subjects and objects that no native speaker would.

        4. This is also the way people who develop pidgin languages talk, as the University of Hawaii's Derek Bickerton showed in the speech of late 19th-century immigrant laborers:

            Gud, dis wan. Kaukau   enikain   dis wan.
            good, this one   eat   any kind   this one

            Pilipin   ailaen   no gud. No mo   mani.
            Philippine island   no good no more money

V. There is some kind of genetic basis for language.

    A. One family in England has many members with hampered language capacity; they also lack a fine enough ability to control their mouths to speak clearly. These members lack one copy of the gene *FOXP2*, which shows that this gene is important in the language capacity.

B. Chimpanzees' version of *FOXP2* differs from ours by a mere two amino acids, suggesting that changes in that gene are connected to the fact that we talk and chimpanzees do not.

C. Moreover, geneticists note that it is rare for a gene to change this much in just the 6 million years that humans split off from the ancestor of humans and chimpanzees, suggesting that it was actively selected for because of an advantage it lent the species, rather than being a random mutation.

VI. Syntax may be the way it is because of a connection between phonology and syntax.

A. Andrew Carstairs-McCarthy at the University of Canterbury in New Zealand asks an interesting question: Why does human language rely on all full sentences having verbs and there being a difference between a noun phrase and a sentence?

B. That is, he asks why a language could not be just nouns, in contrast to how a human language renders the same exchange.

C. He noticed something in common between how syntax works and how syllables are structured.

    1. The basic structure of a syllable, in linguistic analysis, is that there is an *onset* (first sound) and a *rhyme* and that the rhyme is composed of a *nucleus* and a *coda*.

    2. This structure corresponds to a basic sentence, in which the onset is the subject NP and the rhyme is the VP, with a verb as a nucleus and an object NP as a coda.

D. There are various things about syllables that parallel sentences.

    1. Syllables can lack coda consonants (*see*, *ah*) but lack onset consonants much less frequently; similarly, sentences can lack objects.

    2. Sentences often have verbs that have little or no meaning: *Sally took a walk*; *Two and two make four*; *Tomorrow is Wednesday*. This can be seen as an inheritance from a structure based on a nucleus being a key component in syllables, in which sentences retain an element corresponding to the nucleus even when it is no longer necessary to have the nucleus convey a concept.

E. As with babies beginning with babbling syllables, maybe syllable structure was a model for how we came to structure syntax.

VII. Now that you have completed the course, I hope you will see language as used by and around you differently than before.

    A. As we have seen again and again, language is not just words and writing; language is also a hierarchy of subsystems constrained by phenomena such as the underlying versus the surface, hierarchical structure, markedness, regular processes of change, and socially conditioned variation.

    B. Abigail Adams, the wife of second president John Adams, is a useful person to train your new glasses on. In the 2008 miniseries *John Adams*, Abigail Adams is depicted as not using contractions. She utters lines such as, "You do not need to quote great men to show you are one" and "You have overburdened your argument with ostentatious erudition."

    C. From the perspective of phonology, this implies that there was strangely little difference in her speech between underlying forms and their surface ones. That is, for most English speakers, most often what begins as "You have" on the phonemic level comes out as "You've" on the phonetic one: /ju hæv/ comes out as [ju:v].

    D. Part of the reason Mrs. Adams is depicted as speaking this way is because much of her dialogue is taken from the letters she wrote to her husband. People use fewer contractions in writing than in casual speech, but the creators of the series are neglecting something you now know: There is a difference between formal language such as that used in writing and the vernacular that sociolinguists seek. The miniseries writers are having Mrs. Adams mouth the kind of speech sociolinguists elicit via the word list/minimal pair section of a sociolinguistic interview.

    E. One might have a sense that contractions are a latter-day development, but we see them in Shakespeare's plays, such as *Macbeth*—"Call 'em; let me see 'em." (4.1.63)—and *King Lear* (1.1.311–312):

        Regan: We shall further think on't.
        Goneril: We must do something, and i' the heat.

F. Interestingly, John Adams is depicted in the miniseries as using more contractions.

    1. It would appear that the writers are under a tacit impression that women speak more "properly" than men; as we have seen, this is quite often the case.

    2. However, Abigail Adams would not avoid using the contractions that are native to the gender-neutral phonology of English.

G. Abigail Adams's letters themselves are also revealing of basic concepts of linguistics you are now familiar with. For example, she writes, "You was right."

    1. This *you was* sounds Southern or black to us, and yet from the succeeding text we see that Mrs. Adams was writing in a thoroughly formal English (and note, she was born in Massachusetts).

    2. The process of change we learned of called analogy kicked in—speakers tried to make *you* fit a pattern. *You was* made sense in the singular since there was already *I was* and *he/she was*.

    3. Nor was this a chance "mistake"—she uses it regularly. Here is another example: "Mr. Barrel who was sick when you was here recovered but a younger brother of his who lived with him took the fever and died with it."

    4. *You was* is something that prescriptivism ended up chasing away, despite the fact that it technically does make the system tidier.

VIII. Thank you for coming with me all this way. To me, linguistics is a lot of things as well as a lot of fun. I do hope that you feel the same way.

Essential Reading:

Kenneally, *The First Word.*

Supplemental Reading:

Jackendoff, *Foundations of Language.*

Questions to Consider:

1. Back in the day, scholars proposed that the first words happened when people used how things sounded to name them (*bow-wow*) or how they made people feel. This was the kind of thing that led to the ban on exploring the topic in 1866; obviously it can only go so far. However, can you imagine how humans came up with words for things like *lift* or even *go*? If you find Steven Mithen and Alison Wray's idea a bit loopy (as I do), consider the awesomeness of the task of figuring out how language *really* began—with the words.

2. If you were held at gunpoint to create a language from scratch, making up new words, how would you distinguish the past and the future? Would you include a word for *the* or just leave it out? Put yourself in mind of truly growing a language from the ground up. What would *your* language be like?

Lecture Thirty-Six—Transcript
The Evolution of Language

You hear this thing that I'm doing right now, this talking? How did this start? It's one thing to talk about the way it's done now, but how did this start when there are no other creatures in the world that do it on anything approaching this level? No matter how much you love your dog and things like that, I think we can all agree that there is something special about this. Of course people have always speculated about it, and in fact back in 1866 the Linguistic Society of Paris banned all further speculation as to how language emerged because there were all these theories. One of them was the bow-wow theory—the idea that someone heard a dog barking and then figured, "Let's call that a *bow-wow*." Obviously, that can only take us so far. When we're talking about language, we mean a sentence like *He just couldn't have slid in without a connection*. That's a sentence. There's no reason that's not a representative sentence: *He just couldn't have slid in without a connection*. Where did all that come from? *Couldn't have*, the contraction; *just*, "He just couldn't have," *just*; *connection*, the fact that that has so many metaphorical extensions from what connection really means— *He just couldn't have slid in without a connection*. The fact that I say it so quickly and that it didn't take effort, how did that start? It's a very interesting question.

Noam Chomsky is, for various reasons, just not interested in the question. It doesn't interest him. For a good while during the era of modern linguistics—if you date that from the '60s—it wasn't a fashionable topic to address because especially the field of syntax has a pope of sorts, and it's him. Among a representative school of people, but over the past 15 years in particular, there's been a revivification of interest in the study of how this would have evolved, because presumably it's a product of natural selection; that's how things work.

Some things aren't. There is a kind of whale, the fin whale, and its jaw is black on one side and white on the other. It just is. There doesn't seem to be any reason for it. It doesn't have anything to do with whether it's seen from below or above; it's the sides. It just seems to be some kind of genetic quirk that's passed on; it serves no particular purpose. There are things like that that evolve in people, but language? The ability to say things like, "He just couldn't have slid in without a connection"—the fact that that allows us to develop civilization and destroy the world? I think that clearly there must have been some benefit to this originally; it seems to have gotten us pretty far. Presumably it's a product of Darwinian natural selection; but how did it start? How did we get here from there? If it was so easy and such an uninteresting process—if it was really just a matter of we'll call this that and we'll call this that—if that's what it was, why haven't any other creatures done it, especially chimpanzees? I dealt with a chimpanzee once. It was in diapers, and it clearly had something like a soul, and it grasped my hand, and that little thing—which made me very uncomfortable—could not talk. They've been taught to sign somewhat. It's real cute, but they don't talk. How is it that we did this?

The speculations have been rampant, and some of the ones that are being discussed to a certain extent today are very interesting. There's one, for example, about where words came from. We have to go beyond we're going to call this that and this that; obviously there's more going on than that. Stephen Mithen of Reading University and also the linguist Alison Murray at the University of Cardiff have hypothesized that language may come from music. The idea is that our initial propensity for singing may have led to the extrapolation of words.

For example, let's say that according to this theory there is a warbling call that there might have been among early hominids, and it would be something like *tebima*—they have not given it a melody, but that's the melody it has in my head—and if you're going to warble *tebima*, then that means that you want to give something to a female individual. So, *tebima*, like a present or something like that. Then suppose there's some other warble like *kumapi*, and *kumapi*—that one means something like you're telling someone to share something with a woman. There's *tebima* and *kumapi*, and there are these two warbles. *Tebima* and *kumapi* have something in common, and it's the syllable *ma*.

Suppose some mentally enterprising humanoid decided that *ma* must mean something, because *kumapi* and *tebima* both have this thing, and what they share in common is feminine, and so maybe they might extrapolate that *ma* means *her*. The next thing you know, you've got one of the world's first correspondences between a signifier and the signified; so *her* would be *ma*. What starts out as warbles and hums becomes language. That's supported by the fact that mothers worldwide talk to their children in a singsong tone. As charming as that theory is, it might only take us so far.

There are interesting things; for example in the Huambisa language spoken by a South American group, there is a bird called a *chunchuíkit* and there's a fish called a *máuts*. Some American students were shown the words *chunchuíkit* and *máuts*, and 98 percent of them could tell that the *chunchuíkit* was a bird and that the *máuts* was a fish, that the sounds seemed to correspond to the reference in some way. But of course the question is, how do you get from *kumapi* and all of that to *He just couldn't have slid in without a connection*? What's the process? It seems like it would only be the very beginning.

To the extent that we might be thinking that language and music are generated in the same part of the brain, current research suggests that that mainly applies to the intonational aspects of language and the mimicking, and so people who are good at picking up accents might be good at music or singing. But in terms of the mastery of grammar, in terms of the control of grammar in your native language, language and music do not overlap in the brain to the extent that we would expect—or often that many people who are talented in both areas feel—beyond that level of the music of language. It is of course only one small part of it.

That, however, is a theory of how words would have emerged. There are other theories that pull the camera back a little further on how language would have emerged. One theory that has attracted a lot of attention of late is one by a leading linguist at Brandeis, Ray Jackendoff. Jackendoff is arguing against the fundamental place that syntax alone occupies under the Chomskian paradigm. When I give the trees, that is considered the *piece de resistance*; that is where the generation of language begins. The idea, according to the Chomskian paradigm, is that there are these trees, that this corresponds to something that is in our minds, and that first the syntax is generated, then the semantics is plugged in at a later stage, just like the phonology is applied to the words strung into these trees. Jackendoff calls this a kind of syntactocentrism, and his idea is that all indications are that the semantics—that meaning—is the beginning of the process that generates language.

He has an interesting idea of what language and its components are. His idea is that *rules* are something that encompasses all sorts of things; and so a rule can, for one thing, be add the *-ed* suffix to indicate the past. But then for him, a rule is also a word. For him, a rule is also an idiom like, say, *kick the bucket*. When you talk about someone kicking the bucket, there's no bucket that they kick; you mean that they passed into another world. For him, that is a unified thing. It is one way of saying, "to die." That is a rule that you apply. His idea is that a rule would be the set kind of expression, like if you say, "What is Chastity Bono doing in a place like this?" If you think about it, you don't mean what that sentence means. You don't mean "What action is Chastity Bono performing?" What you're saying when you use that expression is, "Why is she here? What thing would bring her here?" with the presupposition that it's unusual to see Chastity Bono, for whatever reason, at that place. "What is Chastity Bono doing here?" "What is X doing here?" That is a set expression that has a particular meaning different from its actual words; that would be a rule. Jackendoff's idea is that all of these things are generated as semantic elements—they are rules; they are applied—and that all these things are brought together in syntax under a grand process called *UNIFY* that has its complexities.

Then, after that, you have the phonology applying to the string of words that results. Phonology can work against the syntax in some ways. If we say, "The man's coming," then actually the *'s*—which is the contracted *'s*— actually is appended to *man* rather than *coming*, despite the fact that the *'s* is a remnant of the verb *is*, such that we think that it would stick to the verbal form. Technically, we would think it would be *the man scoming*, but it isn't; it's *the man's coming*. It divides things differently than what the syntax and the semantics actually are.

But the point of Jackendoff's syntax is that this seems to correspond to what the evolution of language would seem to be like by kind of tracing the tape backwards and looking at its manifestations in damaged human beings or— no offense toward animals—animals and their renditions of what seems to be developed in such a different way in us. In terms of meaning being first, Jackendoff notices that aphasics can lose their ability to lose grammar, but they can maintain a full and even very colorful vocabulary. There seems to be some sense in which the vocabulary, the meanings, are primal rather than the syntactic tree. The concepts are the beginning.

More indicatively, among the Vervet monkeys in Africa there will be alarm calls that correspond to three different beings: one for leopards, one for eagles, and one for snakes. You could think of it as above and on land, but then one for snakes as well. If you think about it, those could be seen as words for those things—talk about warbles and extracting words from them. Those things could be taken as referring to leopards and snakes. Of course the only thing you can say about them is they're coming and you'd better run from them, but still they refer to those things. Those are fundamental units of meaning. The Vervet monkeys, of course, have no indication of syntax and certainly not of levels of phonology.

Or—even to show that I love animals and that there's a level in my mind where I think animals can talk, too—think about dogs. Many dogs master a great many words. I knew one who could take *walk* out from a running sentence. If you just said something like, "Well, she wanted to take a walk on the wild side," that dog would start jumping up and down. It could actually hear the word. There is a peculiar but very insistent account by one person of late that their dog actually recognized 200 words and could respond to them used at full speed, etc. Of course the dog couldn't talk, but it could understand. All of that said, there is no dog that understands that you're talking about the past as opposed to the future. There is no dog that would listen to you say, "My mother had it rough, but she did the best for us," and then kind of nod or wag its tail to indicate that it understands. Whatever dogs are doing, it is only on the level of words. It seems that that definitely would be the beginning of things.

Then in terms of UNIFY—in terms of the process of syntax as Jackendoff has worked it out—it seems that UNIFY, unlike these Chomskian trees, which are just proposed to have come out of nowhere somehow when one day somebody got struck by lightning, something (I mean really, there are people who have that little interest in it), Jackendoff's idea is that if there is a syntax, it should be something where there is an indication that it evolved in steps, because just like first you have some okapi-like being—look in the glossary for okapi; we talked about it before—the okapi grows a neck in steps, presumably. That's how evolution works. In the same way, take the apes: They can be taught sign language. They can signal words by typing them, words indicated on keys, and they can learn hundreds of words, and they can string them together in simple ways. But there's no evidence of noun phrases, verb phrases; no evidence of hierarchical structure; no evidence of any of the kind of movement processes we saw—transformations. They don't do that, and that is a slightly technical way of saying they're not really talking. For example, Washoe the wonderful chimpanzee was going through a park, and Washoe saw a swan—and this is considered the magic moment in terms of ape communications—Washoe saw a swan, and actually signed "water bird." That's pretty amazing, because that's a rare example of the ape actually saying something rather than either repeating what you said or asking for a banana. It just made a comment: "water bird." Nevertheless, we can't really know: Was that a noun phrase where *water* was an adjective and *bird* was a noun? Or was it just that Washoe was capable of saying there's some water and there is a bird? The fact is, that's as far as it went. Never has one of these apes looked up and said something like, "Life hurts" or something like that, even though it may have for said animal. That's as far is it goes.

Or there are pidgin languages in the way that ordinary human beings will often talk if they have to learn a language very quickly—have no reason to learn the entire language. Here's a situation where there's a very elementary syntax. For example, in Hawaii, starting in the late 1800s, there were many laborers brought there working in plantations, such as for Dole (for juices that are too sweet). There were Filipinos, Koreans, Japanese, and various other people in small numbers. There was a pidgin kind of Hawaiian-English that was spoken. If somebody was saying what we can kind of translate as, "It's better than in the Philippines here; here you can get all kinds of food, but over there, there isn't any money," what they have is, "*Gud, dis wan. Kaukau*"—that means eat—"*Kaukau enikain dis wan.*" And so, "Food, any kind, this. Philippine Island no good; no more money"; and so very elementary syntax. There seems to be something that could evolve under Jackendoff's conception.

As time has gone by, it has definitely become clear that there is some kind of genetic specification for language. We're still working out—we, as if I'm doing that research—they are still working out how this would have happened, but it's been shown that there is a family in England who have an interestingly hampered linguistic capacity. You show them a picture of something called a *wug*, and then you show them a picture of several of these *wugs* and say, "OK, what's this?" An ordinary person will say, "Wugs." They have trouble with that, and there are all sorts of indications that their language ability is compromised in some way. It turns out that they lack one copy of a gene called *FOXP2*, which shows that this gene is important in the language capacity. It's very complicated because we've seen that the gene itself has something to do with motor control, but that's not why I can say something like, "She just couldn't have slid in without the connection." Some of the motor control is far beyond the mouth and the tongue. Also, this family had been shown to also have slightly compromised intelligence in general, so it has something to do with that.

Then you see that the marvel of genes in that you look at chimpanzees and they have a *FOXP2* gene, too; it differs from ours only by two amino acids. Just that little difference makes the difference between their cheeping and eating bananas and not really talking and "water bird" and us doing what I'm doing right now. It's quite amazing; it's tantalizing what's going on with that gene. But there definitely seems to be something. That gene starts evolving in the way that it does in us; you can trace back biochemically by looking at markers in the genetic material. You can see that this made this kind of detour, all within just about 6 million years. Once humans split off from chimpanzees, this thing changes. Genes don't change—there's always a little bit of random change—but a gene doesn't change that much unless there's something driving it to it. There's something that drove humans to speak, and that was advantageous. What the mechanics of this were is harder to figure out.

Andrew Carstairs-McCarthy at the University of Canterbury in New Zealand has noticed that there may be, in the evolutionary sense, some kind of connection between phonology and syntax. Often—because syntax is just so yummy—we are interested in looking at how we have syntax or how we develop words, but we also have phonology, and how would that have worked? He asks a very interesting question. You have to really pull the camera back, pull it way back out to like Mars, and think about what a language could have been. For example, here is an ordinary exchange between Bill and Alice—always these bland names in linguistics; those people should be Justin and Bree, but they're not—Bill and Alice:

> Bill: "Hello. I was sorry to hear you had been ill. You're certainly looking a lot better now!" [I think that this is supposed to be in a British accent.] "You're certainly looking a lot better now!"

> Then Alice says: "Yes, I had a nasty bout of bronchitis for three weeks, but I've got over it—" [oh yeah, this is British] "—but I've got over it, fortunately. Just as well, because we've got to get ready for Bridget's wedding next month."

That is Bill and Alice. Why does it have to be that there are both noun phrases and verb phrases? Because it could just be nouns. Why can't it just be:

> Bill: "Greetings. My regret about news of your earlier illness. A definite improvement in your present appearance."

> Then Alice says: "Yes. My three weeks' endurance of a nasty bout of bronchitis, but my fortunate recovery. Timeliness due to the urgency of preparation for Bridget's wedding next month."

Why couldn't it all be in nouns? Because as silly as that sounds to us, it just sounds silly because that's not the way it is. You could have a whole language like that.

Andrew Carstairs-McCarthy notices that there is something in common between how syntax works and how syllables are structured. The basic structure of a syllable in linguistic analysis is that there's an *onset*—that's the first consonant—and then there's a *rhyme*. The rhyme—that's the rest of it—is composed of a *nucleus* and then a *coda*, and that coda is the final consonant. What's interesting is that that structure corresponds to a basic sentence where you could think of the onset being the subject NP, and then the rhyme could be the VP, and then the verb could be the nucleus, and the object NP could be the coda.

The reason that Carstairs-McCarthy has this seemingly eccentric, but actually very ingenious, idea is that there are things about syllables that seem to parallel sentences. For example, syllables do not have to have codas, and so *see* is one where you've got an onset and a nucleus *ee*, but there is no final consonant. But lacking onset consonants, that's much less, and to the extent that you have a vowel beginning a word, as often as not really there's something underneath that we don't talk about. If I say, "alley," I'm not saying [æli] and just starting with the vowel; actually, there's a glottal stop in the phonetic representation. I'm saying [ʔæli], "alley," like that. A Martian might catch it and write our language that way.

That's something that happens in terms of language as well. That's something that happens with syllables. Sentences are the same way. It's easy for a sentence to lack an object: *Billy sleeps*. But then in terms of lacking a subject, sentences tend to resist that. They want to have a syllabic onset, so to speak. For example, if it's raining, why can't we say, "Raining"? But we say, "It's raining." *It* what? What? Is *it* God? Is *it* like the NASDAQ? Is *it* the clouds? It's clear who's raining; why don't we just say, "Raining"? We say, "It's raining" as if we have to fill in the subject in that way. Or often a sentence will have verbs that don't really have a whole lot of meaning, and so *Sally took a walk*. Took? Where'd she take it? Really, we just mean that there was a walk taken, and that it was Sally who did it. Or *Two and two make four*. Really? Why aren't they *are four*? What is it *make*? *Tomorrow is Wednesday*. Why do you need *is*? In many languages, you would say, "Tomorrow Wednesday," and people aren't walking around bumping into walls. That use of the verb *to be* is very peculiar in European languages.

In the same way, the nucleus—which we can see is corresponding to the verb and syllable structure—is key. It seems that sentences are trying to retain some indication of the nucleus even when there's nothing in the meaning to correspond to it. The idea is that maybe it was syllable structure that came first, and we assume—because of the way babies babble; because of warbling like *kumapi* and *tebima*—that that would come first, and that maybe syllable structure was a model for how we came to structure syntax. That's another interesting idea in the evolution of language these days.

In any case, all of those things are speculative at this point. We still don't know how it is that humans have come to do what I'm doing right now. But I hope that in this course—you realize that now we're nearing the end of Lecture Thirty-Six—you will be able to see languages used around you differently than before, and not just as words and writing but as a hierarchy of subsystems, constrained by phenomena that we've seen again and again, such as underlying versus surface; hierarchical structure; markedness; regular processes of change; and socially conditioned variation that we saw a certain amount of.

In order to keep in your heads the sort of things that I hope you would have taken from this course, we're going to use, of all people, John Adams's wife, Abigail Adams. This is what you need to take away. There is a miniseries, *John Adams*—big HBO business, hi-def—and one interesting thing that you see in it is that Abigail Adams almost never uses contractions. She sits around saying things like, "You do not need to quote great men to show you are one" or "You have overburdened your argument with ostentatious erudition." That's pleasant to see, but it would seem to indicate that there's unusually little difference for Abigail Adams between her underlying and her surface forms. For example, ordinarily among even very standard English speakers the underlying form is *you have* (/ju hæv/), but in any kind of rapid casual speech as often as not the rendition will be on the surface *you've* ([ju:v]). You notice that we have our sign of length here for [u]; that length is all that's left of all that material that got lost between the underlying and the surface.

Part of the reason that Mrs. Adams is depicted as speaking that way is because a lot of her dialogue is taken from letters that the actual Abigail Adams wrote to her husband, and people do use fewer contractions in written language than in casual speech. But what you who have taken this course now know is that very innocently the writers are neglecting that there's a difference between formal language—such as the kind that is used in writing—and the vernacular that, for example, we've seen that sociolinguists seek. The miniseries writers are having Mrs. Adams mouth the kind of speech that sociolinguists elicit by having somebody read a word list or to read a list of minimal pairs like *those* and *doze*, if they're looking for people who pronounce *those* as "dose"; roughly like that. There is a lack of overt awareness among the writers that human beings, no matter what their social class, speak on an everyday level—especially to their spouses—in the vernacular, not in the variety that they would use when they were writing letters.

Of course there may be a sense that contractions are a latter-day development, but we see them in Shakespeare's plays. This is Macbeth, and Macbeth is not a man from the streets. At one point he's asking to see the apparitions who are going to tell him what his fate is, and he says, "Call 'em, let me see 'em." That's what Shakespeare has him saying, so there were contractions. Nor was this just a male thing. We can see it in women. In *King Lear*, Regan says, "We shall further think on't." That's a contraction we don't use now, but you see it a lot in Shakespeare. Goneril says, "We must do something," and she doesn't say, "and in the heat"; she says, "and i' the heat." That's what she says. It's not about gender. Nevertheless, if we might think that—I think that that is something that the people doing the miniseries are thinking, too—there is a sense that women speak more "properly" than men. As we've seen, that is true: Women do use more prescriptive forms than men do. However, that is not so much the case that you would have Abigail Adams sitting around not using the contractions that are native to the gender-neutral phonology of the language known as English.

In fact, if you look at Abigail Adams's letters, you can see some things that show that she was very real. For example, it's January 7, 1793, and this is what Abigail Adams with her proper self wrote: "You was right. The chief Majestrate denies his having given permission to the Mobility to pull down the Theatre. His prime Minister." She started out with—I didn't misread it—"You was right." That's how she started. John Adams does that a lot too. That sounds Southern or black to us, but really, notice that she was writing in very formal English and she was born in Massachusetts. "You was right. The chief Majestrate denies his having given permission to the Mobility to pull down the Theatre. His prime Minister." This was formal English. All that means is that this was a time when even a formal writer and speaker was trying to exert what we've seen as the linguistic process of analogy on the language. If you say, "I was," and if you say, "he or she was," and if you're using *you* in the singular, then it should be "you was." That's something that prescriptivism ended up chasing away, despite the fact that it technically does make the system tidier.

Something else: That "you was" is so weird—it is so odd to think of John Adams's wife saying, "you was," given the sociolinguistic situation today—

that I want to show you it wasn't a mistake; there's no blot on it. Here's another one—December 28, 1798—"Mr. Barrel who was sick when you was here recovered but a younger Brother of his who lived with him took the fever and dyed with it." That's Abigail Adams's actual speech, and it shows that in many ways *plus ça change*. She didn't know that she was writing improper English; that was decided later.

In any case, I think that we've come to the end, and I want to thank you for coming with me all this way over 36 half hours of me telling you such things as these. I just hope that now, if you ever have occasion to be asked what linguistics is or if you ever find yourself going back to an old habit and asking it of yourself, you'll have more of a sense of it than you may have had when you began the course. To me, linguistics is a lot of things, as well as a lot of fun. I do hope that you feel the same way. Thank you very much.

Timeline

1786 .... Sir William Jones addresses the
Bengal Asiatic Society and observes
that Sanskrit, Greek, and Latin are
similar in grammatical structure to such
a degree that they must all trace to a
single ancestor, "which, perhaps, no
longer exists." This was the first clear
acknowledgment that languages exist
in an evolutionary relationship to
one another.

1822 .... Jacob Grimm proposes what is later
termed Grimm's Law, describing the
regular contrasts between consonants in
cognate words in Germanic languages
and others of the Indo-European family
(i.e., English's *father* and *fish* are *pater*
and *piscis* in Latin). This inaugurates
the study of sound change as a regular
process, the beginning of what would
become modern linguistic science.

1916 .... Ferdinand de Saussure's *Course in
General Linguistics* is published
posthumously, outlining the analysis of
language not from a historical
perspective but as it exists at the
moment, proposing that grammar
consists of a conglomeration of signs of
contrasting function. This furnished the
basis of modern linguistic description of
languages' grammars.

1924 .... The Linguistic Society of America
(LSA) is formed. The LSA holds an
annual conference, the largest in the
linguistics field, and publishes the
journal *Language*.

1926 .... The Prague School is founded in Czechoslovakia among Czech and Russian expatriate linguists, including Roman Jakobson and Nikolai Trubetzkoy. Among its achievements is a conception of markedness among sounds and its relationship to language production and acquisition, as well as the conception of sounds as characterized by opposing qualities such as voiced and unvoiced. Modern phonology begins here.

1933 .... Leonard Bloomfield's *Language* is published. Bloomfield officially imprints the study of unknown languages' grammars from a purely scientific perspective, using the tools developed by de Saussure, the Prague school, and others to describe languages' phonology, morphology, and syntax. This approach has come to be termed structuralist linguistics.

1957 .... Noam Chomsky's *Syntactic Structures* is published. In this work and future ones, Chomsky develops a theory that sentences as generated at a deep-structure level and as produced at a surface-structure level are often quite different and that there is an innate universal grammar structure in which all languages, despite their surface differences, are founded. Modern syntactic theory begins here.

1966 .... Joseph Greenberg's *Language Universals, With Special Reference to Feature Hierarchies* is published. Greenberg shows that languages do not consist of random conglomerations of grammatical traits but that certain ones are only present when others are, in a nested fashion. This inspires the study of language universals and typology and provides a body of observations that generativists find it useful to attempt to explain in their framework.

1966 .... William Labov's *The Social Stratification of English in New York City* is published. Labov shows that language changes at different rates and in different ways among subpopulations according to gender, class, and race and does so with various ingenious systems for eliciting casual (genuine), rather than artificially "polite," speech. This inaugurates the now-vigorous subfield of sociolinguistics.

2001 .... The *FOXP2* gene is discovered to play an important role in humans' speech capacity. Specifically, the gene produces a protein that activates other genes; currently, these appear to include genes connected to brain development and motor control. Human *FOXP2* differs from that of chimpanzees by only two amino acids, but it would appear that, in a fashion as yet unknown, this determines that humans are alone among the world's fauna in using full language.

Glossary

age grading: When a variable is used more by younger people than older ones; often evidence that the young's choice is a change happening in the language.

agent: A subject that has an effect upon the object (*the boy kicked the ball*) rather than experiencing the object (*the boy liked the ball*) or referring to no object (*the boy slept*).

agglutinative: A language that assigns grammatical functions one at a time to discretely separate morphemes that agglutinate together, like Turkish and Swahili (see *fusional*).

allophone: One of two or more variant renditions of a basic sound (*phoneme*) in a language, determined by what kinds of sounds it occurs near. The [p] sound is pronounced with a puff of air when initial (*Paul*) but not otherwise (*spat*); these are two allophones of the phoneme /p/.

alveolar: Sounds produced by tapping the alveolar ridge, behind the upper teeth, with the tip of the tongue. In English, these include [t], [d], [s], and [n].

analytic: A language in which morphemes are generally separate words rather than occurring as prefixes and suffixes; sometimes called *isolating languages*.

assimilation: When a sound takes on qualities of a sound it occurs near; the *m* in *impossible* is due to what was once an [n] assimilating to the bilabial articulation of [p].

code switching: Using two or more languages within the same sentence or utterance.

complement phrase: A relative or subordinate clause, represented in theoretical syntax notation as a subsentence headed by a comp (C) node.

compound: A word composed of two content morphemes, such as *blackbird* and *streetcar*.

consonant weakening: The tendency for consonants to change into less phonetically robust ones via usage; stops become fricatives, fricatives become glides, and glides disappear: *ripe* is *maturus* in Latin, *mathuro* in Castilian, and *mûr* in French.

constituent: An element in a sentence that may consist of a single word, such as a noun or verb, but can also consist of this plus its modifiers: *a small, black cat* is a constituent—namely, a noun phrase.

conversational implicature: Conventionalized understandings that set requests and statements presuppose responses that do not correspond literally to what was asked or stated; *Do you have the time?* is not understood as a query as to whether one is wearing a watch.

covert prestige: The tacit sense of pride that vernacular speakers have in variables officially considered nonstandard; i.e., "the way we talk in these parts."

deixis: A language's mechanisms for placing a statement in time, space, and attitudinal realm.

derivational: Morphemes that typically change a root to a different part of speech (*happy*, *happiness*) or, if not, create a different word (*friend*, *friendship*).

diachronic: A perspective on language addressing its change over time.

dual marking: In many languages, one can mark not only the plural but more precisely that there are two of something.

ergativity: When a language marks subjects when they are agents of patients with one marker but other subjects with a different marker or not at all. If there is this different marker for nonagents, it is also used on objects. Thus the *ergative* marker marks agents, while the *absolutive* marker marks objects and nonagent subjects.

experiencer: A subject that does not affect the object; e.g., *I like Alice*; *I see a snowflake*.

fricative: "Hissy" sounds involving letting air flow in an obstructed fashion; in English, examples include [f], [s], and [h].

fusional: A language in which grammatical morphemes often indicate two or more functions; e.g., in *walks*, *-s* indicates both present tense and third-person singular.

given information: Content in a sentence that is already known via previous exchange and is thus often abridged; A: *Who took my pen?* B: *That man.* A: *Where did he go?* In the final sentence, *he* is an abbreviation of *That man*, possible because it refers to given information.

glides: Consonants produced with only passing friction, to the point of being almost like vowels; in English, [w] and the sound of *y* ([j]).

grammar: In linguistics, this refers not to "proper" grammar but to the basic workings of sentence structure (as well as, in practice, often phonology).

head: The morpheme that determines the syntactic type of phrase (i.e., noun phrase, verb phrase) of which the morpheme is a member; it is the morpheme being modified by the others; in *the bushy old anteater*, the head is the noun *anteater*.

Head-First Parameter: A syntactic setting in which heads occur either first (when set "on") or finally (when set "off") in their *constituents* in a more-or-less regular fashion throughout the language.

historical linguistics: The study of how language changes over time, as opposed to its state in the here and now.

hypercorrection: A tendency to use forms considered standard to such a pronounced extent as to surpass the habits of even the most typically "proper" speakers; often observed among working-class speakers engaging in the reading of word lists.

illocutionary: Utterances that constitute, in themselves, the execution of an action, such as *I apologize*.

implicational universals: The tendency for certain grammatical structures to occur in a language only if certain others do; e.g., a language has dual marking only if it also has plural marking; many languages have only plural marking, but none have only dual marking.

indicator: A variable with no social significance; i.e., *he's not* versus *he isn't*.

Indo-European: The language family that most European languages belong to, as well as most of those of Iran and India.

inflection: A grammatical morpheme that fulfills a syntactic function but does not change a word's part of speech or meaning; e.g., *-s* in *walks*.

manner of articulation: One of several ways of producing consonants; i.e., stops, fricatives, nasals, glides; contrast with *place of articulation*.

markedness: This is a multifarious term in linguistics, both over time and across the various subfields. As used in this course, *marked* features are sounds or grammatical features that are less common across all languages than those found most commonly in languages (*unmarked* features). Often the marked rendition is found only when the unmarked rendition is found in a language as well. For example, the final sound in Bach (a voiceless velar fricative) is more marked—meaning less common—than the sound of *a* in father. To take a grammatical example, some languages mark not only plurality but the more specific concept of the dual, indicating that there are two of something. Dual marking, which is less common than plural marking and only occurs in languages that also have plural marking, is more marked than plural marking.

marker: A variable that has social significance; i.e., *singing* versus *singin'*.

minimal pair: Words that contrast in only a single sound, such as *those* and *doze*; often adduced to determine what constitutes a phoneme.

morpheme: A unit of meaning, of which a word may contain several; *hunters* contains three morphemes (*hunt*, *-er*, and *-s*).

new information: Content in a sentence or utterance that is novel, marked explicitly as such in many languages with particles or affixes.

nonproductive: A derivational morpheme no longer applied to new words, such as *-dom* in *freedom*.

observer's paradox: The fact that vernacular speakers tend to switch to standard speech in the presence of investigators from outside of their community.

patient: An object that is directly affected by a subject (*the boy kicked the ball*).

phoneme: A sound in a language that can make the difference between one word and another (*bat* versus *pat*), as opposed to a sound that is just a variant way of rendering another one (the pronunciation of *l* in *lick* is quite different from its pronunciation in *oil*, yet both are "the same sound," the phoneme /l/).

place of articulation: Where in the mouth a consonant is produced (bilabial, alveolar, velar, glottal, etc.); contrast with *manner of articulation*.

polysynthetic: A language in which a verb's subject, object, and other associated components must either be compounded with the verb or reflected on the verb in the form of affixes; e.g. in Mohawk, to say, "He likes babies," one must say either, "He baby-likes" or, "He likes them, babies."

prescriptive: The perspective on language stipulating that there is a "correct" and an "incorrect" way to speak, as contrasted with the descriptive tradition, which accepts all generalized speech patterns as legitimate.

Pro-Drop Parameter: A syntactic setting that, when set "on," allows subject pronouns to be omitted (Spanish *hablo*, "I speak"). Also known as the Null Subject Parameter.

semantic role: Classes of meaning that elements of a sentence correspond to independently of their grammatical functions as subjects or objects; e.g., in *the dog bit the man* and *the man was bitten by the dog*, the subject is *dog* in one and *man* in the other, but in both, the agent is *dog* and the patient is *man*.

sociolinguistics: The study of how language varies according to social factors such as class, race, and gender and external factors such as bilingualism and culture.

syllabary: A writing system in which signs indicate syllables rather than individual sounds.

synchronic: The perspective on language analyzing its present state, rather than the *diachronic* perspective, which addresses language as it changes.

syntax: In linguistics, this refers not to the exercise of sentence parsing on paper but to the mechanisms ordering words in sentences after the processes of phonology and morphology have been applied.

topic: In linguistics, an element serving as the focus of an observation, separate from the syntactic subject of the sentence; in *Me, I like pomegranates*, *me* is the topic.

trace: In syntactic theory, a "space" left behind when an element is moved in the pathway from deep structure to surface structure; e.g., in *What did you see?* it is hypothesized that there is a trace after *see*, an empty or "phantom" node (sometimes indicated as T), left behind by *what*.

transfer: The use of native language grammatical features in one's rendition of a second language, resulting in, for example, a foreign accent in terms of phonology.

transformation: Processes involving the movement of words or constituents in the process of generating a sentence from deep to surface structure, such as the movement of *what* to the front of the sentence in *What did you see?*

variable: One of two or more possible renditions of a sound or affix in a language, with one rendition often considered less "proper" than others, such as *singing* versus *singin'*.

vernacular: Casual speech learned as a child without explicit tutelage, as opposed to standard forms often learned through teaching and reading.

Verb Attraction Parameter: A syntactic setting that brings verbs forward in sentences, hypothesized by some linguists to result from ample verb-conjugation suffixes; thus in French *J'embrasse souvent Marie* but in English *I often kiss Mary*; in English the verb stays after the adverb because there is little conjugational morphology in the language. Sometimes referred to as the Inflection Parameter.

Biographical Notes

Noam Chomsky (1928–): Best known in the wider world as a leading leftist political commentator, he was also the founder of today's most influential school of syntactic analysis. He was born in Philadelphia. While doing his graduate work in linguistics on Hebrew grammar at the University of Pennsylvania, he found that the then-reigning theories of how language is structured could not provide a systematic analysis of Hebrew. In his dissertation, published in 1957 as *Syntactic Structures*, he argued that language is generated in the mind first in a deep-structure rendition, upon which various transformations are applied to yield a surface structure. He took a faculty position at the Massachusetts Institute of Technology (where he is currently a professor emeritus) and has developed the hypothesis that humans are born with a hardwired capacity for language, within a larger cognitivist philosophy of the human mind, notoriously opposed to the behaviorist conceptions of B. F. Skinner.

Joseph Greenberg (1915–2001): Trained as an anthropologist at Northwestern University but found himself most interested in linguistics. He spent most of his career teaching at Stanford University. Greenberg noted that languages' grammars are organized according to a flow-chart principle, in which certain features are only present if other ones are; otherwise, these features are never present (i.e., no language has vowels like the *i* sound in *sit* or the *u* sound in *but* that does not also have the basic set [a], [e], [i], [o], [u]) and, in this, founded the subfield of typology. He also grouped the 1,000-plus languages of Africa into four subfamilies and, more controversially, the Native American languages into three subfamilies, as well as grouping Indo-European, Uralic, Eskimo-Aleut, and some other families into a megafamily called Eurasiatic.

Jacob Grimm (1785–1863): Collected folktales in his native Prussia with his brother Wilhelm and is thus best known for the legacy of *Grimm's Fairy Tales*. This collecting, however, was one part of a broader interest in the earlier stages of his country's language and culture. After training in law and serving in assorted administrative posts, he took his place as a professor at the University of Göttingen, where he wrote a seminal description of German grammar. (According to the convention of the period, this was actually a treatise on the historical development of the language). Grimm's most important insight was that the sounds in a language change in consistent fashion over time, demonstrated most memorably by the regular differences in how consonants are rendered in cognate words in

Germanic languages and classical ones like Latin and Greek. This is called Grimm's Law. Grimm was also a fervent German nationalist and served briefly in the Frankfurt National Parliament in the wake of the political upheavals of 1848.

Wilhelm von Humboldt (1767–1835): During his lifetime, he was most widely known as an accomplished diplomat and ambassador for his native Prussia. He was also a political philosopher, espousing classical liberalism ("The government is best which makes itself unnecessary") in *On the Limits of State Action*, a primary source for the ideas that would later influence the Anglophone world through John Stuart Mill's *On Liberty*. Von Humboldt also established the Prussian educational system as a world-class one; as Minister of Education, he was central to the creation of the University of Berlin. He began researching linguistic issues mainly after retiring from politics in 1819. Besides his typologization of languages, his most influential work included foundational research on the Basque language and its history and an exploration of the relationship between languages and their speakers' world views, which anticipated later work in this vein by Edward Sapir and Benjamin Lee Whorf. Von Humboldt's brother Alexander was a world-renowned naturalist.

Roman Jakobson (1896–1982): Born in Russia, he embarked upon the study of linguistics there. After the revolution there, he relocated to Czechoslovakia, where he was part of what came to be known as the Prague Circle. Here Jakobson was central to the formulation—developing the ideas of Ferdinand de Saussure—of conceptions of markedness hierarchies and their relationship to phonology, language acquisition, and typology. After a move to Copenhagen, Jakobson moved to New York City. He then taught at Harvard for the rest of his career, where he collaborated with Morris Halle on a foundational text on markedness theory (*Fundamentals of Language*, 1956). Jakobson's scholarly interests also included the study of communication in the broader sense, as well as poetry and art.

William Labov (1927–): The founder of variationist linguistics, which analyzes how language structure differs according to sociological factors such as gender, class, and race. After spending his younger adulthood as a chemist, Labov took his doctorate in linguistics at Columbia University in 1964 and since 1971 has taught at the University of Pennsylvania. His foundational text was his master's thesis, analyzing how the local speech of Martha's Vineyard was changing due to factors of social identity. He followed this with his signature study, *The Social Stratification of English in New York City* (1966), analyzing the gradual disappearance of the once-prevalent local New York accent via innovative methods of eliciting unmonitored speech from strangers. He also pioneered the study of Black English as a systematic speech variety in *Language in the Inner City* (1972).

Rasmus Christian Rask (1787–1832): Often cited for his astonishing capacity for learning foreign languages, he reportedly spoke about 25. A Dane, he began as assistant librarian at the University of Copenhagen and was soon supported in a two-year expedition to Iceland, after which he wrote the first grammatical description of the Icelandic language. He went on to do foundational research on the relationships between the languages of Northern Europe, Greek, and Latin and the languages of Iran and India, travelling widely to gather data and learning to speak new languages along the way. In his *An Investigation Concerning the Source of the Old Northern or Icelandic Language* (1818), Rask was the first to observe the systematic difference between Icelandic and Greek consonants, which would soon be developed as Grimm's Law.

Edward Sapir (1884–1939): His most tangible legacy to modern linguistics is his 1921 book, *Language*, a readable and lucid introduction to the study of human speech. This book and his other writings include an argument that languages to some extent reflect the thought patterns and cultural outlooks of their speakers, an idea that Sapir's student Benjamin Lee Whorf took further after his death. Sapir was born in Prussia and did his graduate study in anthropology at Columbia University in New York. He taught at the University of Chicago and Yale University. His research focus was on Native American languages of the Pacific coast, especially those of the Athabaskan family; he worked with the last surviving Yahi, Ishi, to document the language. Sapir died at 55 but inspired later prominent followers such as Whorf, Mary Haas, and Zellig Harris.

Ferdinand de Saussure (1857–1913): A Geneva-born linguist, he attained his doctorate at the University of Leipzig and specialized in the Indo-European language family. His monograph *Course in General Linguistics*, although actually compiled after his death by two of his students from notes taken from his lectures, was the foundation of the concept of language as composed of signs encoding opposite meanings and thus of the basic framework of modern linguistic analysis. During his lifetime, de Saussure was best known for his hypothesis that the ancestor of all of the Indo-European languages had a trio of laryngeal consonants now extinct in all of its descendants but deducible via tracing backward from certain particularities of cognates in the languages. The discovery of documents in the extinct Indo-European language Hittite proved de Saussure correct, despite the initial rejection of his idea.

Benjamin Lee Whorf (1897–1941): Despite his renown as a thinker on linguistic issues today, he was during his lifetime a fire-prevention inspector for the Hartford Fire Insurance Company with a degree in chemical engineering from the Massachusetts Institute of Technology. He pursued linguistics as a hobby, and it was while taking linguistics courses at Yale that he came under the influence of Edward Sapir. As a result, he developed and promulgated the Sapir-Whorf hypothesis, proposing that people's languages channel the way that they perceive the world. Whorf was especially interested in the Hopi language and also studied Mayan and Nahuatl. Whorf, like Sapir, died early (at 44), but the influence of his writings on research in linguistics, anthropology, and psychology continues to this day, gathered in the now-classic anthology *Language, Thought, and Reality*.

Bibliography

Arlotto, Anthony. *Introduction to Historical Linguistics*. Boston: University Press of America, 1972. An especially clear introduction to comparative reconstruction of protolanguages, often assigned in undergraduate courses some years ago. Newer books in the vein have come along, but this one is worth seeking in a library for its conciseness, as the newer ones cover the historical linguistics field more broadly.

Bailey, Richard W. *Nineteenth-Century English*. Ann Arbor: University of Michigan Press, 1996. This book, pitched to general readers as well as scholars, gives thorough (but not compulsive) coverage of what English was like two centuries ago, and it gives invaluable perspective on the arbitrariness of what is considered "proper speech" from one era to another, revealing English as, like all languages, a vast smudge of variations on a theme.

Baker, Mark C. *The Atoms of Language*. New York: Basic, 2001. This is a clear and engaging presentation of the parameter concept by a leading linguist who is one of today's leading proponents of the hypothesis. A fine job of translating an often highly abstract and jargon-heavy school of thought into terms effective for laymen.

Baugh, A. C., and T. Cable. *A History of the English Language*. Englewood Cliffs, NJ: Prentice-Hall, 1978. One of those deathless staple sources, a standard accessible history of English for those hungry for the details but not the trivia.

Bauman, Richard, and Joel Sherzer. *Explorations in the Ethnography of Speaking*. 2nd ed. London: Cambridge University Press, 1989. Long out of print, this anthology remains a classic source of studies in the ethnography of communication framework. I include it in particular because of one of the most illuminating and accessible articles on language use I am aware of, the one on rural Antigua by Karl Reisman, which I highly recommend.

Bernstein, Basil. *Pedagogy, Symbolic Control, and Identity: Theory, Research, Critique*. Lanham, MD: Rowan & Littlefield, 2000. For those interested in engaging Bernstein more closely, this anthology gathers his most significant work; this is a new edition that includes works that an earlier one did not.

Brown, Penelope, and Stephen C. Levinson. *Politeness: Some Universals in Language Usage*. Cambridge: Cambridge University Press, 1987. This remains the foundational text of the study of politeness and is accessible to people outside of linguistics and psychology. It is still in print and is especially useful in addressing three very distinct cultures: America (and England), the Tzeltal Mayans of Mexico, and the Tamil of India.

Bryson, Bill. *The Mother Tongue: English and How it Got that Way*. New York: William Morrow, 1990. Unsurpassed as a jolly, often laugh-out-loud trip through the history of English. Baugh & Cable will give the details, but this is a great introduction.

Colarusso, John. *A Grammar of the Kabardian Language*. Calgary: University of Calgary Press, 1992. This is the only full-length grammatical description of Kabardian. I chose this language because it is so complex that it almost beggars belief that anyone actually speaks it, and those with a bent for checking out obscure tongues just for the glory of it might enjoy curling up with this grammar (luckily, available in an inexpensive paperback).

Comrie, Bernard. *Language Universals and Linguistic Typology*. Chicago: University of Chicago Press, 1981. The closest thing to a book for interested laypeople on universals and implicational hierarchies; I recall reading this one as a first-year graduate student before I was familiar with many concepts or much terminology, and yet it came through loud and clear.

Croft, William. *Typology and Universals*. Cambridge: Cambridge University Press, 2003. This book, revised from a well-received first edition, covers in detailed fashion the basic concepts applied to by specialists in typology. Not one for the beach, but by no means too dense for anyone but superspecialists, either.

Crystal, David. *The Cambridge Encyclopedia of the English Language*. Cambridge: Cambridge University Press, 1995. A magnificent, almost imposingly rich trip through English, past and present, in all of its facets, as beautifully illustrated as the previous volume. Captures between two covers a magnificent volume of information, much of it otherwise hard to access.

———. *The Cambridge Encyclopedia of Language*. Cambridge: Cambridge University Press, 1997. An invaluable encyclopedia, lavishly illustrated, on anything one might want to know about language and languages. This has been at arm's length from my desk for 10 years now.

———. *The Fight for English: How Language Pundits Ate, Shot, and Left*. Oxford: Oxford University Press, 2007. Linguists' anti-prescriptivist stance summarized in a pointed yet temperate tone in a single book, well keyed to the world we live in today.

Farber, Barry. *How To Learn Any Language: Quickly, Easily, Inexpensively, Enjoyably and on Your Own.* Secaucus, NJ: Citadel, 2001. A pleasant-to-read and spot-on guide to how to learn a foreign language by yourself, showing how to make the crucial step beyond reciting the words and sentences in your self-teaching book and generating the language on your own "for real." Not a scholarly book, but effective in every way.

Fasold, Ralph. *The Sociolinguistics of Language.* Oxford: Basil Blackwell, 1990. Those who want a closer look at how socially conditioned variation in language leads to change in the language will do best to consult the eighth chapter of this textbook on sociolinguistics. It has not become one of the standard ones, which is a shame because the author, a career sociolinguist, is a born teacher and writes engagingly.

Finegan, Edward. *Language: Its Structure and Use.* 5th ed. Boston: Thomas Wadsworth, 2008. A uniquely reader-friendly linguistics textbook and likely the one best suited for people outside of a classroom who simply want an introduction to the subject.

Gass, Susan M., and Larry Selinker. *Second Language Acquisition: An Introductory Course.* New York: Routledge, 2008. A solid, comprehensive survey of the best of what has been thought and said about second-language acquisition; it is especially useful in that this subfield straddles several disciplines and subdisciplines and thus can be challenging to gain a bird's-eye view of.

Gentner, Dedre, and Susan Goldin-Meadow, eds. *Language in Mind: Advances in the Study of Language and Thought.* Cambridge, MA: MIT Press, 2003. An anthology of Neo-Whorfian work, which I recommend especially in that it contains an interesting and readable study by Lera Boroditzky on perceptions of objects as gendered, mentioned in Lecture Twenty-Eight.

Harris, Roy, and Talbot J. Taylor, eds. *Landmarks in Linguistic Thought I: The Western Tradition from Socrates to Saussure.* London: Routledge, 1989. For those interested in explorations of language over the millennia with a philosophical orientation (as well as other explorations), this is a handy, readable survey of thinkers' landmark observations about language from antiquity through to the 19th century. Each thinker is treated in a chapter, in which a text is cited, followed by insightful commentary by the editors.

Heath, Shirley Brice. *Ways with Words: Language, Life and Work in Communities and Classrooms.* Cambridge: Cambridge University Press, 1983. This is a classic study on how language use varies according to social class and its effects on children's development and their prospects in school, based on detailed ethnographic research.

Hill, Jane H., and Kenneth C. Hill. *Speaking Mexicano: Dynamics of Syncretic Language in Central Mexico*. Tucson: University of Arizona Press, 1986. A classic and well-written study of language use by indigenous Mexicans, including the use of both Spanish and the local language Nahuatl, with an orientation in the ethnography of communication perspective. Not in print but available, especially in university libraries.

Hock, Hans Heinrich. *Principles of Historical Linguistics*. Berlin: Mouton de Gruyter, 1991. A standard, wide-ranging coverage of the basic tools of historical linguistics, including detailed sections on Grimm's Law, analogy, and related issues.

Hopper, Paul J., and Elizabeth Closs Traugott. *Grammaticalization*. Cambridge: Cambridge University Press, 2003. The standard introduction in the field to grammaticalization, written by two of the pioneers of its incorporation into mainstream linguistic thought in the 1980s.

Horn, Laurence, and Gregory Ward. *The Handbook of Pragmatics*. Malden, MA: Blackwell, 2005. This rich and hefty collection of articles on pragmatics will answer any questions one might have, or guide one to where to find them, on pragmatics, which is a wide-ranging field with applications to many other disciplines and subdisciplines.

Jackendoff, Ray. *Foundations of Language: Brain, Meaning, Grammar, Evolution*. Oxford: Oxford University Press, 2002. This signature book is written more for academics than laymen, but more in its thoroughness of argument than in being utterly opaque to general readers. Those with a serious interest in current conceptions of what language is and how it could have happened will find this a useful source to curl up with.

Joseph, John E., Nigel Love, and Talbot J. Taylor. *Landmarks in Linguistic Thought II: The Western Tradition in the Twentieth Century*. London: Routledge, 2001. This is a continuation of the Harris and Taylor volume described above, covering the 20th century and equally useful.

Kenneally, Christine. *The First Word: The Search for the Origins of Language*. New York: Viking, 2007. This is, finally, a book for general readers chronicling the burgeoning study of how language emerged in humans. Kenneally does not as a rule present substantial outlines of scholars' work on the subject but instead gives previews, after which readers can consult the original sources themselves.

Labov, William. *Language in the Inner City*. Philadelphia: University of Pennsylvania Press, 1972. This remains the summary statement about variation in language, consisting of various foundational studies by Labov from the 1960s. It also remains timely in addressing the speech of inner-city blacks. It's no accident it's still in print almost 40 years after its appearance.

————. *The Social Stratification of English*. Cambridge: Cambridge University Press, 2006. This second edition of a book originally published in 1966 preserves a detailed account of the research project by Labov described in Lecture Sixteen and adds a summary statement of the progress of this kind of inquiry in the decades since.

Ladefoged, Peter, and Ian Maddieson. *The Sounds of the World's Languages*. Malden, MA: Blackwell, 1996. The standard reference work comparing sounds in a wide range of the world's languages, shedding light on how common or rare various sounds are.

Lakoff, Robin. *Language and Women's Place: Text and Commentaries*. New York: Oxford University Press, 2004. This is an annotated version of a text originally published in 1975, which founded the modern school of linguistics investigating language and gender. This source is the perfect way to engage the foundational ideas of 1975, given how much American society has changed since Lakoff first wrote the book. It includes her own commentaries from the vantage point of our times plus others from a wide range of other specialists, including students of Lakoff's.

Levinson, Stephen C., and John J. Gumperz, eds. *Rethinking Linguistic Relativity*. Cambridge: Cambridge University Press, 1996. A substantial anthology of studies under the neo-Whorfian paradigm, including the one mentioned in Lecture Twenty-Eight on directional concepts among an Australian group.

Lightfoot, David. *How to Set Parameters*. Cambridge, MA: MIT Press, 1991. Mainly written for academic linguists, this book will be useful to those who want a deeper engagement with the parameter idea, as Lightfoot is so clear a writer that nonlinguists will be able to approach a great deal of the text. The book is also suitably short.

Lucy, John A. *Language Diversity and Thought: A Reformulation of the Linguistic Relativity Hypothesis*. Cambridge: Cambridge University Press, 1992. A flinty and insightful survey of the original Whorfian hypothesis and the experiments testing it up to the early 1990s, including some by the author.

Lust, Barbara C., and Claire Foley. *First Language Acquisition: The Essential Readings*. Malden, MA: Blackwell, 2004. A collection of seminal writings on how children acquire language; a perfect way to get a sense of how modern linguists approach the subject.

McWhorter, John. *The Power of Babel: A Natural History of Human Language*. New York: HarperCollins, 2001. A reader-friendly survey of what has happened when the world's languages have proliferated and then met one another, with excessive digressionary footnotes about the author's hobbyist predilections and neuroses. (Anyone who agrees with the "excessive" assessment should have seen the first draft!)

McWhorter, John, and Jeff Good. *Saramaccan Grammar*. This will be the first full-length grammatical description of Saramaccan and will contain ampler descriptions of the constructions discussed in this course and, of course, so much more. As I write, the work is just short of completion and has not yet been submitted to a publisher. But it will be sometime in early 2008, and luckily there is no such thing as linguists writing a grammatical description and being unable to find a publisher. So, depending on how much further in the future you are from when I am writing this, hit Amazon and ye shall find.

Milroy, Lesley, and Pieter Muysken, eds. *One Speaker, Two Languages: Cross-Disciplinary Perspectives on Code-Switching*. Cambridge: Cambridge University Press, 1995. A collection of scholarly articles on code switching from a worldwide perspective and from the point of view of various disciplines.

Myers-Scotton, Carol. *Code-Switching: Evidence from Africa*. Oxford: Clarendon Press, 1993. Why Clarendon Press didn't publish this together with Myers-Scotton's *Duelling Languages* as one book has never been clear to me, but this book covers the sociological motivations for code switching and will likely speak more directly to laypeople than the other book.

———. *Duelling Languages: Grammatical Structure in Code-Switching*. Oxford: Clarendon Press, 1993. This is the book-length exposition of a leading and clear theory on how code switching works in the linguistic sense. The details will mostly interest linguists and psychologists, but the first few chapters will nicely acquaint others with what I consider a finely argued hypothesis.

O'Grady, William D. *How Children Learn Language*. Cambridge: Cambridge University Press, 2005. A perfect compact introduction to findings in first-language acquisition, written in accessible prose, almost as if it were explicitly designed for audiences of The Teaching Company's courses.

O'Grady, William, John Archibald, Mark Aronoff, and Janie Rees-Miller, eds. *Contemporary Linguistics: An Introduction*. New York: St. Martin's, 2004. Generally considered the finest linguistics textbook; those interested in delving further into topics covered in this course, including engaging with the "problem set" format via which linguistics is taught in the classroom, will find this textbook highly useful.

Payne, Thomas E. *Describing Morphosyntax: A Guide for Field Linguists*. Cambridge: Cambridge University Press, 1997. Although this is technically intended as a tool for linguists describing hitherto-undocumented language's grammars, it is also a concise yet comprehensive survey of the various functions that affixes and other forms of morphology have in languages and is a handy summary in general of grammatical concepts fundamental to the study of language.

Pinker, Steven. *The Language Instinct*. New York: Harper Perennial, 1994. This is the now-classic source for laymen to examine the issue of whether there is an innately specified ability to use language in our brains. Pinker writes with hipness and wit.

―――. *Word and Rules: The Ingredients of Language*. New York: Basic, 1999. Pinker pulls off the achievement of describing various issues and controversies among linguists studying morphology in an engaging fashion. Those who want a rich survey of the most interesting debates surrounding morphology today will find this book just the ticket.

Pullum, Geoffrey K., and William A. Ladusaw. *Phonetic Symbol Guide*. Chicago: University of Chicago Press, 1986. For those interested in a more detailed look at the International Phonetic Alphabet, including indications of which alternative symbols have been used by which schools of linguists over the years, this is the best guide.

Radford, Andrew. *Syntax: A Minimalist Introduction*. Cambridge: Cambridge University Press, 1997. Radford is a gifted explainer, and this is an introduction to Chomskyan syntax as engaged in since the early 1990s, rather different and less layman-friendly than the earlier rendition mainly presented in this set for practical purposes.

Robinson, Andrew. *The Story of Writing*. London: Thames & Hudson, 2007. This is a solid survey of the origin or writing and the proliferation of writing systems worldwide. Some surveys on this subject seek to make in-house cases of various kinds; this one is admirably just-the-facts.

Sacks, David. *Letter Perfect: the Marvelous History of our Alphabet from A to Z.* New York: Broadway Books, 2003. This is the most readable and most up-to-date survey of how the alphabet came to be. It pulls off the trick of getting in much detail while also being hard to put down. For most who are interested in the history of writing, this, although nominally about the alphabet specifically, is the book to buy.

Sampson, Geoffrey. *Writing Systems: A Linguistic Introduction.* Palo Alto, CA: Stanford University Press, 1990. A detailed and insightful survey of writing systems, written from the perspective of linguistic science by a fine teacher.

Sapir, Edward. *Language: An Introduction to the Study of Speech.* Charleston, SC: BiblioBazaar, 2007. This book is now very old (originally published in 1921), but it remains a concise, elegantly written introduction to the basic tenets of modern linguistics. Today's particular frameworks did not exist in the 1920s, of course, but Sapir's is a classic presentation showing what it is to "think like a linguist."

Saussure, Ferdinand de. *Course in General Linguistics.* Translated by Roy Harris. London: Duckworth, 1983. Strangely enough, de Saussure's foundational work (known as *Cours* in French) was not available in English translation until 1983. Those interested in engaging the original who do not happen to know French will find this translation much more useful than the French original, which was in French.

———. *Writings in General Linguistics.* Translated by Carol Sanders and Matthew Pires. Oxford: Oxford University Press, 2006. In the mid-'90s, a cache of new de Saussure manuscripts was discovered, which clarified many questions that had long reigned unanswered by the interesting but fragmentary notes that the original *Cours* book was based on. This book gathers the newly discovered sources in English translation and is in many ways clearer than the *Cours*.

Saville-Troike, Muriel. *The Ethnography of Communication: An Introduction.* Malden, MA: Blackwell, 2002. The standard book-length introduction to its topic, in a third edition including new chapters. Those interested in ethnography of communication should begin here.

Singh, Simon. *The Code Book: The Evolution of Secrecy from Mary, Queen of Scots to Quantum Cryptography.* New York: Anchor, 2000. This book will interest those whose interest in writing systems includes, as it often seems to, an interest in codes and cryptography. It also has well-written accounts of the decipherment of ancient scripts.

Slobin, Dan. *The Crosslinguistic Study of Language Acquisition*. 5 vols. Hillsdale, NJ: L. Erlbaum and Associates, 1986–1997. These volumes examine how children acquire language in a vast number of different languages, lending insight into how children wrap their heads around a wide variety of constructions in languages around the world. A standard reference for scholars of language acquisition.

Tannen, Deborah. *Conversational Style: Analyzing Talk among Friends*. New York: Oxford, 2005. Hands down the most accessible and engaging presentation of the conversation-analysis perspective, with the "hook" of examining spontaneous conversation over a Thanksgiving dinner.

————. *You Just Don't Understand: Women and Men in Conversation*. New York: William Morrow & Company, 1990. Tannen is the bestselling linguist in America other than Steven Pinker, a fact which began with this first and classic book from her pen for the general public. Her popularity does not mean, however, that this book is not a crucial source of information on how linguists have analyzed how gender differentiates the way humans express themselves through language.

Traugott, Elizabeth Closs, and Bernd Heine. *Approaches to Grammaticalization*. Vols. I and II. Amsterdam: John Benjamins, 1991. Benchmark anthologies on grammaticalization, containing articles on the process in several language families; those seeking detailed coverage of the process around the world and through time will value these two books.

Watkins, Calvert, ed. *The American Heritage Dictionary of Indo-European Roots*. Boston: Houghton Mifflin, 1985. This will serve those who want a brass-tacks look at how Indo-Europeanists do comparative reconstruction. This is a book version of an appendix included in the *American Heritage Dictionary*, aimed at a general readership.

Watts, Richard, Sachiko Ide, and Konrad Ehlich, eds. *Politeness in Language: Studies in Its History, Theory, and Practice*. Berlin: Mouton de Gruyter, 2006. The foundational work on politeness in language (Brown and Levinson's *Politeness*, listed above) has been criticized for assuming a conception of politeness as universal when in fact cultures vary in what is considered polite and not. This collection of articles addresses these issues while still taking Brown and Levinson as a benchmark.

Winford, Donald. *An Introduction to Contact Linguistics*. Malden, MA: Blackwell, 2003. An academic survey of work on language contact, an area of inquiry that has only crystallized over the past 20 years or so in such a way that one could compose a useful book on the subject; Winford has done that.

Wolfram, Walt, and Natalie Schilling-Estes. *Hoi Toide on the Outer Banks: The Story of the Ocracoke Brogue*. Chapel Hill, NC: University of North Carolina Press, 1997. A brisk and readable study of the origin of the interesting dialect of the island of Okracoke off of North Carolina, written by specialists in how socially conditioned language variation leads to language change.

Wooffitt, Robin. *Conversation Analysis and Discourse Analysis: A Comparative and Critical Introduction*. London: Sage, 2005. This book outlines the field of conversational analysis in survey fashion, pitched on an undergraduate level and thus not requiring previous knowledge of jargon and previous studies.

Internet Resources

The American Heritage Dictionary of the English Language. www.bartleby.com/61. This dictionary is now online and is the most reliable source on etymologies, including its famous list of Indo-European roots and, more recently, Proto-Semitic ones. Between these features and its submission of usage questions to a panel of linguists and writers, this dictionary is a linguist's friend.

Ethnologue. www.ethnologue.com. This site has an entry on every known language in the world, with data on location, population, names of dialects, etc., as well as detailed language maps of all regions of the world (this last is difficult to find for many areas and online is easily printed out).

Language Hat. www.languagehat.com. This site is more of a "language nerd" site than Language Log, less concerned with the media than with engaging with issues such as translation and the art of writing. Recommended for a nice combination of erudition and spirit.

Language Log. languagelog.ldc.upenn.edu/nll. This is one of the most popular and influential blogsites on language, with daily posts from a stable of academic linguists on topics usually concerning the use of language and claims about language in the media and the light that the science of language sheds on them. Posts are well-written and often substantial, and those by site leaders Geoffrey Pullum and Mark Liberman have been published in book form (*Far From the Madding Gerund*).

Notes

Notes

Notes

Notes

Notes

Notes

Notes